Dennis Barker is a journalist who has worked as reporter, feature writer and columnist for the *Guardian* since 1963. His early career was spent on the *East Anglian Daily Times* and the Wolverhampton *Express* and *Star*, before he joined the *Guardian*. He is a frequent broadcaster and the author of two novels.

Soldiering On

An Unofficial Portrait of the British Army

DENNIS BARKER

SPHERE BOOKS LIMITED
30-32 Gray's Inn Road, London WC1X 8JL

First published in Great Britain by
Andre Deutsch Ltd 1981

Copyright © Dennis Barker 1981, 1983

Published by Sphere Books Ltd 1983

TRADE
MARK

Set in Linotron Plantin

Printed and bound in Great Britain by
Collins, Glasgow.

CONTENTS

Preface

I shall never forget the Clicking Colonel. He clicked his teeth at me with gusto, with threateningly practised skill, at each question I pressed. It seemed that either my will or his jaw must break. I am much relieved to say that neither did.

The clicking sound seemed to say: who is this meddlesome whipper-snapper, and why isn't he on a charge? This despite the fact that my questions (on some quite innocuous topic, with as much of a security angle as the correct time to boil Officers Mess eggs) were not in fact directed at him, but only to a colleague of his who happened to be within earshot.

Is the British Army of today a puny, rumbling remnant of the Boys of the Old Brigade, the Indian Mutiny, the Charge of the Light Brigade, two heroic and expensive World Wars and an often humiliating economic decline? A purely nominal national protection? A snobbish last-ditch refuge for the die-hard and the dolt? Officers burping over their port, Other Ranks touching their forelocks and asking their Betters what they are allowed to think? In short, an institution that can bring succour and satisfaction to only a small proportion of the British and world population — the comedians and the satirists?

There may be those who think so. Certainly there are those who would like to think so.

Even ten years ago Britain and the West as a whole may have felt safe enough to regard the whole question as merely academic, the answer merely entertaining. The answer, I hope, is still diverting. But recent international events have willy-nilly pushed the question to the very centre of the

1

minds of those with an ear finely tuned to menace. It is likely to stay this way throughout the 1980s and perhaps into the twenty-first century. It touches the layman as much as the militarist. Some may see the question as overblown. Others will regard it as a matter of life or death, national independence or a new serfdom. *Will* dangerous times continue to be dangerous only for other people?

There remains a stubborn thread of legitimate humour running through the whole subject of the Soldiers of the Queen, represented perhaps by the officers in the tin huts of Belize, eating their dinner (and wearing neckties, of course) in the company of green lizards and their regimental silver; or by the Guards outside Buckingham Palace, straining to keep those sleeked-down black Bearskins on in a high wind; or even by the Clicking Colonel.

What does my book break ranks to say for itself? There have been books about the Army before. I venture no remark about their general readability. The good fortune of this particular book is simple. For the first time the British Army has opened its doors freely to a non-specialist writer whose stance is that of an interested, but not necessarily uncritical, layman. This is the first time the Boys of the New Brigade have spoken on the record as thinking human beings, not merely efficient robots. I have been allowed to talk to soldiers in barracks and to officers hunting illegal immigrants on the border between Hong Kong and the People's Republic of China. I have braved the plentiful burrowing beef bugs and the rarer alligators of Belize while out on a jungle patrol led by a twenty-one-year-old officer who was definitely post-Kipling — his father was a hotel keeper in a seaside resort — and I have asked the men with him, as I shared their cold food out of tins in the shade of an attap tree, how they liked their job.

On several occasions I have been to the East-West German border, where I once saw a British officer facetiously pose under the scrutiny of the telephoto lens of the East German troops on the other side of the squalid barbed wire, booby traps and scatter guns that the East has presented to the British soldier's most real frontier. I have crawled into and out of dug-outs with face-blackened infantrymen in the cold night of a West German autumn exercise, and aimed a guided missile at thundering 'Enemy' (the Army doesn't say 'Russian' — officially) tanks. I have met, in sportive, fast, encircled and slightly unreal West Berlin, a Senior British Staff Officer who had not had time to get out of his track suit before our appointment in the converted sports stadium that was to be part of Hitler's thousand-year Third Reich.

Most hair-raising of all, I have shared the risks, as a piece of human litmus paper, with British troops in Northern Ireland — both in previously mortared bases surrounded with corrugated iron and out on patrol on the streets, where every face is perhaps not quite what it seems to be, and the soldier may be dead before he knows whether a rifle shot or a landmine has killed him. And I have survived, as many who wear the Queen's khaki uniform have not.

I was allowed to talk to whom I liked and ask what questions I liked. I would have preferred to quote officers and men by name, whether it be on active service or at the selection centres for officers and men; but the Army thought that this might embarrass individual soldiers. I have quoted everyone by rank, but not by name. This has the advantage — since individual soldiers normally change their functions once every two years, more often in Northern Ireland — of giving the book greater timelessness.

Another factor will, I hope, prevent this book becoming easily outdated. I was more interested in the people than in the weapons, suspecting not merely that they changed less over the years but that they would be a more reliable guide to the muscle-tone of the present-day British Army. I was more concerned with first-hand atmosphere than with statistics, feeling that it would better guide me to an understanding of the diverse character of the animal that has replaced Britain's house-dog of the Wellington, Kipling and Kitchener eras. After all, statistics can prove anything.

3

As it takes just as long now to get troops across London by motor vehicle as it would have done by horse before the First World War, we *could* 'prove' that both the British Army and the British capital city have not materially changed.

My aim has been to show a body of 155,000 soldiers, plus Reserves and Territorials, doing their job and talking about it. The result is not a textbook nor a recruiting brochure. Nor is it, I hope, the sort of stereotyped condescension so often displayed by the man of letters and communication (lately fashionable) towards the man of action (lately unfashionable). It has been produced with such official help as I have asked for, but it is in no way an official book. The manuscript was submitted to the Ministry of Defence for corrections on points of fact, scrutiny on points of security and perusal on matters of comment, where I retained the right, in the final analysis, of saying what I pleased. I am grateful to Major General Derek Boorman, Director of Public Relations (Army) at the time I began the book, and more recently Director of Military Operations, for his help; and also grateful to his successor as Director of Public Relations, Brigadier Guy Watkins; to the staff of Army Public Relations, and in particular to Derrick Knight, whose help was invariably cheerful and efficient; and to the very many officers and men who spoke frankly in conversation with me. They must be nameless now, as they are in the rest of the book. I received every reasonable facility from the Ministry of Defence and the Army to see and talk to whom I chose. I would like to thank all who made themselves available on the UK mainland, in Northern Ireland, in Germany and in the remainder of Empire; often when they were actually in the course of their job.

The reportage of the book I would claim to be accurate. Such judgements as I have made may be proved right or wrong as the British Army enters what is an entirely new era for the nation of Wellington, Haig and Montgomery. Whether I have considered it right or wrong on a particular issue, I have acquired a respect for the Army as a collection

4

of varied men and as a disciplined force. Even its multitudinous regimental niceties — whether one stands up or sits down through the Loyal Toast and so on — have a value, even if I (a damned civilian with no more military experience than scant and compulsory service in the Officers Training Corps at school), still can't contemplate it with a completely straight face. Fortunately, today's Army can laugh at itself, too, if not at its *profession*. Can one say the same of perhaps more fashionable callings of the late twentieth century? It would be unkind, unchivalrous and unmilitary to demand an answer.

Civilians may well ask: is the present-day British Army *interesting*? When, at the outset, I asked one officer why he had not made himself richer by going into a merchant bank instead of the Army, he said, 'Because the Army is a much, much more interesting and varied life.' At the time I doubted this point of view. I do so no longer. I am ready to believe that for a young man who likes variety and action, the British Army offers a chance of self-expression, without necessarily penalizing him for being able to think. I never at any time doubted the opinion of an infantry private soldier that the Army could be far more interesting than work on the factory shop floor. There is an element of unpredictability about Army life, at whatever level, that makes it more attractive to many men than clocking on and clocking off. Whether it always makes it more attractive to their wives is a different matter; but, as one lady remarked, 'A man who is bored isn't at all nice to live with.'

The cult of the Man of Action has been out of fashion in Britain and much of the Western world for over a generation. It has been replaced by the cult of the intellectual, the academic, the analyst, the consultant, the media man. It has become fashionable to lend a serious ear to men who watch rather than men who *do*.

In no way does this change express itself more openly, more directly, and perhaps more disastrously, than in public attitudes to the British Army. These most revealingly betray themselves in unguarded moments. In the arts cinema of a university town I watched a short film about an Army patrol party ploughing through the jungle. The leading soldier carried his rifle silently in one hand while he hacked his way through the jungle with a machete. The shots of the silent men of the jungle, never saying a word, their hats jammed down square on their foreheads, their bullish moustaches rigid above stiff upper lips, admittedly went on rather too long as they strode and stumbled silently on and on and on. Suddenly the whole audience began to erupt into wild laughter.

One could well understand the hilarity at an overdone introductory scene which was evidently intended to convey more tension that it could bear. But some of the basis for the laughter was evidently not as sound as this one, or as worthy of intelligent young people. They evidently thought that a soldier diligently doing his duty was ridiculous *as such*. But is a stiff-upper-lipped soldier hacking his silent way through the jungle essentially any more fatuous than an academic pronouncing on national problems that perhaps he himself could not handle for five minutes?

The second pointer (also off-guard) to the causes underlying what could be called a dangerous shift in fashion came in the pronouncement of an American Women's Liberationist. She said that women were now totally the equal of men in everything 'because war, which was once the male preserve, can now be waged by pressing a button'. This statement may have said more about American defence policy errors (now being grudgingly rectified) than it did about Women's Liberation. The theory that war can be successfully waged by nuclear button has been the siren song of the generation that has forgotten the merits of the Man of Action.

If war is to be decided by nuclear button, the Soviet Union has been crassly wasteful in building up its men and armour — its purely conventional military forces — so that they outnumber the West's by two or three to one. The West's vaunted trump card in this situation has been the nuclear ability to commit suicide and take the other side with it. Is it a step that would actually be taken, or that the Russians would really assume would be taken, as they started to move forward with their men and tanks?

The plain fact is that, during the age of the watcher, the analyst and the critic, actual military activity — of which there has been plenty outside our own immediate area of consciousness — has almost always been successfully conducted only with men and armour: in other words, with the armed soldier. The view that war is now to be won or lost by a magic button is a parochial delusion sustainable only in the relatively calm waters of Western Europe and the USA. It goes against what is actually happening — and demonstrably happening — in the wider world.

In short, though he is not fashionable, it can be argued that the soldier is as important as he ever was. The East knows it — and has military conscription, often for long periods, in support of it. The chatter of Western cocktail parties and television coverage had until recently latched on to less challenging topics than the need for strong military defence in an uncertain world.

The British Army is seldom written about. It is even more rarely written about as a body of men living in the same sort of national society as anybody else. But it is there. 155,000 men. It contains a very different cut of man: a man, some might guess, with more relevance to the British 1980s than he had to the 1970s and infinitely more than he had to the 1960s of Carnaby Street, the King's Road and the 'Never had it so good' self-delusion. It is to him that I dedicate this book with respect, goodwill and some reservations.

Certainly I finished up with the impression that the British Army of today is dominated by the concept of professionalism, as the recruiting advertisements more than hint. What does this concept mean? It means, I would judge, that it would be likely that soldiers would carry out *any* orders given them. It means also that it would be *un*likely that the Army would seek to overthrow the civil power by the sort of coup fashionable in other climates.

Only one person I met in my enquiries, that Clicking Colonel, came really close to the caricature so beloved of those who distrust and lampoon the Military. He sat opposite another Colonel I was interviewing behind a Whitehall desk. Every time I fished for a definite answer to a question as sensitive as how many years a Major had to be a Major before he could be made a Colonel, or how many officers were at Sandhurst, he made that memorable clicking noise with his teeth that suggested impatience at not being able to have me reduced to the ranks and imprisoned for rank insubordination, treason and incitement to mutiny. Or, of course, he might just have been brooding over the clues to the crossword he was doing in his newspaper, and resenting interruptions.

In any case, I know why I shall remember him so clearly. He was so very, very rare in Her Majesty's Army of today, an odd man out among (to update that old song) the Boys of the New Brigade.

PART ONE

Where They Are

1

Bandit Country

'I have never regretted joining the Army, not even in Northern
Ireland. I was a solicitor in the City of London, and to join the
Army, I took a salary cut of two-thirds. But there is scope in the
Army. I went to see a man I had known in the City the other day.
His office had a magnificent view of St Paul's Cathedral. Do you
know what he had on his walls? Prints of St Paul's Cathedral.'

> — Captain, aged twenty-nine, in British Army
> base in Northern Ireland which had been
> blown up with mortars a few months previ-
> ously.

'The bad thing about Northern Ireland is not that you might get
killed — that keeps you on your toes. It's knowing who your
enemies are, but not always being able to go out and get them.'

> — Guardsman, aged twenty, at same base.

Unbelievably, it was Christmas Eve. I was shiveringly
crouched under cover of a council house fence with a British
Army patrol. We were picking our way with great caution
through an estate in Newtownhamilton. The village is in
the heart of what is called 'bandit country', a five-minute
car journey or less from the border with the Irish Republic
and the most dangerous strip of land for the soldier and the
civilian in the whole of Northern Ireland.

Icy fog hung around the dim street lamps. We slipped
and slithered on the ice and snow, which seeped into our
clothes whenever we threw ourselves down for extra cover.
Patrols can go on for hours or for days. One might see
merely Noisy Nell, of whom more later. Or one might not
see the bullet that cut one down or the bomb that blew one
to smithereens.

Was this really the time of the year which, elsewhere, is supposed to signify peace and goodwill? In Northern Ireland it is, for the British soldier, the period when his life is at greatest risk from the patchwork quilt of people who want British Northern Ireland to be taken over by the Republican South and are prepared to set aside ordinary human scruples to bring it about.

The experienced Lance Corporal who led the patrol, a veteran of twenty-three, had told me in advance what the form would be. 'I will lead. Walk thirty metres behind me, not closer. That is very important. If one of us is taken out by a bomb, the rest may escape.'

The 2nd Lieutenant who would normally have led the patrol was aged twenty and fresh from Sandhurst. 'He will be behind you,' said the Lance Corporal. 'If we are fired upon, don't fall flat at once, because it is more easy to hit a stationary target. Look for the nearest cover, and go there, running crooked to stop yourself being hit. I will cover you with fire from the front and the Lieutenant will cover you with fire from the rear if anything goes wrong. Don't worry. We will get you out.'

It was not the nicest way I had ever been wished a happy Christmas. I had been in Northern Ireland only four hours. I was having to make very rapid mental adjustments to the atmosphere of the place, just as every soldier must do if he is to have a fair chance of staying alive. I had set myself up as a target like an ordinary soldier, albeit for a more limited time, using my own adrenalin and fear as a barometer of what the fifteen thousand or so British soldiers do and feel when up against the unseen terrorist of an Irish Republican Army which has been so convinced of its own moral rightness that it has been able to excuse, to itself, any atrocities, even ones that include the totally innocent.

Sprawled along the council house fence, overlooking a house believed to have IRA connections and hoping that the machine-gunner, the last man in the party, had crept up so that he could cover the whole area with raking fire if need be (though he was invisible to me), I took my own moral pulse. Stomach muscles tight, mouth dry, eyes flickering watchfully over every window, every door and — especially — every passageway. No longer any thoughts about death, no time for that; only the desire to win some sort of game, the game of staying alive.

The thoughts of death or mutilation come when you first know you are going to Northern Ireland, especially if it happens to be to the bandit country of the border. In my case, they started a fortnight before my arrival, as they are apt to do in young soldiers making their first trip to Northern Ireland. I kept thinking about Northern Ireland when I should have been thinking about other things. My mind kept slipping cogs. It was better when at last I had something concrete to get to grips with: the separate gate used at Heathrow Airport, London, for the air shuttle to Belfast. There is a totally separate channel for the one service, riddled with security guards, body searchers and luggage examiners. They even take hand luggage away from you before you get on the plane, allowing you only a book to read. They tell you you will get your briefcase back at Belfast, and when you do, it is wrapped in a polythene bag, to prevent interference. Or is it to prevent some dark, unearthly contagion?

Such gloomy questions come easily in Northern Ireland. They certainly come easily to the Army. Soldiers know that a moment of forgetful spontaneity, of human carelessness, may cost them their lives.

'Thirty pence for the time we've been parked here? Thirty pence!' grumbled the Sergeant of the Royal Corps of Transport who had been sent out to Aldergrove airport, outside Belfast, to fetch me. We were in a red, but otherwise inconspicuous, 'plain clothes' car with civilian number plates, one of a series which are bought and sold again before their numbers become known to the IRA.

The grumble about the thirty pence sounded normal, as normal as the traffic signs, the telephone boxes and the airport car park itself. What was *not* normal was the fact that the Sergeant, while grumbling about the thirty pence like any Sussex commuter, was pulling out his Browning .9 millimetre automatic pistol, ramming in a magazine of bullets and slipping it down his trouser belt, under his hairy wool sweater.

'We don't get out of headquarters much at all,' he said, as the car proceeded at scalded-cat speed towards the headquarters of the 1st Battalion, the Welsh Guards, at Bessbrook, further towards the dangerous border. 'And when we do, we carry a pistol all the time. There are a lot of illegal road blocks by the IRA in this area, and the only way you are going to get out of one of those alive if you are a British soldier is to get *them* before they get you.'

The accelerator pedal stayed firmly near the floorboards as the car made for the city of Belfast itself, past the British Army's checkpoint for all traffic coming from the other direction into the airport. The car slowed down again slightly as it passed the British Army's first visible base — at the top of the notorious Falls Road, where many squalid side streets have twenty foot high wire mesh fences stopping people coming on to the main road except through a narrow and easily manned gate. Once out of the city and heading towards South Armagh, the atmosphere grew even less psychologically congenial, and the car went even faster over roads covered with snow, slush and occasional black ice.

For safety's sake, the Sergeant and his driver, a Guardsman, did *not* wear their safety harnesses. 'Going through the windscreen is the least of our worries,' said the Sergeant. 'If the car was stopped, you might have to get out quick and engage the enemy. In a safety harness, you are trapped. And we can't go slowly. The faster you go, the less time you stay in the blast area of a bomb that may have been planted by the roadside, or under the road in a culvert.'

The point was not academic. The week previously four soldiers had been killed and one injured when a remotely-detonated bomb in a culvert went off quite unexpectedly under an Army Land Rover, which was reduced to an almost unrecognizable lump of metal. The IRA then fired twenty rounds at the Army vehicle which followed it, but failed to injure any more British soldiers.

The headquarters of the 1st Battalion, the Welsh Guards, for its regulation four-and-a-half-month tour (half completed when I arrived), was in an old linen mill at Bessbrook, twenty miles from the border. In front of it were twenty foot high panels of corrugated iron. Behind the protective and obscurantist iron sheet was a row of cages, each one containing a fierce smeller dog. Such dogs are never photographed for publicity purposes. Nor are their handlers. Their job is to sniff out explosives before they have a chance to injure soldiers. The more anonymous their skills, the safer they are from IRA pre-emptive attack.

In this stockade, with no visibility to the outside world, lived two hundred men, including Royal Engineer search teams trained to clear roads and houses of bombs. The roofs were reinforced with wire netting, but the only real protection against the mortar bombs which the IRA were increasingly employing was under a concrete staircase, where eighty people would have to huddle in a space that would have comfortably taken a dozen.

On the table of the Officers Mess was some nice regimental silver, including two well-modelled statuettes of Welsh Guardsmen. 'Of course,' said the Major who met me, 'one would not employ one's very best regimental silver in these sort of conditions, but a few basic items lend the right tone. It is important to keep morale and standards in this sort of situation. Any fool can be uncomfortable.'

What is felt by soldiers coming into Bessbrook for the first time is not discomfort. It is, rather, distinct and very understandable unease. South of Bessbrook, nearer the border, lies bandit country, where the majority of people are Catholics and, if not ardent Republicans themselves, know that they may be taken away and tortured, perhaps to death, if they give so much as a cheery wave to the security forces, let alone give them concrete help.

'If you tried to go nearer the border than here by road, people would think you were mad,' said the Major. 'It simply isn't done. You could be bombed, shot at, taken — anything at all could happen to you.'

Bandit country includes the small town of Crossmaglen, the most emotive name in an emotive South Armagh. It was manned, at the time of my visit, by the Prince of Wales Company (1st) of the Welsh Guards, an elite company who all have to be over six feet tall. One in six of *all* soldiers killed in the whole of Northern Ireland have been killed in Crossmaglen.

'There has only been one company in the last twelve who have been here who have *not* had a man killed there,' said the Major. 'The last one of ours was a month ago, when a radio bomb killed one of our men by a thousand to one chance. It was probably meant for a police vehicle, but a foot patrol set it off. The man was blown to smithereens.'

So, almost, earlier in the year, was the entire Army base built over the Royal Ulster Constabulary police station at Newtownhamilton. This was the base at which I was to spend a typical Northern Ireland Christmas with the British Army — in a village with eight hundred people; permanent barriers on all roads into the town, save one; and a derelict hotel that was gutted when a mortar overshot the Army base and hit it in March of 1979, damaging it so badly that it was not worthwhile restoring it for the microscopic trade likely to venture into the village in future.

'No one in his right mind would go to Newtownhamilton unless he absolutely had to,' said an Army man aboard the Gazelle helicopter that took me over bandit country, changing course for safety's sake every few seconds. Helicopters had been shot at before, but so far none was recorded as being hit by the IRA, though one came down unaccountably in bad weather.

Why was bandit country considered so dangerous by the Army? There were seven possible escape routes across the border in the section of it covered by Newtownhamilton — main roads, minor roads and earth tracks. This made it a particularly good area for the IRA. They could detonate bombs by remote control, and slip away across the border long before their firing position was discovered. They could set up mortar-firing tubes on lorries near the base, set the automatic firing mechanism for five or ten minutes' time, and be back across the border before the mortars were even on their way. When the attack on Newtownhamilton with mortars was made earlier in the year, nine were fired. One was left in the barrel to kill investigating troops. In the event, five mortars overshot with loss of civilian life, two landed on the Army stockade and two hit the Royal Ulster Constabulary police station underneath the Army in the same stockade — the police station which the Army was there to protect, and did, with its own buildings. One soldier was killed and eleven people hurt, including civilians.

All this information, fed to me before I got there, was not the most encouraging preliminary to a visit. True, by then a surge of adrenalin was beginning to come to my rescue. The knowledge that there is no way out begins to focus the mind wonderfully. There was also the awareness that one was in a situation in which the British Army would take no more chances than it had to. Three Guardsmen with self-loading rifles climbed to the top of the three sangars (concrete and corrugated iron observation posts) around the helicopter landing pad as the chopper landed. The rotors continued to whirl, ready for instant take-off, as I pulled my luggage hastily out on to the ground, slammed the helicopter door behind me and raced for the base.

The word 'base' can be used to describe a whole range of military establishments, from the ambitious to the primitive. Nevertheless, Newtownhamilton was singular. All that was visible was a square surrounded by corrugated iron sheets twenty to thirty feet tall, blocking off the vision of any attacker and giving some slight protection against the throwing of grenades. The holes made by the four mortars that had landed inside were still there.

There was only one entrance to the stockade, through a brick-built structure rather like a built-on domestic porch, except that the door was of two inch thick steel. The group of soldiers who met me whisked me through the steel door as fast as possible. The relief, when the great and well-oiled door closed behind me, was noticeable.

Inside the base, however, there was no discernible sign of relaxation. 'It is probably the most dangerous of all the bases in bandit country,' said the Commander of the Support Company at the base, a thirty-two-year-old ex-Etonian Major, 'but I think the men probably prefer it to Crossmaglen.' At Crossmaglen, there was more protection but less space. Newtownhamilton was far more comfortable.

Which remark showed clearly that comfort is relative. I was shown to the quarters where I would sleep. It was a wooden hut, eight feet by five feet, with a primitive heater, a collapsed shelf unit and a 'dressing table' consisting of a heap of piled-up old steel chairs. There were two bunks in it. I had to take the top one as the officers felt that if I took the lower one I would probably bang my head if I had to get out of it quickly during the night. I very probably would have done.

By Newtownhamilton standards, these quarters were elegant. Only the Officer Commanding had his own bedroom. Officers shared two to a room, in a well-insulated but basic new wooden building which replaced the one destroyed by the mortars, and provided two lavatories and four washbasins. Shaving was done there, in hot brown water. The men slept up to six a room (eight in an extreme emergency). Their accommodation block was covered in do-it-yourself shelves, old steel locker cabinets and new pin-ups — a decor consisting almost entirely of sheet metal and pubic hairs.

'We live today in as great a fear of a mortar attack as we did at the time of the last one,' said the Second-in-Command, a twenty-nine-year-old Captain. 'It unquestionably adds to the strain, because the men know they do not have the same protection they have in Belfast or even Crossmaglen.'

In the area covered by Newtownhamilton, during the

year before my visit, there had been four major incidents. There was the mortar attack. There was an explosion which wrecked a lorry one and a half miles from the village, in order to get British soldiers out of the base, where they could be more easily attacked. Two Royal Ulster Constabulary Constables were hurt. An Ulster Defence Regiment man had been murdered five miles to the east. A two hundred pound bomb had blown up the road between Newtownhamilton and Newry, with no casualties. Only just outside the area covered by the Newtownhamilton base, a Queen's Own Highlander had been killed by a blast bomb connected to the door of a house; a Welsh Guardsman had been killed on routine patrol by a two hundred pound bomb under a farm gate; and a Paratrooper had been killed by a bomb that went off in a derelict house. Eighteen people — a 2nd Lieutenant in the Parachute Regiment, two Queen's Highlanders and some civilians — had been blown up by a bomb in a hay lorry by the roadside, and two soldiers had been killed in a helicopter crash which might or might not have been the work of the IRA. There had been a spate of bombings in Newry, and a cattle lorry had exploded. Then, the week before my visit, there had been the Land Rover incident when four soldiers were killed. On a market day, soldiers might pass at least a hundred cattle or hay lorries. They cannot be avoided. There was no possible precaution, said soldiers, except crossing the fingers and praying.

What does such knowledge make you feel like? Life, even the boring bits, suddenly seems infinitely sweet. Will you be able to hide your fear? If a bomb goes off underneath you or beside you, will you feel ghastly agony as you are blasted to pieces, or will the mind not have time to register anything? Is there any possible way you can escape the coming gamble with your life? All these thoughts and feelings churn around inside the head and nerves, and there is a considerable expense of nervous energy in concealing such fears from other people.

'Life here is a lot different to a soldier's life in Belfast,' said an officer. 'In Belfast, there is a host of small things happening, in which the soldier is not always greatly at risk. Sometimes they will let off a rifle at you, and sometimes they will throw stones at you. Or they will blow up the shop next door to you. If someone is blowing up the shop next door or along the street, it is no great risk to the soldier. Here, in Newtownhamilton by the border, we have a period of uneasy calm, in which nothing at all happens, followed by a very substantial incident. That is the pattern.'

The briefing to the patrol was given in the courtyard of the base, an area of iced-up concrete about the size of a large living-room. Breath came out as freezing vapour. From this courtyard it was only a few footsteps into the gatehouse, where a soldier kept constant vigil on the half-demolished street for any signs of suspicious movement.

'Right,' said the Lance Corporal. The thick steel door was swung open and he stepped smartly out into the street, his rifle ready in the firing position.

I forced myself to wait, then forced myself to walk out of the doorway once he was the regulation thirty metres ahead of me. The sodium street lights seemed unnaturally bright. It felt like painting a target on your own forehead and stepping out into a rifle range. The mist was icy and eerie: who was lurking just out of sight?

'The mist is good,' shouted the Lance Corporal over his shoulder. 'We can't see them, but they can't see us, either. Keep on the other side of the street from me *and* slightly behind. Keep against the wall, don't make a silhouette of yourself, and take advantage of every scrap of cover you can find.' The knowledge that there were two medics at the base, neither of them doctors; that the attitude of local doctors might be equivocal (one doctor from a town nearby is alleged to have walked, laughing, past a seriously injured British soldier: the story has taken on the authority of folk myth); that all casualties would have to be shipped back to Bessbrook by helicopter, like every bit of food and scrap of refuse, did *not* help induce ease of mind.

The regulation patrol is in the form of what is called a

'brick'. It consists of a rectangle, at the four corners of which are the four men who make up the brick. In practice, the formation is rather more like an empty rectangular picture frame which is pulled out of true. The four men are staggered rather than perfectly rectangular, so that no man walks directly in line with another (one bullet might kill them both if they did) or directly behind another. But the formation can provide fire through a complete 360 degrees, if there is trouble.

The first possible hazard to be faced by the patrolling soldiers was Noisy Nell, as they called a lady of the neighbourhood who lived in a near-derelict house and was in the habit of abusing troops roundly every time she saw them. She was also said to have cursed a pet dog of the locality just as roundly, which was why the black labrador the troops called Blackie had attached itself to the base, and was, that Christmas Eve, out on patrol with the Army, instead of growling at them.

The roads and pavements were covered with ice and hoar frost, the fog was getting thicker and the night was getting darker. Noisy Nell stayed indoors, to everyone's relief — including, possibly, the dog's.

A piece of broad tarmac up a hill from the base was called The Common, a cosy enough name for a harshly illuminated open space by a set-back Protestant church. It was in the gateway of this church that I crouched while the Lance Corporal reconnoitred the space, which seemed as large as a desert and as devoid of cover. To cross an open space, any open space, in Newtownhamilton entailed a certain risk if one was a soldier or in the company of soldiers. By this time — and we had been on the streets for less than ten minutes — I had got into the habit of never stopping for breath anywhere near a street light, always looking at every visible window for any sign of movement, and never standing directly in line with any of the darkened passages between houses.

Any soldier crouched in the gates of a church, as I was, would take a chance on the attitude of the incumbent. It was, said the soldiers, apt to be as equivocal as that of some doctors (or some lawyers, who make money by defending alleged IRA men in court). One young officer, scarcely out of Sandhurst, who happened to be interested in old churches, was told by one priest that he could look at the outside of his church, but it would be better if he did not go inside.

There was a narrow and ill-lit street leading off The Common. It was here, in near ideal cover, that the patrol demonstrated one of their major reasons for being on the streets at all. They set up a vehicle check point (VCP) by walking in front of every car that turned the corner, and demanding identity papers. They also questioned the drivers and passengers closely, and with great courtesy, about where they had come from, where they were going to and when they were likely to be coming back.

Armagh Street, with its round concrete blocks and its rows of cars parked up against them (each one a potential container for two hundred pounds of explosive) was empty. So, lower down the hill, was Dundalk Street, a row of grey terraced houses, with icy water leaking down the walls from rusted gutterings, splashing over the pavement and freezing treacherously. In a side street was a public house which had already had the building next to it demolished by a bomb. 'People say the publican is mad to stay, but he is certainly a very brave man,' said one of the patrol, as he sheltered in a shop doorway. Sometimes soldiers have gone into pubs to ask questions about the clientele; but as it was Christmas Eve, and the soldiers had no specific information to go on, this formality was tactfully omitted: care is always taken not to irritate the local population more than is absolutely necessary.

What was the little building set back in darkness further up this road? 'It is called the Orange Hall,' said one of the patrol. 'It is a Protestant meeting house.' In 1975, IRA machine-gunners had walked in and raked a meeting with bullets, killing several people. Every building in Newtown-hamilton seemed to have its slice of IRA history, some

22

major, some minor. It was certainly not an easy environment to live sanely in, or with.

It was a relief to get off the deserted minor streets of the village and into a housing estate, a local authority development of modern grey terraces which the 2nd Lieutenant, the twenty-year-old ex-Etonian, pronounced to be 'palatial in comparison to what you will find in Belfast, with all the litter, filth and slogans — these people are very lucky to live here, really'.

Where was the celebration of the luck? Where were the Christmas trees gleaming with fairy lights in front windows? On the whole of the estate, not more than two were to be seen. From the other houses no lights shone into the road at all, as if the whole population of the estate had decided to pull its front curtains, retreat into back rooms and be as inconspicuous as possible. Perhaps this interpretation was a trick of the imagination, as I crouched down behind a slatted garden fence at the entrance to the estate, taking careful stock before advancing down its lighted streets? Perhaps and perhaps not; there have been few sane certainties in an area where soldiers claim civilians have been shot in the kneecaps or elbows, or both, for merely wishing the Army 'good morning'.

There was, said the 2nd Lieutenant (who had joined the Lance Corporal and me behind the fence, breaking the 'spread out' rule, because we now all had fair cover), a house down the road where one of the sons was suspected of having IRA sympathies. It was the job of patrols to check on such houses, especially at times of the year when families might be returning home, to see what was happening, and to check on numbers of people who could be expected to go into individual houses.

Breaking cover to start moving down the lighted estate (with its plethora of unlighted windows, each one possibly concealing a gunman or remote control bomber) required a distinct squaring of the moral shoulders, and a fairly rigid adherence to the rule that you walk over the paths not in the shadow of houses, taking care not to make a conveniently silhouetted target of yourself. I looked round, and could not see any other members of the brick behind us, certainly not the man with the machine-gun. 'We were behind you and in sight of you all the time,' the machine-gunner said afterwards. But at the time we moved towards the house with a son of suspected IRA sympathies, I could see only the Lance Corporal. He went to the front door to ring the bell, while I crouched down out of sight (I hoped) behind the back garden fence.

Before the Lance Corporal even reached the bell, the dog inside the house started to bark. 'Kill the bastards!' shouted a man inside the house, opening the back door and letting the dog out into the back garden. Was the back gate closed? I fervently hoped so. It was.

All the same, I moved round to the front of the house, to join the Lance Corporal and the 2nd Lieutenant in the front porch, as the man of the house, all affability, wished everyone as Merry a Christmas as they had just wished him. *Kill the bastards?* Had one imagined it?

There was a probing session of rather stilted small talk on the freezing doorstep, with the Lance Corporal and the 2nd Lieutenant trying to converse while keeping out of the direct light streaming out of the front door — not an easy task. The weather was nasty, wasn't it? Yes, it was. What would the householder be doing for Christmas? Staying indoors. Oh, he wouldn't be going out to the pub? No, he wouldn't go out, he was too frightened to go out. ('Sometimes they say the things they think you want to hear. It is not dishonesty, it is just a desire to be agreeable,' said the 2nd Lieutenant afterwards.) Was his family coming home? Oh yes, they would be home for Christmas. So how many would there be in the house? Oh, eight, but one son would not be home. No, he would be staying where he was.

By now the conversation was sounding distinctly strained. But it has been partly from such conversations that the Army has built up its picture of who is where and why. This has enabled the soldiers to decide more easily which is an acceptable face in any particular locality, and which is the unexpected one to watch or stop and question.

Because Newtownhamilton has had all four approach roads, except one, barriered off and made inaccessible to traffic, the risks have been in some respects less than in the other communities near the border — Crossmaglen and Forkhill. Machine-gunning from a speeding car is unlikely when the car would have to leave by the same road as it came in. And it would be less easy for *another* row of mortar bombs to be set up in a lorry 150 yards from the Army base, as the 1979 mortars were.

Such knowledge has not been a complete comfort to the soldiers — at least, not if my feelings were the fair barometer I hoped they were. I was relieved when the time the patrol was due to finish arrived (patrols have started and ended at constantly staggered times, to confuse would-be attackers); and even more relieved when the steel door of the entrance closed behind me with a dull but reassuring clang. It was like suddenly being in a depressurization chamber. The soldiers began to laugh and make jokes as they removed the ammunition from their rifles, pointing the barrels carefully at the mound of sandbags set up near the base entrance especially for this purpose: it would be tragically ironic if a soldier, having survived a patrol, were to die of a spare round left in a rifle.

In the debriefing room, the results of the evening patrol were produced and analysed. The doorstep conversation was repeated: one member of one family would not be home for Christmas. Additionally, one house now stood empty where before it had showed signs of occupation, and the red door of a derelict house had been open, whereas before it had been closed.

A fair crop from a patrol, though rather hard and long in the reaping. The last item — the door of the derelict house being open when it had been closed — was perhaps the most urgently interesting: bombs in derelict houses had by then become one of the worst dangers faced by patrolling soldiers. Some bombs had been set to go off when the front door was opened, others only when it was closed again. Some were set to go off when a floorboard was stepped on; others when the pressure on the floorboard was released. Some had been arranged to be exploded by radio in the hand of an observer in the nearby hills. Some, more dangerous still, had been arranged to go off when a soldier, thinking he was being careful, shone his torch through the window at the bomb — setting it off with the light from his torch. Patrols, therefore, have usually done no more than seal an area off when they have thought they may have a bomb. The experts have been brought in, perhaps with a 'wheelbarrow', an electronically controlled wheeled device that can inspect a bomb, explode it, or even take it to pieces while soldiers remain a safe distance away.

While patrols of one, two or three hours (or fractions or multiples of these times) have been going on, other soldiers have been engaged on much longer patrols, looking at suspect areas, or people, while staying out of sight themselves. The Army, naturally, has not been at pains to advertise or describe these operations, but they have involved soldiers walking through, and then laying up in, waterlogged or frozen ground for up to four or five days, carefully placing their excrement in polythene bags and taking it away with them so that their presence will not be detected later.

Soldiers who have done this duty repeatedly have sometimes complained that they have lost feeling in their feet for up to a fortnight afterwards. One such soldier, a muscular Guardsman well over six feet tall, was hobbling at the rear of a day patrol I joined on Christmas Day itself, covering country as well as town. His failure to keep up was not due to butterflies in the stomach, though ditches, gates and culverts all take on a quite different appearance in one's mind's eye when one remembers that soldiers have been blown up by bombs placed in or near them. Often the bombs have been placed months before the IRA has decided to trigger them.

The delay was due purely to the unfortunate Guardsman's feet. He said he had had to spend two days laying up in his leather boots, which had been soaked through. He had lost the feeling in his feet on the second day and he had not got it back yet, a week later.

Whether the Army has paid sufficient attention to the question of soldiers' boots is a debatable question; what is less debatable is that a lot of grumbles from men in the Army, whether it be in the bogs and ice of Northern Ireland or the fetid jungles of Belize, are about boots. A civilian may well have four pairs of shoes to suit all sorts of weather conditions, from slip-ons to non-skid thick-soled waterproofs; but a soldier is usually more limited in his choice. On the Christmas Day patrol round the countryside of Newtownhamilton, the Welsh Guardsmen had a choice between the sturdy DMS (Dunlop Moulded Sole) boot, which did not come far up the leg and therefore let the water in, or a lighter-weight boot with higher sides called the Urban Patrol Boot, which was not greatly favoured because it wore out much more rapidly, and was also more restrictive of movement. Would it be possible to devise a boot to suit soldiers' foot problems in the specific conditions of Northern Ireland? And another boot for soldiers in Belize, where the present rubber jungle boots, with hard inner soles, are uncomfortable to wear once they are full of water and the feet become like soft sponges?

'I don't think they listen to the right people when they design Army boots,' said one of the Guardsmen on the Newtownhamilton Christmas Day Patrol — echoing what some soldiers had said to me in the vastly different climate of the Belize jungle.

'Men,' said an officer at the end of the patrol, 'do not always take the proper precautions themselves. All men are told, when they reach the point they are going to lay up, to take off their wet socks and pull on a pair of dry ones. It may sound crazy, when their feet and boots are still soaking wet, but it does make a difference. It may make all the difference between having foot trouble and not having it. I have not suffered from prolonged loss of feeling in the feet myself.'

Neither my experience in Northern Ireland nor in Belize could be called conclusive, but I am not positively convinced that the Army's boffins have been versatile enough about the British soldier's footwear. The point is hardly a trivial one. The boot is the most basic tool of the soldier's trade and effectiveness, and may make all the difference between life and death, not only for himself but also, especially in a place like Northern Ireland, for others who rely on him. Perhaps some of the latest developments at the Ministry of Defence's Clothing Research and Development Centre at Colchester (which include electrically-heated garments) may offer a solution?

Such thoughts about boots, so natural on a routine patrol in Northern Ireland, could themselves cost a life. It is dangerous to think about *anything* except the matter in hand. Are there any suspicious circumstances to the bridge, culvert, ditch or gate ahead? Is there any movement on the skyline of the surrounding hills that might indicate the presence of a sniper? Are the two men ahead, both carrying rifles, really the sportsmen, out for a day's sport, that they appear to be? The men were asked to identify themselves while the patrol held their rifles at the ready in case the explanation was not satisfactory. No, one must really not think about anything except the subject in hand. Even when the patrol walked into a half-completed bungalow on a hillside to check it out, and decided to stay long enough for a quick smoke, there was no real relaxation. We were all out of sight, but the bungalow *could* have been mined, and the nine-inch breeze-block walls would have been no protection if a sniper had opened up with a powerful rifle on the offchance of hitting an invisible target. A machine-gun raking the bungalow could have disposed of our entire patrol.

The Christmas Day lunch back at Newtownhamilton base was rather more comfortable. The officers served the men in their own dining-room, putting the stainless steel trays carrying entire meals onto the cracked melamine dining-room tables, and pouring the men drinks. Such is the tradition of the British Army: on Christmas Day the officers must serve the men, not vice versa, at least *once*, and one could imagine it happening in jungle or Arctic or in the middle of the North German plain, provided an actual invasion was not expected.

For the men of Newtownhamilton and places like it near the Irish border, facing an unseen enemy, such boosts to morale, such affirmations of comradeship between officer and man, have been regarded as especially essential, and accordingly prized.

In the mess room, still bearing the pock marks of the mortar attack, the annual Christmas draw was a great success. This was just as well, as the Sergeant who bought the prizes had to make a helicopter trip, and change cars twice, to get them back to base without making himself too conspicuous a target. The base shop, kept by a Pakistani prepared to accept a monastic life and a considerable degree of danger in return for an extra twopence on a tube of toothpaste, did not stock the sort of prizes offered in the draw — a portable television set, two hair driers, some table lighters, records, radios and sweaters, an electric razor and a cuddly soft toy dog. The maladroitness of the officer taking the numbered tickets from the draw drum was an integral attraction of the show; indeed if he had done it without mishap the men would clearly have felt cheated. He spilled at least twenty tickets on the floor when he should have grabbed only one, producing a great round of applause; he dropped the electric razor to the floor, scattering it into its various components. He looked grateful as he handed out the cuddly toy dog, because the Guardsman who won it got as big a round of raucous applause as he got himself.

At least thirty soldiers (virtually all of those not engaged in active duty on or out of base) attended the Christmas Day church service in the television room. Half a dozen men and officers took Holy Communion: it was the sort of context in which issues of life and death could seem very real, even to young men in their teens and twenties. The Padre was new to the Army, and looked hardly more than a lad himself. He was helicoptered in for the service, a young man who had decided that life in his Welsh village was 'too quiet'. So he did a month's Army conversion course for clerics at Bagshot, did another month at Sandhurst, and joined the Welsh Guards — exactly one week before they were sent to Northern Ireland. He now seemed perpetually cheerful as he wished the soldiers a 'peaceful' New Year and told them, 'Strive to be happy,' a far from empty phrase in the reigning conditions.

Christmas passed peacefully in bandit country, although this went against what Intelligence was available, which suggested that some sort of major IRA offensive might be set up over Christmas. For one thing the IRA had, ominously, said that there would be no cease fire at Christmas this time, unlike previous Yuletides. For another, there was a lady who walked out of a local pub and said to a passing British soldier, 'The IRA will get you, and get you when you least expect it.' This cheerful Christmas greeting was interpreted as meaning that the IRA had something big planned for Christmas. It was filed as Intelligence, showing, incidentally, how slender are the signs by which the British Army sometimes has to work in Northern Ireland.

Perhaps the lady was merely being gratuitously malevolent, or perhaps she *did* know something. A two hundred pound bomb was found in a hijacked mail van left in front of City Hall, Belfast and defused over Christmas, though nothing happened in bandit country itself — except for the constant banging of sporting rifles on Christmas Day, which went on so incessantly that it might have been some sort of demonstration of nonchalance or a war of nerves: at any rate, it forced patrols to investigate constantly, to make sure that IRA fire was not going on under its cover.

For evening meal on Christmas Day at Newtownhamilton, the men had their steak and egg and tea, while in their mess the officers had their roast duck, with wine (Beau Palais vin de table), sherry (South African) and Noval LB port — hardly a sumptuous table for a group of men who had come from Eton (three), Wellington (two) and Sherborne (one).

'Some people may think the Brigade of Guards is anachronistic when they see it on ceremonial duties at Buckingham Palace or St James's Palace,' an officer had said before I crossed the Irish Sea, 'but when you see them in Ireland you will see how impressive they are as real fighting soldiers.'

I admit I had not immediately accepted this remark at the time, but it came much closer to acceptance in the squalid and testing conditions of Northern Ireland. Here even the more arrant snob (which I would like to think I am not) would not like to place his life in the hands of an ex-Etonian if he thought the ex-Etonian was a fool. The moral authority of the youngest officers was, in fact, impressive; and if the Old School Tie can make a nineteen or twenty-year-old officer steady under fire, or under the possibility of fire, then the Old School Tie cannot be dismissed as *totally* ridiculous. Even first names like Roddy, Julian and Romilly become acceptable: a man is entitled to be judged by his performance, not by the encrustations of his background.

The youngest officer I encountered was a 2nd Lieutenant aged nineteen, who had been out of Sandhurst for only seven weeks. Out of uniform he could easily have been mistaken for a boy of fifteen. In uniform he had an authority that blended well with his military background: one uncle and one brother *also* in the Welsh Guards, a father who had been in the Navy. Originally, he said, he had wanted to go into the Black Watch. 'They are the classic, the elite Highland Regiment. I could not see myself in a non-elite regiment. You have got to be honest about it. If you have a job you must *enjoy* it. In any other sort of regiment, I would not have the same interests as some of the other people.'

Such a point of view may be dismissed as social snobbery or not, according to personal taste and conviction. In this case, it certainly went hand in hand with extreme determination in carrying out a tough, demanding and dangerous job around Newtownhamilton. At an age when many people from 'deprived' backgrounds would be wondering what sort of living the world would give them when they came out of university, this young man was wading up to his chest in marshes which might be mined, snatching three hours sleep or none, and then going out on patrol again, and bracing himself to do it for the full four and a half months of his stay in Northern Ireland — with only four days midway through for rest and recreation, two of them inevitably sacrificed in travelling.

Whatever the rights and wrongs of Northern Ireland, whatever the rights and wrongs of officer recruitment resting partly on public school traditions, it is plain that life there forges force of character and cements the relationship between officer and other ranks. Any thought that the officers are forcing the men under them to do things against the IRA they don't want to do, and want to escape from, is purely whimsical. Only one soldier, during all the time I was in Newtownhamilton, came out with a bellicose remark about what he would like to do to the IRA if the restraints were taken off him ('Throw a fire bomb through the window of every house with known IRA connections, and machine-gun anyone who comes out'). And that came from an ordinary soldier, not from an officer.

On the other hand, there was ample evidence that officers and men of even a *Guards* Regiment, with its semi-feudal overtones, learn how to pull together and respect one another's different qualities. It manifested itself in large ways and (possibly more revealingly) in small ones.

One of the calls received in the Operations Room at Newtownhamilton on the evening of Christmas Day came from the Officers Mess, where they were having their roast duck. 'Is there any orange sauce for this duck?'

The Guardsman in the Operations Room hesitated.

Then, slowly he said, 'The Corporal has had a slight accident with the orange sauce, sir.'

A pregnant pause. Roast duck without orange sauce? In the *Guards?* Unthinkable! Then the officer on the other end of the line said in a quite human tone of voice, 'Don't worry him. Forget it.'

Northern Ireland in general, and bandit country in particular, is at least a great, if ghastly, instiller of a sense of proportion, a crystallizer of what is important and what is not important in the relationship between officer and man. But at what a disproportionate price.

The tone of Army life for the British soldier in Belfast itself has been somewhat different. What has chiefly caused the difference has been the problem of the Multiple Interface.

That might sound technical. On the contrary, it is extremely practical and basic and has given the British soldier in Belfast a more ready reminder than his colleague in Crossmaglen or Newtownhamilton that when he *first* went to Northern Ireland in the late 1960's, he did so to aid the police in keeping the peace between the Catholics and the Protestants — and that it was the minority Catholics who most welcomed him.

An Interface, in Army jargon, is where a totally Catholic area directly abuts on to a totally Protestant one. In Central Belfast, the Catholic and Protestant areas are much more clearly defined than in country districts. If an area — perhaps only four rows of streets — is a Catholic one, then virtually all, or *precisely* all, of its citizens are Catholic. If it is Protestant, then all its citizens are Protestant. Any attempt to build new council housing, for instance, for the benefit of the opposite faction, would be regarded almost as an invasion, and would be rigidly resisted. And the streets where one faction's territory directly borders the other's is the Interface where the Army can expect trouble.

Soldiers have to discipline themselves, nevertheless, not

to think of the struggle as being between the Catholics and the Protestants, but as being between the people who want Northern Ireland to be swallowed up by the Republic of Ireland (against the present wishes of the majority of the population), and those who wish to remain part of the United Kingdom.

This necessity — and it is in line with the realities of the Northern Ireland problem, which has an underlying political, rather than religious significance — prompts some strange permutations of thinking and personal reaction in the British officer and soldier.

'I would not call them Protestant and Catholic,' said one officer (a Scot), pointing out to me where the Green and Orange areas merged in Central Belfast. 'I would call them Republicans and Loyalists — probably because I am a Catholic.'

Small wonder that British troops based in Northern Ireland as a whole, and in Belfast in particular, have had an air of permanency even while British officers have acknowledged privately, with increasing emphasis, that the British Army can hardly stay in Northern Ireland, helping the Royal Ulster Constabulary do its job, for ever.

British Army headquarters at Lisburn, just outside Belfast, has been the nearest thing to a secure area the British soldier will find in Northern Ireland — a well-fenced and guarded enclosure in which five hundred men live and into which tradesmen can deliver only if armed with the right sort of passes. It is virtually a village that grew overnight. Here men on a long tour — two years rather than four months or so — can live with their wives, unlike the unaccompanied men on a short tour. In comparative safety, visitors can be briefed on the overall situation: 12,000 full-time British troops involved as the 1980's began, plus 8,000 of the Ulster Defence Regiment (2,500 full-time, the rest part-time), all helping the Royal Ulster Constabulary keep the peace, resulting in a growing acceptance of the police, except near the border with the Republic and in the few areas of virtually all-Catholic Belfast.

The Commander of 39 Brigade, which was looking after the Belfast area, was a Brigadier with experience of anti-terrorism in Borneo and Kenya. He said the essential skill for the peace-keeping forces was terrorist recognition. 'In practice, continuity of contact with the terrorist or suspected terrorist means he is less effective. If it is the Ulster Defence Regiment which is going to be the first line of support to the police in future, we must make the Ulster Defence Regiment a very different force from what it is now. We must assume it can conduct the Intelligence operation, in conjunction with Special Branch, that we now conduct. You would have to make this acceptable in hard Catholic areas, which frankly I don't believe is on.'

There were, said the Brigadier, a smaller number of terrorists about. They had consciously contracted into a small, highly-trained professional guerrilla organization: 'I am talking in terms of fifty to seventy-five people in the whole of Belfast. Their resistance to interrogation has been tested. They don't know among themselves who is planning what. But this had had an effect in our favour. It has tended to divorce them from the population. One of the results has been that the public alongside them are not prepared to stand up and be counted *for* them. There have been demonstrations for which very few people have turned out.'

In this situation, as the British Army began its third decade of major presence in Belfast, maintaining contact with terrorists and suspected terrorists became increasingly important. Informers were in short supply, not wishing to have their kneecaps blown off, or worse, by the Irish Republican Army or other Republican (increasingly Marxist) groups.

Belfast had already showed irritation at the signs of military presence (the check points around the whole of the central shopping area, the armoured 'Pig' vehicles touring the streets, the rule against parking cars for any reason in the outer central region) so the method of maintaining contact had to be one which might seem old-fashioned and

35

wasteful of military man-hours: the simple street patrol on foot. The public relations risks of allowing onto often unfriendly streets young soldiers armed with high velocity self-loading rifles are all too obvious. They have been increased by the fact that in Belfast, as in many other military contexts, the pressure for the 'all-out military solution' has come from the men themselves, not from the officers and still less from the politicians. It would be a great mistake for any anti-Establishment forces to think that the modestly-paid British soldier is aching for a chance to join them: it might be more true to say he was aching for a chance to shoot them out of hand. In Belfast, it is made very clear that he is to go on the streets and into all places where people congregate, but that his task is not to shoot anybody, unless he is fired upon or in a situation where his challenge is answered by flight. His job is to compile Intelligence about who is where.

'Soldiers are incredibly well briefed before they come over here,' said the Commanding Officer of 27 Field Regiment, comprising all batteries in the very centre of Belfast. He was a forty-year-old Lieutenant Colonel, who, like most of his staff and his men, often worked an eighteen-hour day in, or from, the old Grand Central Hotel, a Victorian pile which was condemned before the Army took it over, and which has floors so uneven that, to a civilian, it seems more likely that soldiers will break their ankles than get shot.

But the chance of getting shot has always been a real one: the troops patrol on foot whenever possible, rather than in the armoured Pigs, which separate them too much from the people of the capital city of Northern Ireland. 'The people of Belfast are no more likely to swear at a soldier than they are at a red bus,' said the Commanding Officer. 'They are so used to them. None of the men or the officers I have spoken to think there is a possible military solution to the thing. You might think you can go in with commando tactics, but the number of troops you would need would be phenomenal and then wouldn't beat terrorism. And in any case Britain does not produce that sort of Army. It is a far more understanding and compassionate Army today.'

Soldiers certainly need all their understanding as they patrol streets on foot. Often they are a glaringly illuminated target as they walk around their sectors of Belfast (basically the city is divided up into the central compound and four surrounding parts, the first from twelve o'clock to three o'clock, the next from three o'clock to six o'clock and so on). They may not get shot, but they may get intolerably provoked.

The Intelligence patrol operation I joined was for an area of highest risk, the wholly Catholic area of New Lodge (a jam-packed collection of terraces in half a dozen parallel streets) and the Catholic area around the docks. It was near the traffic lights called Shotgun Corner by the Crumlin gaol, so called because a fortnight before I got there three prison officers — Protestants — had been killed by shotgun blasts. The traffic lights are in the middle of nowhere. To all sides spread demolition sites, deeply muddy when it rains, which is seemingly always; or huge high housing blocks from which any sniper would have a commanding view of patrolling troops. I began to see why incidents in Belfast tend to be more frequent but more minor than in the bandit country nearer the border: the scope for free-lance action is much greater and one strange face is not so likely to be noticed by people friendly to the British troops.

Yet it is the face, and precisely where the face *is*, that is important, and makes sense of foot patrols which otherwise would be pure danger, embarrassment and even, sometimes, farce.

The patrol I joined had a generous measure of all three. It began at Girdwood Park military base, an enclosure just off the city centre, where the Battery Commander, a Major, explained that New Lodge was a very 'hard' area. 'It is full of people who have not done anything overt in our time, but whom we regard as being responsible for suspected terrorism — people with activities not provable in a court of law, the planners who are setting up bombings or, more likely, shootings.'

We left the enclosure at the double, to minimize the most risky part of the proceedings. The only place the terrorists know a patrol will *have* to be at some time is at the gates of its own compound. The purpose was to look inside the public houses of the New Lodge and the dock areas, to see who was about, and who they were with. It was at the very first pub visited that the practical difficulties of the job, and the farcical possibilities, became obvious. 'There is a terrorist sitting there at the back,' said the Battery Intelligence Officer. 'I think I recognize his face.' Unfortunately the pub was in total darkness while a Charles Bronson movie was being shown, and it was impossible to get to the back of the audience without blocking the view of everyone watching the film. As the suspected terrorist had promptly turned his back, both on the patrol and Charles Bronson, his feeling of guilt had to be inferred rather than checked.

A few seconds later, in any case, there were other problems of the sort which tax the good nature of the British soldiers. A very large man, in his thirties or forties, walked deliberately out of the pub, as if in protest, brushing the face of a soldier as he did so with his jacket, which was swinging over his shoulder.

He was asked to identify himself. 'It's my — — -ing country, so - — — off,' was the pleasant response, as Charles Bronson struggled masterfully but unsuccessfully for attention. The man walked out on to the pavement, where he started to lean on the soldiers — much smaller men — until they told *him* to clear off. 'It's my — — -ing country, I do what I like in it,' he said, forgetting that it was *his* decision to — — - off when the troops came into the pub. Eventually *he* — — -ed off. No one else got up from their seat. Everyone continued to watch Charles Bronson, whose conflicts were not so inhibited.

In the second pub, there was a mainly young clientele listening to a guitarist (pubs in Belfast have found it takes some positive inducement to get people out after dark). As attendance was sparse, the soldiers were conspicuous. Within two minutes the proprietor, a Catholic, was very politely asking the senior officer when his men would be leaving, and holding open the door to speed them on their way. The third pub contained, in a back room, a group of twenty-five young girls holding some sort of celebration. Giggling, they invited the soldiers in. Remembering their training, the soldiers remained polite and distant. A friendly girl today could be terrorist bait tomorrow. The fourth pub was unrecognizable as such. The tiny neon sign reading 'Bar' was unilluminated. The small windows had been blocked up with breeze-blocks. No light came from inside: the place could have been empty, derelict. But in the front bar was a group of women drinking beer. In the larger bar there was a group of middle-aged people playing cards; a barman, who said he was off on holiday to the USA shortly, and looking forward to it; and a pile of breeze-blocks, should more be needed. 'This is quite smart compared with some of the bars,' said the Intelligence Officer.

The next pub had 'Welcome' written above the darts board and a two inch thick steel door with a thin observation slit at the main entrance. It was not until the patrol had been recognized that the landlord unlocked the door from the inside and let us in.

'That little chap with the moustache over in the corner,' said the senior officer, 'is probably IRA. A very nasty character. Always swearing at you. Probably upstairs there are some more of them.'

Apart from the big man competing with Charles Bronson, no one swore at the Army on the patrol I joined. Was I imagining a degree of sullen hatred? Perhaps I looked rather military myself. Why did everyone I met on the pavements when with a patrol conspicuously fail to move aside to let me pass, forcing me into the gutter? Why, on the occasions when I made it obvious I was going to stand firm, did they pass me with averted eyes, sometimes looking at their shoes, sometimes at other people who weren't there? Impatience? Dislike of soldiers as such? A desire to hide their embarrassed awareness of their own inner hatred? Or just an unwillingness to get involved with British soldiers in any way, even eye contact, lest they lose a kneecap at the hands of the IRA? It was not easy to measure attitudes, certainly not by what people said — they tended to give the sort of answers they thought you wanted to hear.

The whole patrol, superficially considered, seemed hard and dangerous work for very little result. But the senior officer was not discouraged as we made our way home to base, via an almost entirely deserted social club, where a group of young people playing snooker were asked to identify themselves.

'Some of the positive benefits of foot patrols are negative,' he explained. 'You may learn something by seeing who is *not* around. Is a familiar face missing from its usual haunts, and if so what is it up to? This could be vital information.'

For some of the soldiers, the results may seem irritatingly small; and their gun fingers may at times itch. 'They know,' said the senior officer, 'that someone who shoots a British soldier in a Catholic area gains some kudos. It shows that the terrorist can still function, and it makes him a hero to the neighbourhood.'

What makes one slightly more at ease when patrolling in Belfast rather than in bandit country is that a system of *multiple* bricks — teams of four men in the shape of a rectangle — has been operated. By not operating behind one another, but by circling one another in an apparently erratic way, the bricks put the terrorist in a dilemma. His first priority, before he decides to open fire, is to assure his escape route. He cannot be sure of this if he can see only one or two of the multiple bricks at the same time. The other bricks may be right behind him. It is a technique that has required sophisticated handling, and it has not totally prevented soldiers being shot, but it has served to keep alive many men who would otherwise never have come back to the British mainland.

Fortunately, too, not all contacts between the British Army and the civilian population of Belfast are fraught with danger and the social embarrassment of apparently idle chit-chat in the pubs and on the streets. The Army has built up over the years a reputation as a sort of unofficial welfare agency. From the Grand Central Hotel, the resident Medical Officer and his half-dozen emergency crews have treated not only military casualties but also civilians who have been taken ill. Recent benificiaries have included a man whose heart stopped directly outside the hotel, who was saved by the immediate use of oxygen; a nurse who had an hysterical collapse because she was worried about examinations; and a seventy-year-old man who had a stroke after walking two and a half miles to the nearest bus stop and was treated by a passing Army patrol and Army medical team.

There was also (since, even in Belfast, military life has lighter moments) the strange case of the eighteen stone lady. She was propositioned by a man, who pushed her over in the road when she declined his advances. She was so heavy, and had been celebrating her virtue so well, that she was unable to get to her feet again.

The British Army *did* get her vertical. It was surely one of the strangest of the strange ways that the British Army, hitherto a purely fighting force, has been inveigled into assuming a policing and protective stance by the strange situation in this equally strange part of the United Kingdom.

Certainly no one can begrudge the British Army in Northern Ireland its lighter moments. At the end of my visit there, that point at least was very clear. I took my own emotional temperature and asked myself how I felt. I had coped with some of the strains and dangers faced by British soldiers there with apparent equilibrium. Was it a composure held together with adrenalin and will power? Two days after my return to the easy safety of London, I was left suddenly feeling like an old wrung-out dish rag. The feeling, which took a few days to wear off, is not unknown to British soldiers in Northern Ireland, however excellent their morale may be while actually in the danger areas. Young men in their late teens or early twenties certainly earn their money on their comparatively brief tours there.

Fortunately, Northern Ireland is not typical. Usually today's British soldier labours in more spacious settings, where there is a more encouraging relationship between Britain's Imperial past and her future in the modern world.

2

The White Man's Resurrection

'In Hong Kong, you are expected to have an amah (maid) and this can cost you well over £20 a week. The British Army arranges our accommodation, which is just as well, because my entire salary wouldn't pay the rent of a three-bedroomed flat in this colony. But Hong Kong is still regarded as a very good posting.'

— Captain just returned from a patrol of the Hong Kong-Chinese border.

For the British Army, Hong Kong is a bustling bagful of ironies. The central one might be observed, until recently, through a pair of binoculars on a sunny morning. In Britain's only remaining major colony, her Army did its regular twice-a-year basic physical fitness tests on a hill path it hacked out for itself, called Bowen Road. It is dead flat, stretches two miles around the side of the hill and overlooks the vast blue waters of the world's largest harbour. Soldiers in this hot and damp remnant of the British Empire, enduring humidity which is often as high as one hundred per cent — so that moisture automatically gathers over everything, human beings included — face a demanding test. They must first run one and a half miles in PT vest, combat trousers and boots, in not more than fifteen minutes. Then they must immediately turn and run back in an allotted time, varying from eleven and a half minutes to twelve and a half, according to the age of the soldier. This still goes on, though the venue has been changed for the sake of military and civic convenience.

Admittedly it is not quite so punishing as in the 1840s, when the grip of the British Military on the colony was tighter but when half the men in 'the white man's grave' at any one time died of cholera, bubonic plague or other diseases. Yet the physical fitness test, and Hong Kong life in general, demand from today's defenders of Empire a donation of perspiration and effort that few civilian workers, in or out of the tropics, will be asked to make.

And here is the central irony. In the process, the soldiers — officers and men — command a magnificent view of opulence from which their present status often excludes them. Like Hong Kong harbour itself, which brings in and out of the colony the great wealth in which they do not share. Like the Connaught Centre, built as the highest commercial office block in Asia, in which executives of banking and commercial interests earn money that makes Army salaries look derisory. Like Happy Valley Race Track, in which the seven thousand or so British soldiers, in Hong Kong to help stabilize the place, can scarcely afford to bet.

'The only thing I can afford a bet on,' said a Major, 'is the British general election.' He was ruddy-faced, bald and with an imposing paunch; the sort of man who, in a different age, would have fitted without change of style into the routine of whisky after sundown. 'And all I would bet on *that*,' he added, 'would be a Hong Kong dollar.' (10p or 20 American cents.)

The Major, of course, was being more than slightly whimsical. In any case, to portray the British soldier in Hong Kong as one of the high-caste new poor, assisting the security of an Asiatic new rich (though it might be true as far as it went), would be to draw attention only to the negative side of the irony.

The positive, and far more intriguing, side is this. In an age where colonies are frowned upon by the newly-powerful countries, in which Britain has gracefully relinquished almost all her former Empire, and is seen by many on the international scene as a backer of losers, she is *still* in Hong Kong, and is increasingly welcomed there by China. And she is participating, thanks largely to the British Army, in a highly complex and prosperous area in which East and West, communism and capitalism, meet and interact peaceably at an international crossroads. At best, the British soldiers, sweating their dogged way through their fitness tests, may command a view of a new hope and *modus vivendi* among countries of different systems; a way of life in which the sterile battle of crudely competing social systems may grow into something more mindful of human needs. Even at worst, the British Army's presence will have helped keep open the path for British trade in invisibles — chiefly banking and insurance — for a longer period than those hostile to Britain would have prophesied.

Whatever Hong Kong is, as a sign or portent, it is certainly *not* an easy 'laze about in the sun' for the British soldier. He is apt to become rather touchy if relatives at home see his work in that rosy light.

'The last British battalion we had here had a nasty shock,' said a Captain, who had just come back from patrolling the Chinese border. 'They came from Northern Ireland, and they thought Hong Kong was going to be a rest cure. They found it wasn't. An infantry battalion here probably has as much separation from wives as in Northern Ireland. We spend four months on the border with China or on training exercises. If you add it all up, the average soldier in Hong Kong spends six months away from his own bed out of twelve months. This is a fairly high proportion. You also have a multi-racial problem as well. You have the Chinese, and you have the Gurkhas — 6-7,000 Gurkhas, 2,000 Chinese and about 1,500 British. Then you have problems of pay. But I still like it here.'

Is this because there is an air of newness and optimism about the whole place? Little tailoring, electrical and food shops are jammed into every conceivable corner, so that a frontage of ten feet seems spacious. Is it because a tailor will make you a suit for a third of what the soldier would pay in the United Kingdom? Is it because the atmosphere of Empire (if not the extremes of servility) remains in the local population, so that taxi drivers (charging about half UK prices) will put themselves out to help even a private soldier, and be content with a tip half the size expected in the United Kingdom? Whatever the reason, the British soldier in Hong Kong — and *sometimes* even his wife — has a high morale. And very visibly so.

There is now even a sort of monument to this aspiring mood, clearly visible on the Hong Kong skyline. It is one of the most immediately recognizable landmarks on Hong Kong island itself — a totem to hopes for the future, breaking tactfully some of the links with the past.

The building is HQ British Forces, in the grounds of HMS Tamar. It stands in Edinburgh Place, near the Connaught Centre, the Hilton Hotel and the main Post Office — indeed, could be mistaken by a casual visitor for any of these imposing skyscrapers. It is the Joint Headquarters of British Services in Hong Kong, and takes the name of the Royal Navy depot ship which used to stand near that point on the quay. The whole imposing white block stretches its way through low clouds that often roll down over the craggy hills which make up Hong Kong island. It is just up the road from the equally new Hong Kong police headquarters. This is appropriate. Most of the work of British soldiers in Hong Kong consists of reinforcing the civil power.

HQ British Forces is more than a building. It is a pointer in two respects. It is the first, and perhaps the last, custom-built *Joint* Services Headquarters of the British anywhere in the world. As such it is an exercise in inter-Service co-operation, social mixing and extreme delicacy in matters of conflicting protocol. The customs observed in the Officers Mess are alternatively Navy and Army on succeeding dinner nights, except when a dinner is held to celebrate a particular day — such as Trafalgar Day or Waterloo Day. It is also a reminder that British military presence in the Far East is far from a museum piece. It is a modern reality, streamlined to meet the future.

'A much more efficient and pleasant place to work in,' said a Major chatting with some Naval men in the twenty-sixth floor mess bar, which is as impersonal and unmilitary as the social club of a large company such as ICI or Unilever. The bobbing junks and berthed trading ships of Hong Kong harbour could be seen through the window. 'But less atmosphere of *soldiering*, wouldn't you say? Swings and roundabouts, what?'

It was a hot, humid and drizzly March day in 1979 as he spoke. He was looking down with me on to the densely forested hills where the British Army's Union Jack was being hauled down, for the last time, from the roof of sprawling Victoria Barracks, the home of the British Army in Hong Kong since the 1840s. The graceful collonaded block that housed the old Officers Mess stood empty. So did the nearby car park where, in his war-time underground headquarters, Major General C.M. Maltby decided there was nothing for it but to surrender to the Japanese. Today, however (despite the two ominously mournful bugle calls sounded by a bugler in Victoria Barracks), was no ritual British withdrawal from a former colony. Almost simultaneously, the Union Jack was going *up* on Tamar, both built and manned in a slicker, more modern manner quite in keeping with the new identity of Hong Kong itself — based on commercial adaptability, adroit hustling and the relegation of racial differences to the background.

The new and old buildings reflect the different scale of values. Victoria Barracks has Flagstaff House, home of the Senior Resident Military Commander since 1846: a colonial-style residence, the oldest in Hong Kong, flanked by Chinese stone lions. Tamar has a podium containing car parks, chapel, squash courts, gymnasium, shooting range, storerooms and some offices, all cheek by jowl. Victoria Barracks has an Officers Mess with collonades that speak of polo ponies and whisky under the Flag at sundown. Tamar has eight lifts, air conditioning and a rooftop aerial tower for sending out sophisticated signals. It is small wonder that some officers, who had been moving into it gradually for a year before Victoria Barracks was closed and handed over, felt themselves a little lost.

Tamar, however, for *most* soldiers in Hong Kong, remains a totem rather than a place of work. Essentially, it is a Service headquarters and, like any other headquarters, it does not see the real action. The job of Britain's seven and a half thousand or so soldiers in the colony takes them far from the central district of Hong Kong island, far away not only from HMS Tamar, but also from the finance houses such as the Hong Kong and Shanghai Bank, and smart Oxford Street-style department stores like Lane Crawford, Sincere, Dai Maru and Wing On.

Their main job is to assist the police in internal security, to help the Hong Kong government maintain stability and to show, by their presence, that Britain intends to stay in Hong Kong. 'Any doubt about the latter point,' said a Hong Kong government official, 'and the Chinese would end the whole arrangement with Britain very smartly indeed.'

I have to admit that when I first arrived in Hong Kong, I did not really know what the colony consisted of: a not unusual ignorance among United Kingdom civilians whose way of life is as different from Hong Kong's as a faded governess's is from a young and newly-rich courtesan's.

First, there is the island of Hong Kong itself, off the southern tip of the mainland of China. It is small, much smaller than an English county, and it contains over five million people. Facing the island, and on the coast of the mainland of China itself, is Kowloon, a less fashionable area of Hong Kong, which contains slab after slab of tall government housing blocks — beside which British blocks would look small and demure, especially as the Kowloon versions have washing hung out from almost every window. North of Kowloon, even deeper into the mainland of China, are the New Territories, rapidly being developed. To the north of them is the People's Republic of China, separated from the New Territories either by a wire fence, or by sentries at the most likely crossing points.

Hong Kong island was *ceded* to the British. So was the lower, southerly, half of Kowloon. The New Territories and the half of Kowloon nearest communist China was granted to the British on *lease*, which expires in 1997. Theoretically, the British could hang on to Hong Kong island and half of Kowloon even if the Chinese did not renew the lease to the northern parts of the colony. But, in practice, a Chinese thumbs-down to any part of the Hong Kong deal would mean the end of the British presence. The British are in Hong Kong with the consent of the Chinese and will remain there because it pays the Chinese to have them. They are guardians of a valued trading post with the West. More and more Chinese money is being invested in Hong Kong, and more Western money is being invested in factory development on the communist side of the border.

Three Gurkha battalions guard the border in the New Territories while a rotating United Kingdom battalion (The Royal Green Jackets at the time of my visit) are stationed at Stanley Fort, at the very southern tip of Hong Kong island, originally intended to resist Chinese pirates sailing towards the mainland.

'It is very different from the days when you could see boats coming round the straits, after they had been taken over by the British, with half a dozen Chinese pirates hanging from the yard arm,' said a British officer at Stanley Fort. 'But we are still here.'

The main point of the Stanley Fort siting today is that the presence of the British fighting man is thus discreetly played down. Stanley Fort is half an hour's bus ride from the centre of Hong Kong island itself, and a still longer one, through the new harbour toll tunnel, to Kowloon. For almost every other purpose, including the manning of the Chinese border, the soldiers at Stanley Fort could not be worse placed. It is rather as if the only battalion available for the protection of the UK mainland were to be situated in Cornwall. But soldiers maintain the arrangement is adequate for internal security.

Are there any more paradoxes surrounding the British Army in Hong Kong? There are. It might have been assumed that the easing of tension between communist China and the West would have produced less work for the highly-stretched British soldier. In fact, it produced more. It meant a great rush of both legal and illegal immigrants from China to Hong Kong, later complicated still further by Vietnamese refugees.

I took two trips towards the Chinese border to see for myself the principal reason: the illegal immigration, from communist China, to the New Territories. During my visit to the colony this rose to an all-time peak of over one thousand *per day*. And this figure represented only the number caught and fed back to the Chinese, *not* the unverifiable number who actually crossed but were not caught. I also made a trip across the Chinese border into the ancient southern Chinese city of Canton — once an enclave of British colonialists in houses of British design, and now an agricultural centre with one department store in which (to Western eyes) perfectly ordinary ivory, bone and jade necklaces attract four-deep crowds of sightseers in the same way as the Crown Jewels might do if put on display in Selfridges in London or Gimbels in New York.

From these visits it was all too obvious that a low standard of living (often less than £200 or 400 American dollars a year), plus puritanical fashions in clothes and severe limits to recreation, were potent forces thrusting more Chinese towards the neon-stripped man-made paradise of Hong Kong. It was equally obvious that the extreme difficulty of the terrain was the principal reason that illegal immigrants could lead the British Army and the Hong Kong police such a time-consuming dance. Certainly the British Army in Hong Kong today needs a far more sophisticated mode of soldiering than would serve in the days when it seemed the sun would never set on the British Empire.

My first view of operations against illegal immigrants was in the Sai Kung peninsular, halfway up the east coast of Kowloon — a length of coast with many convenient small islands on which it was easy for illegal immigrants to beach their boats, before swimming to the mainland of Kowloon, or before setting out in their boats again after drying soaked clothes. It meant a drive past Hebe Haven, where the staff of Cathay Pacific have their yachts and where millionaires' large white houses (some of the few single-occupation private houses to be seen in a community almost exclusively given over to high-rise flats) are side by side with an old open sewer.

The joint military police operations in Hong Kong are carried out from what are called Pol-Mil headquarters. Several of them are spread around at strategic points throughout the colony. The Pol-Mil headquarters of Sai Kung was the local police station on the seashore. It had a pepperpot observation tower pointing seawards from the roof, a legacy of the days when marauding pirates frequently tried to land. Now the only people trying to land were the illegal immigrants. It was a sorry spectacle. Some of them had tried to land near the police station itself; others were noticed by Joint Services helicopter patrols in the act of beaching their vessels on nearby little islands; still others were noticed only because of clothes left to dry on the beaches, and had to be winkled out of woods nearby. Many of them were picked up, hauled into a Wessex RAF helicopter and deposited, under guard, on the emergency helicopter landing pad. This was a muddy, churned-up and waterlogged football pitch at the back of the police station itself. Pigs and cows, which had been grazing on the grass of the football pitch, made way in the rain for the demoralized helicopter cargoes. They were mostly under-sized and undernourished Chinese in faded blue or grey dungaree suits. They came seeking money, colour and greater freedom. Instead they ended up crouching, hands on heads or wrapped around chests, on the floors of the police station, before being taken to the border and handed back to the Chinese authorities.

'We started at eight-thirty this morning and we've been going ever since,' said the Naval pilot of a Scout Army helicopter (an example of Joint Services co-operation) as rain stopped play at half past four in the afternoon. 'We have covered all the islands to the east and the area further up to the north, towards the border. The weather has been foul up there. We did an arrest by putting down a Company Commander and his two men. The immigrants ran but were caught. They are never pleased to be caught, you can bet. We sometimes get some resistance, but usually there is nothing for them to do but come along quietly. Combing these islands would take a whole day on foot, but the helicopter can do it in fifteen minutes, and we can be in contact with the Hong Kong police launches all the time. It is probably the most interesting thing we now do over here, from the military point of view. It is more demanding than the routine "taxi service" sort of work we do a lot of the time out here.'

The men with the final responsibility for the way these helicopter parties operated were the Company Commanders of the particular Army unit involved. One of them, a Major of the 1st Battalion, The Royal Green Jackets, said: 'If you see immigrants on the mainland, they usually run like mad, but on the islands there is no point in resistance because there is nowhere for them to go. We have had to use force today. The more of these operations we have, the less time we have for training. Everything had to be dropped today. I was told at eight yesterday evening that we might have to mount a patrol against illegal immigrants, but I didn't know for certain until one this morning. It does cause disruption to personal and military routine. I don't think that any wife particularly likes such separation either. They get six months a year separation in Hong Kong, and the battalion has been in Northern Ireland six times in eight years, for four months in each case. The wives have had quite a bit of separation before they came to Hong Kong. Hunting for illegal immigrants is accepted, but the more there is of it, the less acceptable it becomes.'

Other soldiers agreed that doing one's duty when it involved cold and wet refugees required more skill and diplomacy than a shooting war. 'You have to remind yourself of certain things,' said one soldier as he stood in the rain outside Sai Kung police station, competing for space with the cows and the pigs. 'Of course you feel sorry for immigrants, when they arrive wet and hungry. But then you remember that a lot of the crime in Kowloon comes from recently-entered immigrants. They may be misfits in China who are going to be equal misfits in Hong Kong. Our team have been catching an average of thirty-four a day — which is good going or bad going, depending on the way you look at it.'

Most soldiers were sure the way they were handling the illegal immigrants situation was enhancing their standing in the eyes of the civilian population of Hong Kong, just as their standing in the United Kingdom had been improved by the job they were doing in Northern Ireland. 'When I came down from university in 1967,' said one young officer, 'there was a much greater anti-military feeling than there is now. People are beginning to see soldiers *do* have a value in the modern world.'

The British soldier's tact and diplomacy becomes more valuable the nearer the Chinese border he gets. My second expedition was up the Fan Ling Road to the village of Sha Tau Kok, at the very eastern end of the twenty-mile border between China and the New Territories. I was the first writer allowed to go there, following the easing of Sino-British tensions. I arrived (via the resettlement areas around the hills of Sha Tin village, where people were housed in shacks after their old homes had been knocked down, preparatory to having new tower blocks built for them on the sites of the demolished shacks) at a moment of especial tension. It was the worse for being totally unexpected and out of character.

The officer escorting me had only just said: 'The border at the point we are going to has no fencing, and when the Irish Guards were here, some soldiers went across the border and were held for some hours. But it is much better now.' In the light of this assurance, the slight jumpiness of the armed Hong Kong police at the concrete road blocks at the beginning of the 'closed' border area was rather mysterious to me. Beyond this point, no civilian could enter without a pass. A mile or so up the road, under the shadow of the China Mountain in the People's Republic of China, there was the police station of Sha Tau Kok, standing in its own wire compound and commanding, from its flat roof, a perfect view of the street one hundred yards to the north. The centre line of this street was the border between the People's Republic and the New Territories.

The only visible sign that the far side of the street was different from the near one was a single Chinese Army sentry in typical green uniform, with no badges of rank. He was marching up and down. The Commander of a Company of the 2nd Battalion/2nd Gurkha Rifles, a Major responsible for observation of the area of China stretching from the sea to the east to the vast China Mountain to the west, explained to me calmly enough the role of the Army at this border point.

'First,' he said, 'it is an observation task. We observe the Chinese side of the border. We are interested in all aspects of Chinese military training or militia training. That includes equipment, dress, visitors, the general day-to-day behaviour and training patterns of the country across the border. It remains at the same level after the relaxation of tension. They have a fair number of visitors — they come to see what the British are up to. They all wear Mao jackets so you don't know whether it is a dignitary from Peking.'

The Major, too, seemed a little tense as he pointed out the pillboxes from which the British watch the Chinese, and the pillboxes from which the Chinese scrutinize the British. I asked him why. The previous day, he explained, a Gurkha soldier had found himself just inside Chinese territory; had been surrounded by the Chinese Militia (politically-conscious community police of the People's Republic of China) and ordered to squat on the ground. It was some hours before the soldier was passed back across the border into the New Territories.

There were two conflicting stories about how this happened. According to the local newspaper, the *South China Morning Post*, the Gurkha soldier had unknowingly crossed the border line to buy a pair of underpants from a stall on the wrong side of the street, and had been seized by the Chinese Militia. This story was offensive to the military Top Brass, because it implied that a Gurkha soldier had behaved in a silly way. But the version discussed privately by the British military was just as irritating because it could not be stated publicly without offending the Chinese. According to some eye witnesses of the whole incident (which was in view at all times from the roof of the police station of Sha Tau Kok) the Gurkha had been on the Hong Kong side of the border when he had been jostled and nudged in the direction of the line by a Militia man, after which more Chinese Militia men arrived on the Hong Kong side of the border and asked him to sit down on the road. After the man had been released, a high-ranking Chinese official had arrived with an apology. In short, the Militia men had been over-zealous, possibly not believing too firmly in the new Sino-British accord. The trouble with this explanation was that it would pose more questions than it would answer, not to mention cause more trouble than it would avoid. The British Army bit its lip, and let matters rest as they were, rather than embarrass the communist Chinese further. Soldiering was indeed easier in the days of the Charge of the Light Brigade, when there was a clearly defined enemy and anything done against him was acceptable.

The Major at the border (a very responsible looking thirty, in spite of his fair mop of hair, schoolboy face and disabling handshake) even managed to insinuate that the train of events had been positively encouraging. 'Twelve years ago, the slightest event on the border would have been turned into a statement by the Chinese that the Hong Kong side was to blame. You would drive along in your Land Rover and a woman would overturn her cart and accuse you of knocking it over. I first came in 1971. Since then there has been a lessening of tension on both sides. Incidents can be settled in a way which is very amicable. Before, guards would have spat at us. Now they don't. We no longer have to patrol with rifles at the ready. You will see soldiers today walking back through the fields in rolled-up sleeves. Seven years ago, they would have had rifles, live rounds and a very high degree of readiness ... This time, after the Gurkha incident, local dignitaries from the other side came and apologized. A few years ago they would have said it was our fault. Today there was a more rational appreciation of what happened. Everyone shook hands and dispersed.'

It was just as well that such mutual trust had developed. It was needed when dealing with illegal immigrants from the China side. There had been reports of some immigrants firing on British troops, and other reports of Chinese guards firing on immigrants. Officially there was, at the time of my visit, no contact between British and Chinese troops at the border. Unofficially, each side was helping the other by gesticulating in the direction where illegal immigrants had been spotted. To old-stagers who remembered the Chinese border a decade previously, it must have been almost as remarkable a sight as British and German soldiers in the First World War drinking toasts in the same trench at Christmas time. It created the optimistic hope in some soldiers that eventually the brisk traffic in illegal immigrants would be a thing of the past as each side of the border grew closer culturally, socially and even financially.

The sight of Canton province in the Republic, I have to say, did not convince me, or many soldiers who have also seen it, that such a hope is very near to realization. Foreign visitors doing their shopping are stared at by rapidly-forming groups. Large concert halls may be filled with peasants talking through classical music from countries of the communist bloc (an unbalanced diet of Tchaikovsky, Rimsky-Korsakov, Enesco, Chopin and so on), and attending closely only during dance routines involving brilliantly colourful traditional costumes in very marked contrast to their own grey conformity. Old women sweep 'main' roads which are little more than loose gravel tracks. The sight of all this can add up to a vivid statement that Chinese-Hong Kong economic and cultural parity, which alone might finally remove the illegal immigrant problem, is a great deal further away than is the more limited goal of mutual respect.

With China investing in Hong Kong, and Hong Kong interests investing in the Republic, is it at least much nearer than it was? Economic observers are cautious. Western investment in China is being made in industry, whereas Chinese investment in Hong Kong is mainly in the form of property and real estate. The two do not balance one another out. In the areas near the border, on the Chinese side, the Chinese are building small assembly factories for goods such as electronic components, using labour drawn from the Hong Kong side of the border. The Chinese appear to be raising the wages of agricultural workers and establishing light industry rather than going on a spending spree — establishing heavy industry with Western help — as was originally forecast. In these circumstances, the day when Hong Kong will no longer seem relatively so rosy to Chinese immigrants is still distant; and while it remains distant, the presence of the British Army to deal with illegal immigration will be imperative.

The equalization of life in Hong Kong and China is indeed a 'long way away', according to one observer, Anthony Rowley, business editor of the *Far Eastern Economic Review*, which has its headquarters in Hong Kong: 'Hong Kong is a little enclave at the bottom of what is still a very undeveloped country. There is a long way to go yet before China and Hong Kong have anything in common economically. China is not going to match Hong Kong's standards overnight; it will happen over a period of time.' Illegal immigration, he thought, was 'going to be a problem for a long time'.

There have certainly been signs (even if illegal immigration has not again reached the thousand-a-day mark it passed during my visit) that the British Army need not expect an easier life in Hong Kong. It has been called upon to build a sixteen foot tall barrier fence by the border. At the same time the 42nd Commando, Royal Marines, were launching high speed Rigid Raiders (a sort of raft) to head off illegal immigrants while still at sea. Vietnamese refugees have also made the problem much worse.

It was by this time very obvious to me that whatever soldiering in modern Hong Kong is, it is *not* a sunny holiday. It often requires great stoicism as well as great diplomacy. It is no accident that three of the four British Army battalions in Hong Kong are Gurkhas. These tough and traditionally loyal soldiers from landlocked Nepal on the Indian sub-continent are probably the last tangible left-over from the days of the British Raj in India. It was then that some (the 2nd Gurkha Rifles, the Senior Gurkha Regiment of the British Army) won their right to swear their oath of loyalty to the Queen (be it Victoria or Elizabeth) *not* on the usual regimental flag, but on a great decorated truncheon given to them by Queen Victoria after they had fought successfully, on two fronts at once, while defending the North-West Frontier of India. The truncheon is of bronze, about five feet long, and portrays, at the top, the British crown being supported by three Gurkhas.

Their headquarters is at Sek Kong, a mile or so away from the Chinese border and roughly in the middle of its twenty-mile length. To reach it entails travelling up the Route Twsk to the west side of Kowloon and the New Territories, and then turning into less-used roads towards the interior.

The administration block and the Officers Mess are both built around a square, with a patch of green, bearing sub-tropical trees, in the middle. All this is very foreign. But in the Officers Mess the Gurkha waiter wears a uniform designed by the mess committee: white cricketing flannels, white cricketing shirt, white tennis shoes and a regimental stable belt of his own regiment. Meals in the bar are served on circular bronze tables. The offices are air-conditioned at a suitably English temperature. There is a reassuring

British lady secretary, who might have stepped straight out of Cheltenham, to administer cold drinks or Indian tea to visitors. The air is full of clipped stiff-upper-lip English public school accents. These turn out, as often as not, to belong either to British Officers who are in fact Gurkhas or Queen's Gurkha Officers (a somewhat different breed, usually Nepalese, who have come up through the ranks instead of, like the British Officers who happen to be Gurkhas, through Sandhurst).

At the border, another Major, who was in charge of the inland section of the border itself, had given his estimate of the Gurkhas as a people and as a military force. 'We have a strong colonial influence in the Brigade of Gurkhas. We have more Kenyans and New Zealanders than any other unit. What we end up with in terms of military character is a reflection of it: people who are used to living in a rural atmosphere and quite often with a background of living in foreign countries. In this regiment we are very strong in the father-son syndrome. We have quite a lot of officers whose fathers also served. The roll looks exactly the same as the one in the 1930s — the same surnames. The Prince of Wales, who is our Colonel-in-Chief, came out recently. On parade was one Gurkha whose father got the VC. Beside him was another Gurkha whose father had commanded the section in which the *other* chap's father got the VC. It all adds up to welding us together in what is very much a family regiment.'

Other officers said that the Gurkha was invaluable because he was less liable to boredom than his British counterpart, even if slower on the uptake. He might have very little formal education, but he was less likely to abuse the friendliness of his officers.

There was certainly no trace of racial discrimination as such at the headquarters of the Gurkha Field Force in Hong Kong. All the proof needed was in one cheerful upper-class voice. It belonged to a Captain of Nepalese extraction. He was a thirty-year-old British Officer (Sandhurst 1969-71),

•

an officer of the 6th Gurkha Rifles who was at that time doing duty on the staff.

'My father was in the Army, actually,' said the Captain ('Bugs' to his colleagues). 'He was a GCO with the 1st/2nd Gurkha Rifles. GCOs went out ten years ago; they correspond with the Queen's Gurkha Officers, who have become very good, actually. I was going to be a doctor, but I got fed up with the books and threw them away. I have always been an outdoor type of man, you see. The Army offered me these things. I was in pre-medical school at Katmandu. After a week I backed out and went home. My father just said, "It's up to you." The British Army has been everything I expected.'

There are thirteen British Officers from Sandhurst with Nepalese skins in the Brigade of Gurkhas. This particular Captain said he certainly didn't see the phenomenon as an out-of-date left-over of the British Empire. 'No, I consider myself very much part of today's British Army. The men feel the same. My experience of Sanders? Most enjoyable two years of my life. You worked hard, played hard. Certainly being a "foreigner" — in quotes — didn't matter! I was accepted in every way as a British cadet.'

The Gurkhas are of practical benefit to the British in guarding Hong Kong. There are also strong sentimental ties that serve the Nepalese, as well as the British, rather well. The Gurkhas may have been formed in 1815; they may have been used to protect the no longer significant North-West Frontier of India from 1863; but they still have an impact on the international scene. There are five battalions of them, each of just under nine hundred men, plus units of Gurkha signalmen, engineers and drivers, serving in places as widely separated as Belize and Korea. To the United Kingdom itself they may be largely invisible: there is one battalion based in Britain, but its use in Northern Ireland has been judged inexpedient.

But in their own villages in the remoteness of Nepal, the Gurkhas continue to be admired figures and family providers. They send home much of their wages, diligently learn English by oil lamp, and when they go back to their native village it is quite possible that the village has been enriched by the welfare scheme operated by the Brigade of Gurkhas. This helps with matters as various as schools and landslips, and is privately funded.

I met the Brigadier, Brigade of Gurkhas, in his Hong Kong headquarters. When he started the conversation by telling me the story of how he, as a young 2nd Lieutenant, had taken disbanded Gurkhas from six regiments back to Nepal after the Second World War, I thought he was laying the emotion on a bit thick. But his attitude was reflected in much younger British Officers, including the senior officer who said, 'If we wanted another two thousand Gurkhas, we could get them tomorrow.' Plainly he would have liked to do the recruiting himself.

Hong Kong is a good catalyst for the mixing of races: suburbia and its values seem very far away. It is also a place where different ideologies can sniff one another cautiously. It is thus another of the paradoxes of Hong Kong that the growing ease between Britain and China (once the most militant of the egalitarian powers) has created a glut of illegal immigrants to Hong Kong, and that this glut has indirectly helped to prolong the effective life of jungle scouts like the Gurkhas in the post-Imperial British Army.

To help him withstand the often unexpected strains of service in a colonial territory which is not a holiday paradise, the British soldier has opportunities of relaxation which are denied to many others. They would make soldiers in, for example, the sparse and struggling country of Belize think they were in an Oriental heaven.

Officers are able to sun themselves beside the Causeway Bay swimming pool of the Royal Hong Kong Yacht Club. The pool is surrounded by green plastic imitation grass, and its outdoor bar not more than waiter-summoning distance away from any customer. 'It is nice here because you can let the children swim and know they are safe,' said one officer's wife drinking a poolside Gunner — a drink made of ginger beer, lemon juice and other fruit juices which give it a gaseous kick belying its totally non-alcoholic content. 'There are so many other mothers around, watching their own children. And in any case, we have a lifeguard always on duty.'

Imperial pleasures, indeed. It is poetic justice that the British Army — or at least its officers — should still be able to enjoy the privileges of the Royal Hong Kong Yacht Club as it was by their initiative that the club was founded. But gratitude is not everlasting, and now the Army has to pay the full club subscription — the same one as the Hong Kong bankers and merchants who are among the civilian members.

'It's only right,' say the Army officers piously. Perhaps they are anxious to meet the democratic spirit of the times. Possibly they are too humbled to argue, now that it is obvious from bar takings that they can no longer be regarded as the big spenders. They, at any rate, spend more than the non-commissioned ranks in Hong Kong, who have to do their swimming at the excellent modern outdoor pool of HMS Tamar, or take their chance on one of the beaches. These are not only overcrowded but also polluted by refuse in the summer season.

The 'in thing' for the Army is to get off the island of Hong Kong itself at the weekend and enjoy the comparative quiet of the adjoining islands. Both officers and men can — and do — take themselves off on the ferry (first-class, of course, for Europeans, which means entering the air-conditioned cabin or sitting on the boatdeck with other Army personnel or well-off civilians). One of the favourite trips is to Lantau, an island no more than an hour away by slow ferry. The roads over the rolling hills are still incomplete, and bathing is possible from the obscure and rarely-visited bays.

Lantau island is distant enough from Hong Kong island, but not completely cut off from the Imperial tradition. In some of the roadside cafés, on the roads that wind their way uphill from the ferry quay, the beer the Army men drink may have to be the Chinese Tsingtao, because they have never heard of Watneys or Courage or Adnams; but pictures of the Queen are apt to be displayed — pinned, if necessary, on to canvas awnings.

There is little incentive for soldiers to spend their spare time gambling. I did not discover a gambling casino on Hong Kong island; the two race tracks (the only places where the placing of bets is legal) are not conveniently near the various barracks; and to gamble in any other way means taking a trip from Hong Kong itself. Even so, the guardians of British colonial rule who venture further afield for gambling at gaming tables are at a disadvantage to the civilian population of Hong Kong, who must be among the best-financed and most ferocious gamblers in the world.

Macau, the Portuguese colony on another tip of land on the mainland of China, one hour's fast hydrofoil ride away from Hong Kong, has seen many a routing of the British Army gambler. At the roulette table, a soldier may chance chips worth two dollars (20p) on a number and a colour, when prosperous Hong Kong civilians are making the same bets in thousands of Hong Kong dollars. Small wonder that wives are apt to urge their husbands to stay away from the biggest of the gaming casinos — the art deco-style Hotel Lisboa — and instead buy them some Chinese antiques from quayside places like Yee Chai Curios, claiming it will be a good investment back home in the UK. British soldiers tend to keep clear of the north half of the island. Here Chinese-run curio stalls just on the Macau side of the China Gate (which separates Macau from the People's Republic of China) sell 'bone' and 'ivory' items which look remarkably like plastic. Here, too, Macau frontier police, standing near a grim black notice reading 'No photographs' in four languages, look menacingly at anyone merely carrying a camera. The ease on Hong Kong's border with China is not discernible on Macau's.

There is general agreement that British soldiers in Hong Kong are far better behaved than the rude soldiery of colonial myth. The Wanchai area of Hong Kong island, west of the central area, is the colony's Soho, or 42nd Street. It is full of girlie bars, brashly touting for custom. It is nevertheless rare for the British Military Police, who are strategically stationed throughout Hong Kong, Kowloon and the New Territories, to make arrests because of trouble. There was only one disturbance when I was in Hong Kong. From the fact that the British Military Police merely stood in the street outside a club until Canadian Naval officers arrived, I deduced that the incident did not concern a British soldier but crew members of a Canadian frigate moored at HMS Tamar at the time. Another factor assists the virtue of the average British soldier here. The local bar girl syndrome is expensive for him. It is likely to involve buying out the girl from the bar at about £15, paying her £40 or so for two hours, and then paying another bar penalty of £15 if she is kept away from the bar longer. At these prices, the most randy British soldier tends to find virtue attractive.

David Stevens, a mechanical engineer and ex-multi-national company executive in the Far East, was running, at the time of my visit, an English pub quaintly called the Rose and Crown, in Stanley Main Street, Stanley Fort. Stanley — the village with Stanley Fort Barracks nearby — is practically a European enclave at weekends. Walking down Stanley Main Street is rather like walking down the main street of a Cornish or Connecticut seaside village. Mr. Stevens established the Rose and Crown in the bottom storey of a tall new apartment and office block in 1978. He had become fed up with the bureaucracy of large multi-national companies and wanted to 'do his own thing'. He had the pub built with dark oak beams, exactly as a good old English pub might *appear*, and sat back wondering what sort of custom he would get.

'Three quarters of my custom comes from the British Army, and almost all of them are not officers,' said David Stevens in the quiet and decorous bar filled with British Army men. 'We get very few senior ranks coming in. But — and this is a very interesting point — by and large the behaviour of the men is very good. At first some of the civilians didn't come in, because they figured it was *not* going to be good. But in fact, a drunken civilian is worse than a drunken soldier, especially in Hong Kong. The chaps in the British Army are very used to discipline. If there is any sign of trouble you just go up to them and say, "Now look chaps. . ." and they quieten down. Civilians will say aggressively, "What the bloody hell do you mean?" The difference is noticeable.'

Of course, the tone did vary with the particular regiment which was posted at Stanley Fort. At the time we spoke, The Royal Green Jackets were there. 'The main body of them just want a local. After their work in the evening, they change into civilian clothes and come here for a few beers before going back to barracks or going up into Wanchai for the bars there. While they're here, their drinking is fairly moderate. This regiment is a lot better behaved than a previous regiment, an infantry regiment I won't name.'

Was *part* of the British soldiers' comparatively abstemious ways due simply to lack of money? He thought not. 'By some Hong Kong standards, the British Army people get quite a lot of money. A Corporal would probably be getting about three thousand dollars (about £300) a month, I would guess. That's a lot of money by some Hong Kong standards. If you compare that with a young Inspector joining the Hong Kong Police, the Inspector is lucky if he is getting the same amount, and he is much more experienced.'

One of the oddities of life for the Army in Hong Kong is, indeed, that, though the lower ranks are better off than Hong Kong Chinese at *their* social level, the British officers and their wives are financially well below the highly paid Hong Kong business community with which they are expected to mix, if they mix at all. It is the private soldier who, more justifiably than the officer, feels himself to be the aristocrat of local life in Hong Kong. Many officers try their best to impress this on their own children, so they will not give themselves airs their parents' income cannot sustain. 'You will see some children of officers in the Royal Hong Kong Yacht Club shouting orders at the waiters because they think that is the way Daddy shouts at his troops,' said one officer's wife. 'It will make it very uncomfortable for them when they go back and try to live in the United Kingdom. Some of the children stand with their hands behind their backs like officers are supposed to do, and they are only ten or twelve.'

One of the rare disadvantages of the Hong Kong presence — apart from the very hard work — is the fact that the supposedly traditional Officer Class expectations of life are reinforced. There are allowances for amahs (maids) and other perks not handed out in the United Kingdom. 'It is something to be watched,' said one officer sunning himself beside the swimming pool of the Royal Hong Kong Yacht Club. 'But I think most of us do watch it.'

The sheer wealth of the civilian population around them may sometimes tempt the British Army men and women into small *social* snobberies, but it is hardly likely — mercifully — to tempt them into arrogance that would endanger goodwill towards the British in their remaining jewel of Empire.

In any case, it is in a rather different, much less sophisticated and much less potentially corrupting setting, that the British soldier of today gets his most direct reminder of the world of Kipling, the Raj, and the British as masters of the world's hottest places and most threatening jungles — Belize.

3

The Last Real Jungle

'Is Belize ours? You can hardly tell. All the signs seem to say Coca Cola, most of the cars are American, and the place looks Spanish. The people of Belize are very proud of their new internal independence, even if the country is still British.* And yet when we sent in the Harriers, and more troops, because the Guatemalans next door were making threatening noises, Belize people shouted and danced in the streets.'

— Major in British Army Officers Mess just outside Belize City.

I was in the middle of the thick Belize jungle with a patrol of twelve Royal Highland Fusiliers. Possibly they were among the last of the British soldiers who will carry on the Kipling tradition of jungle patrol *anywhere* in the world — except, perhaps, for practice or as part of a United Nations force. Almost certainly, most of them would have preferred a larger Empire in which to operate.

'Our Empire is shrinking,' said one of the Fusiliers (who are otherwise known as Princess Margaret's Own Glasgow and Ayrshire Regiment), as he threw his heavy pack on to the ground of a dark clearing and wiped his dripping forehead. 'And our job is shrinking with it.'

As they all sat down in the fetid shade of an enormous attap tree, its branches rising like ferns forty feet high, they looked carefully around for snakes — especially the dreaded fer de lance, whose victims rarely live to tell the tale. Then they began brewing up tea in their billy cans and

* Later its independence was formalised, though British troops remained.

67

eating a tasteless though nutritious concoction of processed meat straight out of the can, cold.

The temperature was getting towards one hundred degrees, and the humidity made it seem even hotter. The humidity of this southern part of the tiny British colony, just south of Mexico on the Atlantic side of Central America, is as legendary and as inviting as the fer de lance. The shade given by the surrounding trees was imperfect. The Fusiliers jungle boots, and mine, were full of water from the river we had just waded through up to our navels, keeping a careful eye out for water snakes and alligators, which *do* exist in Belize, though not in large numbers. Their tropical kit was soaked either in river water or rancid sweat. And they had encountered these conditions many, many times before, even if they might not encounter them many, many times again.

It was small wonder that, though the underlying morale would have been more than enough for any emergency, there was some minor mumbling and grumbling in the party. One soldier advised me that the food wouldn't seem so bad if I closed my eyes; the man with the machine-gun said it could fire two hundred rounds on one belt of ammunition but it still *felt* like a ton though it was only thirty pounds.

I accepted this mild grumbling as the routine protest of the healthy soldier who is not especially interested in shaping himself up for promotion. The officer in charge of the party, who was twenty-one years old that day, and understandably anxious that I should see he had command of his men, reached the end of his patience and went on the counter-offensive. 'Well,' he said to the men, 'you'd rather this than Northern Ireland, wouldn't you?'

It was a valiant try by a young officer still feeling his way into the techniques of man management, by which the Army now sets such great store. As a rhetorical question it nevertheless failed — failed disastrously at one level and, more importantly, revealingly at another.

'At least in Northern Ireland, you can *shoot*,' piped up

a Royal Highland Fusilier who was scarcely younger than his senior officer. 'This is unreal.' There was an angry buzz of assent from the rest of the men, though they were plainly amazed at their colleague's temerity in actually saying it.

It would be a mistake, I then realized, to assume the British soldier of today is a tough pug-nosed oaf who does not have a feeling for the relevance of his job; just as it would be most definitely a mistake to assume that a slightly browned-off soldier in difficult conditions, born and bred into the British welfare state, would not be eager to fight. The *absence* of a fight is more likely to worry him, especially in terrain he cannot easily relate to.

The Guatemalan Army at that time numbered over thirteen thousand men in six Infantry Battalions and supporting Arms, some of them trained by the United States' Green Berets in counter-insurgency and commando techniques. But they could, normally, be relied on to stay on their side of the border.

A soldier needs an enemy; and heat, mosquitoes and beef bugs, which enter the skin and grow into the size of a human finger while still inside you, do not in themselves constitute a big enough enemy to keep the adrenalin flowing. This fact, rather than the irritations of life in a tropical climate as such, was, I became sure, the worst irritation — a manageable one — faced by the British Army in Belize. The risk of possible invasion is, of course, always there; but it does not *dramatize* itself to the ordinary soldier as much as it does in some other parts of the world. Unless, that is, the jungle stimulates his sense of history.

Of all the present-day theatres of Army activity, Belize gives the soldier the nearest approximation he is ever likely to feel to being a Kipling hero. He will patrol the jungle, not as he would do while on exercises in Borneo, but for real. He will live in a camp where the Union Jack on the flagpole of a jungle patrol post and a palm tree can both be in the photograph he sends home. And yet it is also a place where remaining signs of Britishness are few and far between. Indeed, the serving soldier has to remind himself continually that the place is British, so parted has the tiny country become from visible British influence. Britain is still responsible for defence and foreign policy, but the serving soldier sees a country which could be American or Spanish rather than British, in which his relations with the local people can be only skimpy.

Certainly many soldiers going there have little idea of what they will find. I talked to some of the men who were on the same plane as myself, the once-weekly Belize shuttle. One of them said, 'All I know is that it's out somewhere hot, and I shall be there for six months. I came because some of my pals were going, so I thought I'd join them.' I had no cause to feel superior: I had had to look the place up on the map myself. Very few British civilians I asked could say with certainty where Belize was.

On arrival, the young soldier is apt to be puzzled by the environment which claims him. The aircraft will land him on the only airfield in the country which can take large jets: Belize International. This is rather a grand name for a modest single strip of tarmac with a reception lounge the size of a large drawing-room, containing cold drinks machines which can be as temperamental as the hard-pressed staff.

The air strip is used for ordinary civilian aircraft as well as for delivering servicemen to the little nation. In addition, it doubles as a military airfield. Harrier jump jets take off and land. They are housed, with defending soldiers, including the RAF regiment and local volunteers, within easy reach of the airfield, but not on it. Though it is thought of as Belize City airport, it is in fact much closer to British Services Headquarters at Airport Camp than it is to Belize City itself. The City is about six miles away, and not invariably popular with British soldiers who go there hoping for bright lights. Mess life is limited; but Belize City is not, for the British soldier, an ideal home-from-home.

The centre of the city is really a shanty town with wooden hut houses and shops built on stilts; open sewers running along almost every street, with walkways above them leading to the few available hotels; a really wide open sewer bisecting the town and dim street lighting. It must be a relief to the serving soldier when he realizes that the Belize citizen, though prickly about any insult to his country, is nevertheless not prone to the knife fights and gun-play that sometimes boil up in the capital cities of the main islands of the Caribbean.

It would almost be possible to believe that every shop and café in Belize City was called Pepsi or Seven Up. These signs are above almost all of them, and constitute the nearest thing to the positively immaculate to be seen in public. Otherwise it is only well out of the centre of the city, along the coast road, that elegance is to be found; and then it is in the Spanish lines of the large houses with balconies commanding magnificent sea views. They are probably owned by Indian traders. Neither in the impoverished city centre, nor in the handsome houses of the Atlantic coastline, will the British soldier find evidence that the place counts as 'ours'. It came as a distinct shock when, after being there a week, I found myself posting a letter in a cast iron pillar box that might have been found at any street corner of Hendon or Huddersfield.

Neither can the serving soldier relate with any great certainty to the local environment by listening to Belize Radio. Its tone is as proselytizing as Jamaica Radio, with talk of the implications of national thrift and self-respect. But its accent is American: the Sunday Bible session is conducted by men with Transatlantic voices, and the exhortations could be from Martin Luther King or Dr Billy Graham rather than, say, the Archbishop of Canterbury. There is no trace of Englishness. The soldier, one feels, is most at home when he is at work.

This can be arduous and demanding, and must at least *assume* that an invasion could happen the next day. Invading Guatemalan troops could move in easily only on two roadways, and the route could easily be made virtually impassable, or very difficult, by the Harriers. The RAF Harriers command the field and, in these circumstances, guarding them has high priority; a higher priority, one imagines (though Army men might demur) than the foot patrols of the jungle of the Blue Creek Mountains further down in the hot and humid south, or than the observation kept through binoculars, from a mountain top, of Guatemalan outposts.

Much of the soldier's time is therefore spent on exercises in which 'enemy' planes try to land on the airstrip of Belize International and are destroyed with self-guiding missiles or machine-gun fire from carefully prepared positions. At the same time all personnel not actively fighting go to allotted half-submerged bomb shelters. Anyone trying to get near the Harriers is challenged and interrogated. The regularity of these exercises is not especially popular, but it is regarded as necessary. It is good, for instance, that camp cooks who may never have to fire a rifle in anger are nevertheless aware that danger may await them in the bomb shelters if they are not careful. The warm, protected atmosphere of the shelters is as popular with snakes as it is unpopular with the personnel who, without warning, may have to leave what they are doing and get inside a hot and crowded shelter in about a minute, and be hotly cursed if they are too long about it. This is the working life of headquarters; and the senior officers spare no effort to instil into the men the feeling that the situation is a 'real' one, and that the mere presence of British troops will not necessarily be enough to deter any aggressor.

There are a number of Army camps stretching down southwards. All have the atmosphere of little outposts of Empire, where officers walk about in khaki drill in the daytime but wear neckties religiously at dinner in the nissen hut mess. I only came across one officer who looked like a college lecturer and talked like a radical, actually disagreeing with a leading article in the *Daily Telegraph*. He did it in such an upper-class voice that his colleagues, one felt, were disarmed and regarded it as a minor eccentricity — rather like that of the Sergeant Major who kept a large collection of dead spiders, each one more large and horrific than the last, loaning them out to visiting journalists who desired to be photographed with a large tarantula nonchalantly on the bicep. It was rather a surprise to find that the radical was actually on a Long Service Commission: even a generation ago, one would not have rated such a man's chances of promotion highly. He was in fact already a Captain, though quite young.

Militarily, the geographical and topographical difficulties of Belize cut both ways. On the one hand, the jungle is notoriously difficult to patrol. The palm or mahogany trees are up to one hundred feet tall. The roots stretch out like gigantic snakes to trip the unwary into undergrowth which may, in fact, conceal snakes or spiders. There is a great deal of less imposing bush which needs to be hacked away with a machete. It is the sort of terrain to appeal to an active Empire-builder rather than to the more humble policeman which the British Army has, in effect, become. Though I was assured, before I crossed the river at Blue Mountain Creek, that the rivers are virtually alligator-free, there are poisonous water snakes; and the bottoms of the rivers can be treacherous to walk on. I was warned that the worst part was when the water level reached the crotch, but it wasn't, it was when I found the bottom of the river consisted of boulders like footballs, slippery and liable to roll away when trodden on. The thick jungle boots may have saved my wrenched ankle from being actually broken: they were worth wearing, even though they were difficult to get on and off, and neither flexible enough to be comfortable in easy conditions nor stiff enough to be fully protective in difficult ones.

But the terrain makes things difficult for a would-be aggressor, too; and one must hope their jungle boots are no better. The actual border with Guatemala is a straight line drawn through thick jungle without any relevance to natural features. It would be as difficult to attack as to defend. And the main Guatemalan post near what would be the *real* frontier lies, obligingly, directly underneath the mountain peak of Cadenas, from which observation is easy.

Constant watch is maintained by soldiers in a post cut out of the mountain top and sandbagged. Reaching this commanding crow's nest would not be easy for an enemy. It is not particularly easy for the British Army, either. It is possible only by helicopter, which has to land on a surface (of loose stones) no larger than an average living-room. Allowing the helicopter to come to a complete rest, with the rotor arms stopped, would make it vulnerable to high winds, landslip or attack. So the blades are kept turning all the time personnel and provisions are off-loaded. The result is that getting out of the helicopter means jumping into a swirling mass of flying stones and bric-a-brac, while trying not to stumble through the ropes which are the only protection from the precipice, *and* not to get one's head cut off by the whirling rotor blades.

Such routines are hazardous but necessary. Invasion by land, as distinct from sea, has possibly been made more likely by the decision to hive off the seat of government from Belize City and locate it at Belmopan. This is virtually in the middle of the country: or, in atmosphere at least, in the middle of nowhere.

A few years ago, Belize City, which faces the Caribbean, was flooded and virtually brought to a halt. The government prepared against a repetition by following the example of Brazil and building a governmental centre, almost from scratch, in the very centre of the country, where it was not likely to be flooded, and where (at least from the map) it was equidistant from all the main centres of the country. Thus Belmopan now stands well away from the sea at Belize City but half way towards Melchor de Mencos, the site of the Guatemalan commando bases — a matter of a mere thirty miles, over the best roads that the country can boast.

Hence the importance of Holdfast Camp near San Ignacio, the small community twenty miles from Belmopan on the Guatemalan side. The theory is that an invasion by road could be held by British troops and the Harrier jump jets before it got to Belmopan and that Belmopan could still stand if Belize City were taken from the sea.

The thinking may be real, but the feeling of Belmopan was scarcely real when I visited it. Acre after acre of low grey government buildings stood literally in the middle of parched fields, with no other habitation visible. A cinema, roughly made of concrete, stood on its own a few hundred yards away. An open air market offered Seven Up, bread rolls, sweets, and hardware like pens and pencils. There was no other visible trade. The place had not yet caught on; it was, like some other similar centres in the Caribbean, a piece of Adelaide or Houston built, with every sign of professionalism, in a surrounding vacuum — puzzling and slightly unfriendly to the local people who use it. British soldiers are not seen there in their dozens, either; and the life of the Governor, who lives in a bungalow whose modesty is nicely calculated to reinforce the self-esteem of the Belize civilian government, faces a life of some monasticism in the cause of (gently) showing the British flag. When I visited him, his second-in-command brought me a cup of tea personally and the Governor himself slid the sugar towards me, with every sign that it was an established ritual. In these difficult days Britain cannot make herself felt by brawn alone. Diplomacy is at least as important as military strength; and there was every indication that the government of Belize is, in practice, quietly allowed a greater range of freedom than the British international committment implies; provided that stability is maintained. As the local population welcomes the presence of the British soldiers; as the Guatemalans are determined to broaden the small land channel which is their only link to the Caribbean; and as the Belizeans are as determined to resist the slightest contraction of their already small country, the British presence could be indefinite, at least in theory.

In practice, the British taxpayer could become restive long before then, and British troops might be more urgently needed elsewhere. There must come a day when manoeuvres as arduous as manning the Cadenas observation post in its mountain eyrie will be carried out by the Belize people themselves.

I did not, however, get the impression that this day is near. If patriotic feeling automatically led to military effectiveness it might be otherwise. The pride of the Belize people in the integrity and independence of their country is heartfelt. I overheard one fierce argument. A prosperous Belize citizen thought that many well-off people in the country would *like* a Guatemalan take-over because it would be the only way the country could be made economically sound, it having little in the way of natural resources or industry to make its way in a competitive world. He was angrily attacked by another, a sophisticated woman in appearance, who said: 'Not a foot of Belize territory must be given up! Not an inch! I think we must all be prepared to die for that if necessary!' Such ferocious sentiments are widespread. No wonder that, when the Harrier jump jets first arrived, Belize people danced in the streets and waved at them, shouting, 'Guatemalans don't come now!'

But the problems of self-help are considerable. The British soldiers are trying to encourage this in ways both military and civilian.

When I was there, the Belize Defence Force consisted of some eighty Belize servicemen, looking rather uneasy in a green version of British Army uniform. They exercised with British troops, and were especially deputed to guard the Harriers. This most crucial task was a compliment, a way of throwing the young local servicemen in at the deep end. It was a compliment difficult to live up to. This was sometimes due to a rather offhand attitude by the junior ranks of British troops.

One rather unnerving experience of my own illustrated the point. I was in a Land Rover being driven by a British driver from Belize City to headquarters near the airport. The route took us past the Harriers. We were therefore liable to challenge. An exercise was actually in progress, and it was assumed that we would not only be challenged but also interrogated by the Belize Defence Force before being allowed to drive on past the Harriers in their camouflage netting. The sentry was a member of the Belize Defence Force, probably still in his teens and armed with a British standard rifle. As we came to a halt, he rested the barrel of the rifle on the sill of the open window of the passenger seat, where I was sitting, and asked the driver who he was.

It was burningly hot inside the Land Rover; we had, a few miles back, hit a huge snake in the middle of the road, which had been no good for anyone's nerves; and the driver's patience was wearing thin. He curtly told the Belizean sentry who he was. The Belize soldier then asked him for his identity papers and who *I* was. He was still standing there with his rifle pointing into the Land Rover. Unfortunately he asked in such a mumbling and apologetic voice, and looked so self-effacing and generally unsure of himself, that the British driver either did not hear him or did not care. He revved up the engine, as if about to drive off. I had visions of being shot through the head. The Belize soldier then asked where we were bound for, but again so quickly and bashfully that even I, right beside him, could hardly hear, let alone the driver on the other side of the vehicle. He was the furthest away from the Belize soldier, and, moreover, busy revving up the engine even faster. Just as I was saying, 'I think he wants to know. . . .' the driver impatiently let in the clutch and drove off, leaving the local Belizean soldier with his gun still pointed in our direction.

It was possibly not the happiest day for the Belize Defence Force, nor for me. But it did illustrate the difficulties in establishing adequate local defence forces in the remaining quarters of Empire. It all happened so naturally. Who was so terribly wrong? The British driver for being impatient during an exercise, with an only partly-trained soldier? The soldier, for not speaking up for himself more aggressively or at least assertively? Or, as I rather suspect, several hundred years of colonial history, during which both black and white men conspired to perpetuate the view that the white man gave the orders and the black man carried them out? It may not be a popular thing to say, that in parts of the old Empire, the old view *still* holds in blacks as well as whites, albeit unconsciously. But it must be said, and faced, if any improvement is to be made in the future.

Whoever was in charge of the exercise obviously decided that an improvement could and should be made. The next day the Land Rover followed the same route, with me in the same seat. This time the Belize Defence Force soldier put his rifle in through the window again and, when the senior man in the Land Rover found he hadn't got his pass, politely but inexorably ordered us all out of the Land Rover and into a guard hut for interrogation and search. The young Belize Defence Force soldier looked very pleased with himself. I felt a lot safer as an individual and, as a Britisher, somewhat safer politically.

The second area of help is purely civil. It has an obvious political and humanitarian value. The Army helps visiting civilian experts (on everything from agriculture to building work) to travel about the country, and be quite safe while doing so. The Army co-operates closely with the RAF in this process. While I was there, an Army Land Rover took an agricultural scientist from Leeds University to an Army camp, from where a helicopter delivered him to isolated villages. The entire populations came out to discuss what crops they could grow, and how to get the best results. The Mennonites, a religious order who operate strongly in Belize agriculture, have done much to educate the Maya Indians — the principal farmers — in modern methods of crop management, as well as supplying nuns to service isolated clinics. (I visited one clinic staffed by a cool American beauty who could have been presiding over an immaculately-kept medical centre in Boston.) But British agricultural expertise is keenly sought, and is comparatively cheap to offer. The scientist was accompanied by one British Army man with a rifle. He travelled on RAF helicopters which would be flying anyway, and dined in the evening, and slept, in Army Officers Messes. In one such mess, a barrel-roofed nissen hut open at one end, we had dinner with officers of a Scottish regiment. The Colonel was in a kilt and the rest of us were in our cleanest available shirts and neckties. Crickets sang and lizards slithered outside.

'You say you're from Leeds,' I said, making suitably decorous conversation. 'Did you happen to know a cousin of mine who was a student there?' I gave his name.

'Taught him. He and his wife used to stay with us a lot.'

'Good heavens!'

It was all very cosy. We were all in the same club, so to speak, while all around us lay the jungle. Was it like that all the time, perhaps, in the days of Empire? Very cosy — for those on the 'inside'? Unfortunately for the average serviceman, the original magic of Empire — holding a plot of land that is 'ours' — hardly applies. He may be excused for seeking occasional distraction.

Before I set off for Belize, a senior Army officer took me to one side, looking rather embarrassed. 'Look old man, I wouldn't dream of telling you what to write, you know that, and we don't mind honest constructive criticism, but there are one or two sensitive things we'd prefer you not to . . . well, give undue prominence to.' I was naturally intrigued. Had the Guatemalans made their first atom bomb? Were the troops in such a demoralized state that they were quite likely to say they couldn't stand it all for another moment? Had we ourselves some Secret Weapon that must not be disclosed?

It transpired that the sensitive area was the brothels. A national newspaperman (nay, two or three) had previously been to Belize and written reports which suggested that the place was seething with brothels. Parents got worried, said the officer; and the Army wasn't like bosses in civilian life, they really *did* like to keep their men *and* their relatives happy and not unnecessarily worried.

Naturally, (such is the professional perversity of a writer's nature) I made a point of investigating the available brothels. They were not numerous, they were not large and they were anything but impressive, except perhaps to a writer in search of material for a seedy novel.

There were two: or at least two I could find. I visited them in ascending order of social standing, without temptation at any point to stray from the path of unsullied virtue. The first was a two-storey wooden building in a state of some decrepitude, with an exterior wooden stairway of uneven and broken stairs leading to the first floor bar. The bar, which had a wooden plank floor liberally christened with cigarette butts, was perhaps three times the size of a modest living-room, and was so dimly lit that it was impossible for some seconds to get a clear view of the groups of ladies who sat around at the tables, swopping stories and evaluating chances. The visual impediment was presumably carefully arranged, for none of the women there — perhaps thirty of them — would, it seemed to me, entice any soldier with good eyesight to anything except escape to the life of a monastic order. A few were local girls. Most were from Mexico or Honduras and looked excessively battered by their travels. I drank Pepsi Cola and asked for it to be served straight out of a previously-unopened bottle. It was brought to me in a jug. I left shortly after pretending to drink it. A serviceman who availed himself of the services of this establishment would have needed, it seemed to me, treatment for defective eyesight as well as treatment of a more intimate and embarrassing kind.

The second was rather more tolerable. It was an ill-lit black-walled hall, with relentless music and the occasional half-caste colonial-looking type in alpaca jacket acting in an erratic way, talking loudly and for effect to black men or women who stared morosely and tolerantly back. The available ladies were more presentable and for this reason no doubt more confident: I was determinedly approached by a Puerto Rican lady of some charm who simply would not accept that I was too poor, too hot, too drunk, too tired or too effete to avail myself of her invitation. 'You are upper-class English eccentric,' she said. I allowed all the mis-statements of fact in this sentence to stand.

'You should come on a Saturday night when the place is humming,' said a soldier in civilian clothes.

I imagine that some British soldiers do; but there were very few in the place the evening I went, and none disappeared upstairs with any of the ladies.

Later an officer with medical experience said, 'If any of the silly baskets get it, I'd like to let them keep it.'

This might have been unnecessarily blunt. But it could be true that ordinary boy-girl relationships, based on some social, intellectual or aesthetic foundation, must be difficult, if not impossible, to come by in Belize. At one point I found an officer wondering into his locally brewed beer if he dared ask the rather nice girl behind the bar out; and deciding better not. 'I don't think anyone would understand,' he said. 'It would just be nice to have a woman around — you know?'

Perhaps I then began to sense the strains the British Army man must have faced when Britain ruled a third of the globe, and how some of the monastic rigidity and sexual stultification inspired by formative years in a public school must have had — then — a utilitarian value. The British soldier in Belize is a living and occasionally uncomfortable example of how much not only Britain's international sway, but also her emotional tone, has changed. It is a change the British soldier in Belize has absorbed with some patience, restraint and honour. But if the demands of Belize are the most direct reminder of Great Britain in the days of her Imperial past, it is in modern Europe that the demands are the most tightly linked — sometimes alarmingly so — to the crucial interests of her more modest present.

4

The Border of Fear

'Where would the Russians attack? Probably through the North German Plain, into the Ruhr and the Rhine, which is good tank country. When would they attack? Probably just before lunch on Christmas Day. The average British soldier here knows it *could* happen and the average German knows it could happen. Do people in Britain?'

— Captain on exercises near the East-West German border.

The Major General had just got off his personal Thunder Box. Squatting on it in the dank early-morning West German woods he might have seemed, to some comfortable civilians, a figure not devoid of comedy as he bent his grey-haired and aquiline dignity to the difficulties occasioned by calls of nature in the field of battle.

His personal loo was no different in design to his men's at the tented field headquarters of the 2nd Armoured Division in the Osterwalde Woods in the north of West Germany. With one small exception. It was over a shallower hole. This was because it was for his exclusive and personal use, and therefore did not have to cope with heavy demands. In all other respects — the square of plain wood, the hole cut in the centre, the tarpaulin stretched vertically around four posts to give just sufficient room to sit down, the gusts of biting Teutonic winds up the exposed legs — the Major General and his men were equal. Definitely *visibly*.

The Major General, who had received me courteously at nine on a freezing October morning (in his slightly more roomy nine-feet-by-nine operational office tent) was nonetheless strangely sensitive on the point. At the end of our interview, he *ordered* a junior officer to show me his personal Thunder Box, so that I could see for myself that he was prepared to put up with the same petty inconveniences in the field as his men. At the time I found his request baffling. But I was to come to understand how important the spirit of brotherhood between officer and man is among the 55,000 troops Britain has stationed in West Germany — a force largely forgotten at home, but a force facing potential invaders of Warsaw Pact countries who have a superiority of nearly three to one in tanks and two to one in soldiers.

The Major General's Thunder Box had an air of the Theatre of the Absurd. A quite different sort of theatre, which the Major General and I were both shortly to see and hear, was the Theatre of the Serious Message: the rumble of heavy invading 'Russian' armour that shook the ground and violated the air, ear and mind; the thunderflashes in lieu of shells and grenades; the red, grey and blue smoke; the diving and screaming jet aircraft; the juddering helicopters and the crackling of radios, which all combined to produce a vision of hell which rivalled Ypres and Mons; a vision which, it is hoped, would become an enemy's Charge of the Light Brigade before it became our version of Napoleon's Waterloo.

The autumn exercises which caused the Major General's discomfort are the annual climax of the soldier's year in Germany: a never-ending statement about readiness on what is still considered to be the most critical frontier of the West. They last from September to November; they are regarded very professionally indeed, because they are near the East-West German border, where the adrenalin circulates somewhat liberally in the blood; and they are even welcomed by the German people themselves, such as the seventy-year-old retired German miner who sat weeping in a beer house in the Sibbesse valley as 'Russian' tanks drummed past — because they recalled his parents' farm in the Eastern zone. 'We must all fall in with what the military wants us to do,' he said with tears pouring down his cheeks. 'If the military were not here, the East would run straight over us. My son-in-law is from the Eastern zone and can never go back. The Russians would have eaten us up, used us like animals if it had not been for the British and the Dutch getting here first. The people round here were very frightened and people of my age still remember it. The Russians were only thirty miles away.' Rightly or wrongly, the lives of West Germans near the Eastern border are still tense and easily susceptible to fear.

The sacrifices of the exercises are not all petty and amusing. During Exercise Keystone, the one I saw, involving twenty thousand troops with armour and heavy guns, there were six deaths by accident. With one exception, all the victims were German civilians. One German doctor was killed when his car ran into the back of a tank which had all its lights on. A German family of four had been killed when they ploughed into a trailer which had become detached from its lorry and was resting in the middle of a road. The Army driver, who was waving a torch in the middle of the road to stop traffic, was cut down and killed by the car. On the exercise that preceded Keystone, one soldier had been killed when stepping out from between his lorry and trailer after fixing the tow bar.

The German people, who are not the most plodding and cautious of drivers, put up with all this, and with the damage caused to fences, pavements and crops, with significant stoicism. As one senior officer who has had to deal with German claims for compensation put it: 'It would be interesting to see what the reaction would be in England if these sort of exercises went on there. People here understand the threat.'

The Army certainly has its own clear idea of the military situation: an invader needs resources of three to one to make success possible in the face of the better-placed defender, and this is about the advantage the Warsaw Pact countries have *actually* got in the items which are thought to be 'the name of the game' today — men and armour. The Army cannot quite understand why this elementary piece of mathematics has not created more attention at home. There is a distinct element of the Army which believes that if it had, they would be able to practise with more than, say, the *three* £3,000 Striker tank-killer guided missiles they are permitted to fire *per year* now, and would not have to do all the rest of their training, including exercises, by means of a simulator.

When I asked the Major General, an Argyll and Sutherland Highlander, at the field headquarters of the 2nd Armoured Division at Osterwalde wood, twelve or so miles from Hamelin, whether the exercises could be anything more than a form of play (which is what some civilians at home would assume), he bristled. 'It is taken very seriously indeed. A major exercise like this takes place every two or three years for us, and it takes a year to plan,' he said. 'We test out a great many of the procedures and techniques that may have to be used for real. I am responsible now for a damn good piece of ground for defence. I don't say I could stay there for ever, but we could give a good account of ourselves. No one is going to walk straight through, however many tanks they have got.'

Exercise Keystone took place in the Sibbesse valley, a plain a few kilometres wide sandwiched between opposing wooded hills and containing the small town of Sibbesse. It followed a series of exercises with exotic-sounding names and even more baffling series of passwords; exercises like Pack Saddle, Steel Trap, Red Dragon, Full House and Aintree Task. It came just before the last exercise of the year, Red Gauntlet. All these exercises used different divisions, of which there are four in Germany.

It was not a game and the aim was realism. Two facts made the realism relatively easy. The Sibbesse valley is just the sort of territory over which Warsaw Pact tanks would rumble, in their battlefield formations of ten tanks wide and ten deep, if they wished to sweep westwards to the River Weser, the first major barrier to an enemy advance. And secondly, the whole psychological atmosphere of Germany near the border is tense and sensitive enough to allow even a visiting civilian to feel the hairs rising on the back of the neck, fanned by the very sight of the East-West German border itself, only half as far away from the exercise itself as London is from Brighton.

The border is like a long, obscene and sinister worm which trails a thousand miles (1,393 kilometres) across Germany, splitting half a dozen towns and two ideologies. It is a reality which makes the regular autumn exercises understandable. It is also an education which it is very easy to ignore completely in the United Kingdom — a fact which makes soldiers very edgy. 'Tell people what it is really like,' is the gist of what they say. 'Some of the people in the UK think that because the war has been over for nearly forty years we must be having a comfortable swan here.'

A comfortable swan it certainly is not. It is not easy to be complacent near that ugly worm. It is true that its vehicle pits are dug so that they prevent vehicles getting *out* rather than in; and so, in one sense, the wall can be regarded as an instrument of internal security rather than of external aggression. But not many miles behind the border's many murderous traps are the Warsaw Pact tanks and men, not to mention over twice the number of our fixed wing tactical aircraft and pieces of artillery.

What does one normally expect of a frontier? Perhaps barbed wire and a few trenches. The East-West German border fortifications (which are all on the East side) are as like this as a black Alsatian is like a Pekinese. They can all be seen near Helmstedt, a German town almost exactly in the middle of the section of the border which is the responsibility of the British and near the only road on which it is possible to pass from West to East. Near Helmstedt is the village of Hotensleben. It can be seen clearly from the Western side, and many large families have members in both communities. Visiting is a major operation. One woman whose husband kept a shop just on the Western side, and who looked quite capable of jumping the narrow stream which is the exact border line in this area, nevertheless had to travel thirty miles there and thirty miles back every time she wanted to see her relatives in the East. The border is exactly in the middle of the stream. In theory, anyone who fell into the four foot wide stream from the Western side, and toppled over the half-way line, could be fired upon without warning from one of the gigantic control towers that abound on the East side, like weird mushrooms between thirty and ninety feet tall.

The fortification nearest to the Western side at this point is a barbed wire fence put there by the Russians and now woefully rusted. Some way back from this is an eight foot tall wire mesh fence, and further still a twelve foot high concrete wall with a pipe of large diameter running along the top to make it more difficult and dangerous to climb. Then there is a four foot deep ditch to stop any vehicles coming out from the East. Back beyond that is a ploughed strip of sandy earth which is regularly examined for footprints or other disturbance, before being meticulously raked over again. Then there is a concrete track for patrol vehicles. Behind this is what is called an early warning fence, wired with alarms. Beyond *that* is another twelve foot high concrete wall, harshly lit at night like a football pitch. The whole worm has a thickness of perhaps four hundred feet or more. It trails all across Germany without becoming thinner. Indeed, at various places it thickens up with the aid of two parallel wire fences (which allow fierce dogs to run around between them) and scatter guns which automatically blast, from several different angles, anyone touching a fence.

Some Army wives are fond of bringing visiting relatives to the border and it is not officially discouraged. The Army view is that it is healthy for people from home to see it. But visitors are always warned about the risk of getting too near the first fencing, because the official border line is well to the West side of it. The actual line is marked by a line of concrete posts bearing crosses and East German emblems. Often they are so covered in bracken and grass that they cannot easily be spotted, and people from either side carelessly cross over. Usually any friction is minor — one East German soldier sitting on one of the border blocks was simply told to take his backside out of the Western zone. Most of the discernible unease is from the Eastern side. All visitors to the border are photographed through enormous telephoto lens cameras by East German soldiers in the control towers. An irritated British officer went into a tap dance routine for the benefit of the waiting cameras. The smiles from the West were not returned.

There is really not much to laugh about near the East-West German border, though soldiers of the British Army try. But the atmosphere does keep their adrenalin flowing, especially during exercises, making work stimulating where it might have become mere routine. Germany is a favourite posting, as wives will confirm, but most entertaining is done in quarters rather than in German beer houses. In the German equivalent of the British pub near the East-West border, the subject of the position of British troops is likely to be introduced by strangers — followed by, first, the evasion and then the tactful departure of the soldier or family thus approached. 'The subject *does* tend to come up,' said one NCO. 'You have a few pints and suddenly you notice they are rather *too* interested in you, and you don't know the true sympathies of the people you are talking to. Suddenly you are very sober. That can be a bore.'

On the other hand, at the official level, relations between the apprehensive Germans and the British Army are good — so good that they can absorb even the constant sight and sound of military vehicles and the concentration of that sight and sound during exercises, even the unavoidable damage to property done by the armoured vehicles: the broken fences, smashed pavements and ruined crops. Without this mutual understanding life during exercises could be even grimmer.

In this favourable psychological climate, the Major

General with the responsibility for holding the Sibbesse valley in the face of 'Warsaw Pact' troops (actually Danish troops and the British 4th Division) could not begrudge putting himself on a spartan war footing in the woods near the exercise. Not even if it meant — as it did — giving up his comfortable house, an old German tax authority building at Lubecke ('a rich German industrialist's sort of house') for its duration and sleeping in a converted ambulance with a canvas extension, a hard bunk, a small cupboard for clothes, a tiny washbasin and a bottle of Teachers. His batman, a Rifleman, who had been with him nine months, hugged his rifle like a long-lost child, and said that he regarded looking after a General as 'a marvellous change'. The batman, like other men and officers, could hardly have been dazzled by the Major General's life style, because, like everyone else, the General used the campaign Desert Rose urinals — funnels attached to lengths of pipe stuck into a bed of rubble.

'I suppose,' said the Major General, with a composed enthusiasm that put these primitive details in their place, 'you could say this is the climax of my military career. I have never commanded nineteen thousand troops in this sort of area. It happened in Belfast when I was a Brigade Commander. I am now due to leave for another job and I don't anticipate being allowed to come to Germany again.'

Such being the case, the Major General threw himself into his duties touring the battle area, keeping in touch with the Chief of General Staff (who at one stage was turned back at a barbed wire barrier by zealous Territorial Army soldiers because he didn't know the password) and keeping up the morale of his men.

The eleven tents pitched in one complex around the Major General's contained a seedy muddle of desks, papers, rulers, charts, refuse bins, maps, Gestetner machines, typewriters, telephones, teleprinters, and also some more singular additions, like sub-machine-guns *and* Wavell —

the computer which reads out essential information on to a television screen.

The whole operation was being controlled from what *was* the bowling alley of a local pub in Gehrenrode, a first-floor room large enough to contain the Intelligence, Air Support, Military Police and German Police sections. Raised up on the stage (a fact which many might see as politically symbolic) was the Damage Control Centre, whose aim was to keep German causes of complaint down to a minimum. This department was under the control of a retired Lieutenant Colonel who had been at a German Staff College for two years and was admired for blending very inconspicuously into the German scene. In fact, he even *looked* rather like a youngish German executive.

'The older type of German, who knew the war, is dying off now,' he said. 'The younger generation have done National Service, but they are not so military-minded as the older generation. I saw one man watching the Artillery shelling the exercise ground. He was watching with a great deal of interest. He said, "I know what this is all about. I have two metal legs." This sort of person is dying out.'

Under the Status of Forces Agreement, signed after the war, NATO forces can exercise over any ground in Germany they regard as necessary. But, in practice, great care was being displayed on Keystone to be as agreeable as possible to the local population — keeping off their crops wherever possible and being as lenient as possible with any local citizens waving a camera about (a comparative rarity, as military exercises have been a way of life in Northern Germany since the time of Bismarck).

'There are some sensitive questions,' said the Lieutenant Colonel. 'If a British soldier sees a German photographing military equipment, what are the powers of arrest? This is a problem which has raised its head. Someone was seen taking photographs of positions. He turned out to be the local landowner. He was entitled to take pictures, but one is not always clear about the position. We are allowed to detain a German whom we suspect might be endangering our security, provided we immediately hand him over to the German police, who will follow it up.' This is rarely necessary.

One officer on the exercise said he regarded himself as 'a technological vandal in a good cause, able to give vent to the boyish anarchism which is in us all.' This was romantic hyperbole. With the British government paying seventy-five per cent of the claims for damage, compared with the German government's twenty-five per cent, there is no incentive, even in the heat of mock battle, to charge through a front garden when the roadway would do, or to turn a tank round in a field of crops when a broken pavement edge would be cheaper.

'In a good crop year, you may get sworn at by a farmer,' said an officer. 'But on a bad year for crops, farmers have been known to stand in the road and direct you into their fields as if they were traffic policemen. They know they will make more from compensation than they will from a bad crop.'

The 1st British Corps (the only one Britain has in Germany, though some officers believe that two would be needed to do the job properly and without strain) consists of four divisions, of which the Major General's (the 2nd) was only one. The 5th Field Force, working with the 2nd Armoured Division, had been given the job of blocking off the crucial Sibbesse valley, and it was to their headquarters that I went for a sight of how officers and men function one step down the chain of command.

On the ground floor of a beer house in Brugen, the headquarters had a parquet floor beginning to disintegrate. Half a dozen sleeping bags were grouped by the draughty and ever-open door, three of them filled by sleeping soldiers. They were snatching a brief couple of hours' sleep before moving once more into the curtained-off Operations Room. The 5th Field Force Commander, a Brigadier in the Scots Guards, was directing his staff in the Operations Room and waxing enthusiastic about the support he was getting from the 5th Light Infantry Regiment, a Territorial

Regiment with headquarters at Shrewsbury, which had come over voluntarily to help the defence of the Sibbesse valley.

'They fit in quite remarkably well,' said the Brigadier. 'They are ninety-nine per cent like us, because of their enormous enthusiasm. It is amazing sometimes to think of the sacrifices they make personally, and sometimes financially, to go to camp. It is such an enormous comfort in this day and age to find people who are actually serving Queen and Country. There is no one *forcing* them.'

Normally, in war, such a regiment would have a role in the rear area of the 1st Corps. But for Exercise Keystone, the Brigadier got them near the 'sharp end'. Said the Captain who was in charge of the Intelligence section: 'The aim is to make the plan as plain and simple as possible. We do it by looking at the problem and finding the easiest solution. Instead of saying, "You will move at 23.46 hours," we say, "You will move at 23.00 hours."'

Further still down the chain of command, where the officers and men were kept (deliberately) in greater ignorance of the 'enemy' plans, the clinical simplicity dissolved in the sort of grime and uncertainties there would be in actual war. At a company command post in the village of Sibbesse — the old barn of a farmhouse near the village crossroads — a Major commanding a Company of the 3rd Battalion of the Parachute Regiment was briefing his men on how they would help get friendly Chieftan tanks and other armoured tracked vehicles back from their present forward position. The French forces, to the north of the British, had had to withdraw under heavy enemy pressure, which left the British 2nd Armoured Division too far ahead of the rest of the front line, and vulnerable to a pincer movement. Here faces were blackened with thick grease, hands were given similar treatment and the air of tension was even more noticeable. So was the intense cold, broken only by the calor gas cooking stove. Only the Commander of the attached French platoon fastened his mind on to such mundane matters as food. Stroking his neatly trimmed black beard, he asked: 'When is breakfast?'

He was assured that men would be available to take *his* men their breakfast in hayboxes. The Frenchman looked a little mystified until two enormous steel boxes, like gigantic thermos flasks, were pointed out to him. The British Army hangs on to traditional names with the same tenacity it hangs on to its singularities of uniform or to a piece of the battlefield. It is many, many years since a box with hay as an insulation has been used to carry food long distances; but the huge, heat-insulated barrels of the 1980s are still called hayboxes, as they were in the old days. The food, even out in the exercise field, is on the whole rather better. The men in the barn were having liberal portions of Menu G.

A good understanding of forms, and a can-opener, is the prerequisite of gastronomic survival in today's British Army. Units are issued with a copy of DOS Form 492 (Rev.1977), entitled 'Menu Sheet and Cooking Instructions 10/4 Men Composite Ration Packs', and sub-headed, 'LOOK Before You COOK'. There are seven complete menus and each comes in tinned form, the tins packed into cardboard cases about the size of two bricks, and given a title letter from A to G. It is claimed that one unit, not quite understanding the system, decided to take all Menus D for a ten-day period of special duty in Northern Ireland, and after eating chicken curry for ten days went off the dish for life. The story may be apocryphal, but is used to persuade units that they should take a mixture of menus with them when they are in the field, as Menu A will give them goulash, Menu B corned beef, Menu C casserole steak and onions, Menu D chicken curry, Menu E steak and kidney pudding, Menu F chicken supreme and Menu G stewed steak. Sweets are also varied from fruit salad to chocolate pudding, and each box contains coffee, tea, sugar, milk chocolate, sweets, matches, salt, mustard, a can-opener and, as the Army believes in intensive follow-through, toilet paper.

I restricted myself to chocolate bars and oatmeal blocks. The blocks can be either watered down, when they make a sort of porridge (I was told), or eaten as they are, in which case they taste like a rather superior kind of shortcake. After being exposed for a few hours to the biting winds of Northern Germany in the autumn and winter, sitting on the top of armoured vehicles whenever they can (so that the escaping warm air from the exhaust blows up the trousers), soldiers in urgent need of calories do not turn up their noses at such a diet, or at hamburgers, tinned salmon, baconburgers and sausages. No, not even at beans in tomato sauce, which are included in *every* menu. If eating in the modern British Army can be summed up, in field conditions, as the misquoted title of an Arnold Wesker play — Tins With Everything — the important fact is that such food is nutritionally balanced, will keep practically for ever in the most gruelling conditions, and takes up very little space.

The Major mentioned to his men that the Chief of General Staff would be in their vicinity at some time during the approaching long night, watching the withdrawal of the British forces to a consolidated line. There was a *very* sharp officer in his entourage, so there had better be no mistakes. 'He has an Intelligence Quotient of about 420,' warned the Major, in tones of deep reverence.

'And no bloody common sense,' piped up the Sergeant Major, to a gust of laughter.

It is a mistake to imagine that the Army is less capable of ribald irreverence than a civilian organization: on balance, the exact reverse would be more nearly true.

How does a French platoon fit into the exercises of its allies? — an important question in estimating the effectiveness of co-operation in the face of the Warsaw Pact countries. There seemed to be some feeling among British soldiers that the French had a different outlook, relying more on their officers and NCOs to do the serious thinking, whereas the British soldiers were encouraged to have more initiative — they were given an outline and told to get on with it.

The Major and some of his men then discussed the difference in efficiency and morale between a conscript and a professional force. None of them were keen on a reintroduction of National Service in Britain. 'There is a different feeling in a professional force,' said the Major. 'Even our soldiers near to the end of their service don't seem to count the days. They are still interested and involved.'

Would the fact that the Warsaw Pact countries had national service mean that their forces would be *less* efficient than they could be? 'That,' said the Major, with a brief laugh, 'is what I would like to think.'

Working from the barn command headquarters, the soldiers managed to cope on precious little sleep, just as they would have to do in battle. A Sergeant said he had managed one and a half hours the previous night. 'One night I had no sleep at all,' he said.

'It makes the blokes *better*,' said the Sergeant Major. 'You get used to going without sleep. I had four hours last night, which is about average. Three to four hours is quite sufficient. Even in war, the adrenalin would keep you going. You get a fatigue period, usually at eight or nine o'clock in the evening, and then you wake up again.'

It is at barn and trench level, far away from the gold braid on officers' hats, that soldiers emerge most uninhibitedly as men with decided, and often sensible, views of their own. The Sergeant Major, a youngish man with a well-trimmed moustache and a chin that would have been useful for battering down doors, was personally dubious about Milan, the new anti-tank guided missile that can not only be manually directed at an enemy tank, but can be pulled back to start again if it overshoots.

'Personally,' he said, 'I think it would be better if you had a gun rather than a guided missile, because the missile takes twelve seconds, and twelve seconds is a long time if you are being fired upon.' I was later to fire a guided missile, by simulator, in the battlefield. I saw what he meant.

The trouble was, said the Sergeant Major, that the Army did not always go to the right people when it wanted to test out new equipment: 'It gave the new Army boot to the Royal Artillery to test, and they don't do much marching. They didn't give it to the Infantry. There's something funny somewhere; they must give it to the people they think will accept it.'

He had his personal views on what should be done to stand up against the Russian tanks. 'I would like to see an infantry battalion formed especially to fight tanks, since armour is what the Russians are going to use. It should have every sort of weapon necessary to fight armour, and be formed especially for that purpose.'

The soldiers in the barn felt that limitations in training, rather than difficulties with discipline, would be the main problem in facing an attack. 'Training is supposed to be realistic, but it can't be,' said one soldier. 'You are out on training but you are afraid to fire the bullets, because they are in short supply. People get so that they would be frightened to fire a bullet even if the Russians came. It's training for a peacetime Army, really — hemmed in by civilian rules and regulations.'

The deeper into the freezing field of battle I went, the more philosophical the soldiers were prepared to be. The icy winds blowing down from the North German Plain, the stumbling about in the darkness of dense woods without a betraying torch, the eating from billy cans, can be great levellers in some dimensions, if not in all. In a three foot deep dug-out in a dark beech forest on the hills to the north of the Sibbesse valley, I found the 1st Battalion, The Royal Hampshire Regiment's forward command post. It was by now pitch dark. It was a miracle that I found the post without incurring a broken leg; indeed, I might not have found it at all, but for a chink of light through the canvas entrance to the dug-out, for which someone was given a ritual tongue-lashing.

The Lieutenant Colonel, in charge of four hundred men, was a large and companionable man who admitted cheerfully that all his yearly reports said: 'Overweight.' He and his men were up at the front line, he said, because the bosses thought that to have Regular Infantry way back was wasteful: the traditional jobs in the rear area could be done by TA soldiers. He was cheerful 'because we have the best anti-tank shoot in the whole of Europe', wooded hills commanding at least six miles' visibility. As he drank tea and joked with his men, the reason for the Major General's earlier insistence that I view his spartan loo became more comprehensible: he wanted to show me that in battle there is, at one level, a rough equality between officer and man, a common attitude vital to morale.

The conditions, the Lieutenant Colonel owned, were not exactly those that would apply in war. He would like to fire illuminating shells, but someone might be set fire to, or be hit on the head by the burning remains. 'The limitation is that we can never simulate the enormous amount of obscuration there would be when our plan was sprung. If you can imagine two hundred smoking tanks, it *could* be that we were hard pressed to see a hundred metres.' I was later to see and hear what he meant.

Despite the limitations in realism, the Lieutenant Colonel was insisting that his men take the same precautions in their hillside dug-out as they would do if they were expecting an enemy barrage. Nothing white must be dropped outside, on any account, because it might be seen by an enemy reconnaissance aircraft. And every man must mentally prepare himself for a Soviet Artillery 152 Fireplan descending on their position. It could be shattering.

What kind of man could best withstand it? This is the question that every Commander asks out loud and every soldier asks of himself in his heart. 'One tends to be, perhaps, very pro the soldiers you recruit from your own part of the country,' admitted the Lieutenant Colonel of the Hampshires. 'The British southerner is a fairly phlegmatic sort of person. You will rarely get a southerner saying, "It's bloody good." He will say, "It's not so bad." Your Welshman and Scotsman and Irishman are very much up and down people. When things are going extraordinarily badly, Welsh morale will be extraordinarily high. It is a curious thing. But if you get a fairly phlegmatic, level approach to life, you are likely to have a fairly level approach in action. A General like Montgomery used different types of troops for different sorts of operations.'

The Lieutenant Colonel didn't think that the Hampshires were a particularly quick-thinking outfit, but they were particularly suited to digging in and holding a position. 'We thrive,' he said, 'on "Dig in and don't move".'

What would help the ability of men like the Hampshires to hold on if there was a real enemy attack? The Lieutenant Colonel pointed out that the 5th Field Force had no armour at present. 'If I could wave a magic wand, I would ask for a squadron of fifteen Chieftans. That would probably increase my effectiveness three-fold. But a Chieftan tank is about £500,000. Well, we are in a secondary rather than primary position. More resources must be put into the first crust, and we must accept our role as a lorried infantry brigade.'

Such stoicism, thought the Lieutenant Colonel and his men, was rather more than one could expect of today's British civvy street. 'Whenever I get depressed about people in England, I am glad I belong to a body of people who are disciplined and are pleased to do their duty. We are commissioned by Her Majesty and I am glad to say we are proud of that.'

Morale was slightly less sanguine in a Striker combat tracked vehicle further down the hillside, but only because there was nothing for the crew of three to train their night light intensification sight on, except civilian cars passing along the Sibbesse Valley. The sight gives a light magnification of two thousand, and the vehicle can fire a cable-controlled Swingfire missile that would hit a tank before a tank could hit it with its own gun. There is a price: the vehicle is claustrophobic, fitting the soldiers like a glove. The slightest wrong move can smash the head against hard metal. The twelve seconds necessary to guide the Swingfire seemed a very long time indeed; but in battle the man who fired the missile could do so by remote control from 150 metres away from the vehicle.

Down in Sibbesse itself, as the evening turned to dark and excruciatingly cold night, men of the 9th/12th Royal (Prince of Wales) Lancers Cavalry Regiment manned the crossroads of the small town which would be the withdrawal route for the British tanks and other armoured vehicles. By midnight, these were rumbling through so fast that one of the worst dangers in real battle was readily illustrated: two 'enemy' tanks attached themselves to the back of a column and tried to get through. They were spotted and disqualified. Friendly tanks continued to retreat down the two possible routes, code named Plum Duff and Custard Pie. (One Colonel refused to sanction the use of the word 'Custard'. 'All yellow and runny,' he protested.) Men played the old soldier by warming their hands and feet on the tank exhaust pipes. So did I. If it meant clambering up the side of the tank so be it. In war, such measures can make the difference between death and survival.

On the Lieutenant Colonel manning the crossroads post fell an onerous responsibility that would be baleful indeed in time of war. 'I have to advise the Brigadier,' he explained, 'when I think I have brought back everything I can from forward. The Royal Engineers need twenty minutes before the anticipated arrival of the enemy to mine the remaining paths; and after that our tanks could not get back either. The Brigadier makes the decision when to start mining the gaps, but on my advice.'

A troop of three Chieftan tanks, halted at the crossroads, awaited instructions. Fifty-six tons of tank is a difficult thing to approach, even when stationary, and there is no disputing the courage of an enemy who manages to get close to one with a hand grenade.

'In time of war,' said the Troop Commander, a man in his twenties, 'I would say you would have the difficulties of an exercise ten times over.' The Troop Corporal, of the 5th Inniskilling Dragoon Guards, was asked what it felt like to be inside this massive object. 'Bloody cold. From the point of view of comfort, I would prefer to be an infantryman outside, because you are less of a target. This would be a death trap. But it is better if you want to hit the enemy. For that it is good.'

By three in the morning, most of the tanks had been pulled back. I went to bed in a guest house near the front line, and at seven-thirty opened the bedroom curtains to see 'enemy' (Danish) tanks screaming past, shaking the road and the hotel. It was the first probing thrust of the day and it was repulsed by quick action from the 2nd Armoured Division.

The major attack was expected around midday. I took up a vantage point in the middle of the Sibbesse valley, against a row of houses standing in the middle of sugar beet fields. I felt safer, standing against easily visible houses, though in war a blinded tank could drive straight through a house and out the other side without damaging itself. Nearby were the signs of resistance: the red triangles denoting a minefield, a Chieftan with its gun towards the enemy positions and numerous trenches covered with corrugated iron or fencing stripped from nearby houses. There was some agitation because, earlier, a Danish tank went literally, and all too realistically, straight over the top of a trench containing Frenchmen. They scrambled out unhurt, though one of their rifles was bent like a hairpin.

As he waited for the next thrust, a Sergeant noted that the early morning invaders had worn gas masks. At their second thrust he thought they might be using blood agents: things which produced blisters and a tightness of breath. This could produce a choking sensation that made men want to rip off all their protective clothing, in which case they would suffer serious injury.

Near the East-West German border such possibilities do not seem as fantastical as they would in England's green and pleasant land. There the horrors of science fiction are brought to one's doorstep. The advance of the enemy tanks, when it came, did nothing to dispel these horrors. Soldiers estimate that, though the Western powers are outnumbered by Warsaw Pact tanks three to one, the outnumbering on the section of the border which is the British responsibility could be as high as *seven* to one. Though armoured vehicles that were not technically tanks deputized for tanks in the mock attack, there were enough of the real thing to set every bone and nerve trembling as they appeared over the skyline from the East and charged towards the minefield in close formation. Each tank sought a way forward until it struck a mine; and then other tanks took over from where the first tank left off, until one *had* found its way through the minefield. Then all the other tanks burst through in the same set of tracks, while helicopters overhead machine-gunned them, Harrier jump jets strafed them with rockets, and the tanks let off smoke flares to disguise their position.

In real battle this smoke-filled Bedlam would probably have been preceded by forty minutes of Russian preliminary bombardment. The enemy's arrangement, on its own front line, of one gun per ten metres would have left hardly any of the defensive positions above ground untouched, though soldiers in their deep trenches might have survived everything except a direct hit. But a Major who was a member of the umpiring team thought the conditions of the exercise were flattering to the enemy. 'In a *real* minefield,' he said, 'the enemy would have suffered heavy casualties, at least sixty per cent, and their attack would have petered out. I don't know whether we would have sustained heavy casualties, but the whole thing would have been a massive dustbowl and for weapons to take out the enemy wouldn't be all that easy. You wouldn't actually *see* as many of them as we are seeing today. On a nice clear day like this, you get the wrong impression.'

A nice clear day it might have been before the attack started. But the attack itself was so frightening (soldiers admitted being caught up in the plausibility of it all, even though it was only an exercise) that the need for the minor as well as major exercises in Germany (forty-nine in the year

1979 alone) was all too clear. To make such massive displays of war machinery familiar enough to take out at least part of their sting is one of the purposes of the exercises.

It would be misleading, but not *very* misleading, to give the impression that the 55,000 British troops in West Germany spend all their time on exercises. One Troop Corporal in a Chieftan tank obligingly gave an outline of his past year, a year in which he saw his wife in their four-bedroomed flat for only eight months out of the twelve. November and December: getting tanks ready again after the ravages of the previous exercise. January and February: training for the annual firing tests. March: camping. April: working to get tank in perfect condition again. May and June: maintenance and adventure training in Bavaria or Norway, which was not compulsory; he hadn't gone himself this particular year because his wife was expecting a baby. July: three weeks' leave spent with his parents in the North of England. August: more tank maintenance: 'You can never stop.' September: to Canada for tactical exercises and learning how to kill enemy tanks. October and November: the annual major exercises.

What did wives, I wondered, think about all this separation? 'She married me when I was already in the Army,' said the Troop Corporal, 'and so she can't push it. I have thought about civvy street, to be honest, but there is damn all there, isn't there? I mean money and opportunities for interesting work. For a married man with four children a civilian job would have to be a very good one to compete with the Army. And I don't fancy the dole. I have never been on it, and I don't want to be.'

But the major complaint among Army men in West Germany is not separation or any other type of family problem. It is shortage of training materials. An eighteen-year-old West Indian of 32 Guided Weapons Regiment, the controller of a Striker anti-tank vehicle given the task of commanding the Sibbesse valley from wooded hills to the south, expressed the nature of the problem when he said the exercise hadn't 'left much impression' on him. He was rather blasé about taking out tanks with an electronic simulator in his sights. He wanted to use a real missile. But he was one of those Controllers of Swingfire who find themselves able to fire only *three* unarmed, though otherwise real, guided missiles per *year*.

'It is a great pity that more politicians and taxpayers don't come to the East-West German border to see for themselves,' said one officer. 'An exercise is different from a real war, of course, but it is more revealing than nothing.'

It certainly is. It dramatizes what many Army officers think of as the real possibility of attack — though in this there would be no German civilians patiently building new houses in the very path of the tanks, no German small boys playing in the fields and triggering off blue smoke mines by merry accident, and no German farmers making more out of compensation than they would have done out of their ravaged crops. There would only be a smoke-filled hell.

It is a concept any European under the age of fifty may find it difficult to imagine. But in Germany there are those with memories of the last war, who take a peripheral part in the autumn exercises, to whom the concept is all too real.

At Bielefeld Army Headquarters, in the middle of Germany, I drank early morning slivovitz (plum brandy) with a group of central European refugees — members of the Mixed Services Organization. This was an organization of civilians put together just after the last war to do security and other jobs on Allied bases, where German civilians would have been a security risk.

At the beginning of the 1980s there were about 2,500 of them in Germany as a whole — chiefly refugee Poles, Czechs and Yugoslavs whose unquestioning devotion to the Allied, and now Western, cause is both touching and useful. And a little sad, because there is no forseeable way in which this spirit can go on undimmed for ever: it is the heritage of a very different past, with death and retirement thinning out the ranks.

The men from the Mixed Services Organization seemed

more British than the British in their blue version of old-style British Army battle dress. They keep a stiff upper-lip in advancing their cause. The Chief Superintendent, a trim man with a slender, very British, moustache once went to Nuremberg to recruit more workers for the Mixed Services Organization. 'There were articles in the newspapers in Yugoslavia, saying that I was trading in white slaves at ten dollars a head. Absolutely untrue, of course. It was so laughable that when I came back I jokingly asked our Colonel to give me the money, and we had a big laugh about it.' It is hardly a surprise that new recruits are vetted by British and German Intelligence and by the CIA.

A British officer, who was also drinking breakfast-time slivovitz, told me fiercely that I mustn't expect *him* to be objective about them: 'I am biased in their favour.' Another said that when the Poles moved tanks, as they did on non-operational journeys, 'they cry when they bring their tanks in. They polish them so hard you can see your face in them ... They have achieved something we shall never see again.'

It was easy to see that the refugees from the last European conflict could easily sense the realities behind the drill. Often on their lips was the phrase, 'The Mixed Services Organization is dead; long live the Mixed Services Organization.' They are men with a profound respect for survival and survivors.

British soldiers certainly respect *them* profoundly. The soldiers think about the present realities before their eyes, and are disturbed because they suspect some people back home in modern Britain don't want to know. 'Frankly I would not necessarily expect to survive,' said one Parachute Regiment officer. 'But if I did, I would become a guerrilla and keep on fighting. I don't think we believe in final defeat.'

Understandably, it is in West Germany that the realities, and grim potentialities, of the British soldier's life *as* a soldier are more evident and oppressive. In comparison, in terms of numbers and techniques, Northern Ireland can b seen as a one-off minor policing operation.

One hundred miles further forward, across the East-West German border and into the territory of the Eastern bloc, the British soldier's job is cast in yet another mould. One with more diplomatic niceties.

5

The Encircled Fun City

'One has to be very careful in Berlin, because very minor incidents can easily blow up and become much more major. I suppose I see a lot more trivia that would not reach me in a more normal place. If it is trivia in Berlin, it has to be taken seriously.'

— A British Army Staff Officer, Berlin.

The incident certainly didn't seem, on the face of it, to be one that required the serious attention of the British Army. It involved a bit of banging on a car roof.

In Berlin, the Russians tour the West's area of the city to show the flag and confirm their right to be there, just as Britain, the USA and France tour the Russian sector of the still-occupied and divided city for the same reasons. Usually the Russian flag tours (as they are called) of the British sector take place at the rate of seven a day, though in times of awkwardness there have been as many as fifty a week.

On this particular occasion, the Russian vehicle was going very, very slowly — perhaps accidentally. Accidentally or not, it blocked the path of a local West Berlin bus. The driver got out and, when shouting availed nought, started banging loudly on the roof of the Russian car.

The result was a protest by the Russians, received the day before I arrived in Berlin. 'The protest came down an *un*official route,' said a senior officer, 'so theoretically we haven't received it. So now we will probably protest ourselves, at the behaviour of the Russian flag tour. But we will do it by the *official* channel, through the Russian Embassy. Their protest came down the military net to us, which is *not* the official channel. This was an instance of a little thing that blew up a bit, as they are apt to here.'

Jokes are definitely out when it comes to East-West relations in the former German capital, which was divided up between the four Allied nations at the end of the Second World War and has been curiously frozen in that situation ever since. The Russian sector is almost as big as the British, USA and French sectors put together; but the population there is apt to feel that it would be less claustrophobic in the West. Hence the Berlin wall, which prevents break-outs from the East, though people still manage to escape from time to time. While they are not turned back by the West, the British Army is always very careful indeed not to offer more provocation than it need — even the provocation of humour. When some escapers from the East arrived at Gatow airport in the Western part of the city in a light aircraft, the RAF took it to pieces and then solemnly delivered the pieces back to the Russians. No one smiled. When other East Berliners escaped in a glider, it was also solemnly handed back to the Russians. But this time someone had written on a label attached to the wedges that kept the rudder steady during freightage: 'To be removed before the next escape.'

Berlin, over a generation since its division at the end of the Second World War, is a place of sensitive incongruities and glaring inconsistencies which must somehow be taken with a straight face by the three thousand British troops there. They remain inconspicuous — scattered outside the city centre, in barracks at Spandau and other suburban points — and come into the city centre itself only for an occasional evening out in a night club. Or they may occasionally show a family visitor from Britain the four foot thick white wall, built in a half-moon shape by the Russians around the Brandenburg Gate, which would otherwise be the easy link between East and West. The Gate and the statuesque charioteer on top of it are facing East, as if dramatizing the East's stony rejection of the West. There are lights focused on the Gate itself, showing up the white-painted East German observation post, which patiently watches and photographs all Western visitors who mount the viewing platform on the Western side. These platforms are to the right of the old Reichstag building. East Berlin itself is dimly lit behind the glare of the Brandenburg Gate. The atmosphere, at what used to be the centre of Berlin, is rather like that of a deserted cemetery. Some may think it appropriate that the Russians have their own war memorial inside a restricted area in West Berlin; for the whole funereal border is a memorial to the defensiveness of Eastern psychology at a time when it might have been more warranted than it is today.

Is the Eastern stance merely defensive? All Allied soldiers going to West Berlin are briefed with a thoroughness which attempts to take stock of them as thinking and motivated human beings rather than military machines — a move that would perhaps have struck Wellington (much as he approved of military innovations if they worked) as too egalitarian by far. They are told that within twenty miles of Berlin there are ninety thousand men of the Warsaw Pact countries; that disconcertingly near are half a million men under arms with eight thousand tanks; that tons of coke, building materials, clothing and food are always stockpiled for any sudden emergency. They also know — which can be a bit bewildering to some — that when Russians are met in the course of military duty, relations are expected to be amicable.

There are examples of this strange two-sided mood of caution with friendliness every day. Every morning, a British military train sets off from a West Berlin station whose platforms have weeds sprouting lushly through the old and cracked concrete blocks — a platform more evocative of East than West Berlin. A few miles out, at Potsdam, the East German locomotive is changed for another East German one, which takes the trainload of soldiers, wives, families and visiting officials on until the engine is changed *again* for a West German one, which takes the train over the border. Here three British soldiers take all the passports and travel documents of everyone on the train and present them to Russian soldiers for examination. The length of the delay to the train can be a fairly accurate barometer of Russian-British relations. The average is twenty minutes.

On the day I made the journey, it was only ten minutes — roughly the time it took to make the last change of locomotive. 'The sun is obviously out today,' said one fairly regular passenger on the train, as a young British soldier walked up the corridor with an unloaded automatic pistol at his hip, telling everyone to please keep in their seats and not gape out of the windows. Outside on the platform, three British soldiers walked with a briefcase full of documents to meet the stolid Russians. 'But,' he added, 'you can't always tell. I was quite worried one day when there was a half-hour delay. It turned out that one of the Russians in the station office was ending his tour of duty. Our people brought out a bottle of vodka for a little goodbye celebration.'

But still the huge Warsaw Pact military build-up goes on around Berlin; and still the British remain with the French and Americans to keep the Western flag flying one hundred miles inside Eastern territory. The three thousand British soldiers are the only British Army personnel in Germany who are not part of the NATO forces in Europe. The diplomatic reasons for this are fairly obvious.

Why is the British Army in a Berlin that would be difficult to defend in time of war? Because to pull out any peg of the arrangement that now holds the former capital in balance would be to risk precipitating adventures that the East might not want, but might be tempted to launch if they were faced by weakness. Britain has a right, under the terms of Germany's surrender, to military occupation of its own sector; and where Berlin is concerned, all rights are rigorously exercised — by both sides. The balance of power is intricate, and in need of constant lubrication.

Understanding the Army's chain of command alone requires a computer. It is as topsy-turvy as the siting of the headquarters of the British Army itself. This is a handsome stone building called London Block by the British but Eagle Block by the Germans, who remember the gold eagles on grand pillars by the entrance, put there by Hitler when he built the place, next door to the Berlin Olympic Stadium. There is a display case of historical photographs in the foyer of this imposing building, and the captions, neutral in tone, show a willingness to let bygones be bygones. One of them reads: 'Adolf Hitler, Führer and patron of the Games, walking in the Stadium with leaders of the World Sports.'

The General who commands British forces, from the building that was a pride and joy of the Nazis, wears two hats. He answers to two masters — to the British Ambassador in the new capital of West Germany, Bonn, and to the Commander-in-Chief, Germany. He heads the British Military Government, and he is General Officer Commanding, British Forces, Berlin. He has a Chief of Staff — a full Colonel, who is in effect the general manager of his military staff in the headquarters.

When I met the Chief of Staff, he apologized for being in his track suit. He had been playing hockey. The atmosphere was quite relaxed, more so than at many Army dispositions on the main East-West German border. Initially, I found this strange. West Berlin is 110 miles from the nearest point in West Germany; only fifty miles from Poland. The Russians encircle it completely, leaving the three air corridors and the main road and rail routes to Helmstedt as the only available lines of communication, for the Allies, with the West. The routes are rather like an umbilical cord joining the mother to a thirty-five-year-old baby; a baby which is regarded as an important advertisement of Western values and achievements. The relaxation of West Berlin, compared with the adrenal edginess of the real East-West border over a hundred miles back on the Western side, may be (think some soldiers) because the Russians are seen face-to-face, not as a vague and mysterious presence, as they are in East Germany.

British soldiers in Berlin have to be diplomatic and the diplomacy must be exercised from the lowest level to the highest. An example. When I made my visit, the trees near the runway of Gatow airport were a matter which had reached attention at General level. Flying into Gatow airport is difficult enough in any case, involving flying all the way up the narrow air corridor from Helmstedt to Berlin at a regulation height. This is the height at which the old Dakotas originally flew, and which no one since has cared to vary, because everyone is suspicious of *any* variation when it comes to Berlin. The trees near the end of the runway made the whole landing operation even more difficult than it need be. The trouble was that the trees, though they affected aircraft, were not on the airfield itself, but just outside it, and the West Berlin Senate (city authority) have strict rules against cutting down trees. Though the Gatow field is run by the RAF, the Army's General, as Commandant of the British Military Government, was naturally called in to look after their interests. Plans were made to cut down the trees, and demonstrators were due to come and interrupt the process. Not the stuff of World War Three? Perhaps not, but a wrong word from any soldier could have caused great ill-feeling.

'In the sector headquarters side, we work very closely with the British Military Government, because almost *everything* has political implications to some degree or other,' said the Chief of Staff.

In these delicate, if not usually fraught, circumstances, every soldier is in effect a diplomat as well as a protector. He discharges this unofficial function in a very rich city which spent 800 million Deutschmarks (about £200 million or 400 million US dollars) on a new conference hall in 1979 — though it is subsidized by an even richer West Germany to the tune of 10,000 million Deutschmarks a year, fifty-two per cent of the West Berlin budget, but less than one per cent of the gross national product of the Federal Republic (West Germany). He discharges it in a very fast city, where the pace of life is reflected in the way people

111

drive their cars — easily measured by the dents; where it is scarcely more easy for him to 'get out into the country', if he feels like it, than it is for the West Berliners themselves; and in which, therefore, a feeling of claustrophobia sometimes creeps up on him. All the raw materials for manufacturing industries and all the food for the civilian population and troops have to be *brought* in through or over East Germany, and there are two hundred flights a day coming into, or going out of, West Berlin.

The soldier of Wellington's, Kitchener's or even Montgomery's day did not need to get to grips with such a complex situation and keep it always in mind. If a soldier is involved in a motoring mishap with one of the hard-driving Germans while on a flag tour of East Berlin, he must *not* deal with the East German police, because that would mean Britain recognized East Berlin as a separate city, which she does not. The soldier, bruised and shaken as he may be, has to ask for the immediate presence of a Russian Army officer (whose presence we *do* recognize in East Berlin) and deal only with him. If he is driving in West Berlin and is in collision with a large Mercedes, he must keep his temper — as he must in bars where the superior purchasing power of the West Berliners may not always please him.

The fact that foodstuffs have to be brought in from the West may not create strains for the soldier, but it may sometimes create problems for his wife. 'It means that a very large stockpile of meat has to be kept in reserve in case of emergency,' explained a Sergeant encountered in a hotel bar. 'They have to sell it off before it goes bad, so they let us have it at a reduced price and our overseas allowance is lower because of it. This sounds a great idea, and sometimes you can get some very good cuts for very little money — which is something when you consider that every time the government gives us more money in salary they usually find some way to take it back off us. So the meat is appreciated by the wife. The trouble is, you have to give in your orders a week ahead, which ties you down a bit — which I suppose is fair enough. But then you don't always get what you ask for, and have to make do with the next best thing, which can be particularly disappointing if you have your family visiting you, or something like that. Wives get irritated about it.'

Irritated wives tend to lead to tense husbands, and West Berlin is not a good place in which to be tense; it is too much like a gold-rimmed goldfish bowl; a gleaming, almost entirely modern city where practically everything costs the soldier just short of double what he would pay in his home country. If a soldier wants to drive in the country with the same freedom he has at home, he has first to drive 110 miles out of West Berlin and along the permitted road to Helmstedt; it is only there that his *relaxed* motoring can *start*. If he wants to take his family to Britain for a few days at Christmas or during other school holidays, he may well find that all his savings (and because of the overseas allowance men *can* save in West Berlin) have to be poured into the operation.

Still, British soldiers in Berlin are not poor; and they are certainly put on their guard about how to react to any attempt to exploit their modest circumstances relative to the local population. They are carefully briefed before and after their arrival on what to do and what not to do. Since they enjoy Berlin more than West Germany (because their accommodation is better and because they are not liable to be sent to Northern Ireland suddenly from Berlin, as they are from West Germany) they take heed.

'Obviously,' said an Army officer, 'sitting here as one does, a hundred miles behind the NATO lines, subversion is something that one has to guard against, but I don't think it is a great problem. All soldiers are briefed on arrival that if they are approached in any peculiar manner, they are to report it. Of course, no one will approach you and say, "Photograph some secret files for us." It won't start like that. It would start with a more mundane sort of thing, but once they had got you, they could try for something further.'

There are iron gates at strategic points in London Block corridors and identity passes are rigorously scrutinized: it was one of the few atmospheric signs in West Berlin that the place was an island and not part of an ordinary thriving Western country. Careful briefings go on at high as well as low levels. Periodic talks are given to visiting politicians, soldiers and journalists. They are normally a two-headed operation between the Army and the British Military Government and they bring out facts that the average visitor to Berlin, let alone the man in the UK street, does not know.

The Major who was at the lectern when I visited, a tall and stately man with a crisp manner and a talent for oblique meanings, kicked off by saying that although Berlin was almost destroyed at the end of the war by Allied bombing, ten thousand old men and boys had succeeded in defending the city, in the closing stages, against advancing Russian troops. Later, when asked by one visitor whether the British Army's presence in Berlin could be regarded as a sort of diplomatic mission rather than a defence force, he returned to this point. 'No, I don't think we are a diplomatic mission. We are quite convinced that if anyone starts shooting at us, we will start shooting back, and that makes us an *Army*. The people of West Berlin would rather expect us to shoot back. Otherwise there is no basis for them carrying on living here.'

The British, with 3,000 soldiers in West Berlin, are the middle force in numbers: the Americans have 6,500, the French 2,500. Some officers in Berlin estimated that the Russians would be able to put seven men into an attack against every British soldier; but the Major once more pointed out how two Russian Armies had been held up at the end of the war by the old men and boys. 'I don't think it would come into the Mafeking or Ladysmith category. Nevertheless I am quite confident that if a military attack were made on Berlin — which is unlikely because there is nothing to be gained — we could hold it for as long as necessary. On the basis of Suez, I think we could hold up any aggression into the city for two weeks, when world opinion would step in to condemn the aggression. At least, I hope so.'

If the average British soldier in Berlin is more concerned with showing the flag than showing his rifle, it may well be because it is by no means certain — according to the men on the spot — that the Russians would trouble to take Berlin, thus holding up their advance, when they could simply invade West Germany itself, and mop up an even more isolated Berlin afterwards. But the East could make things awkward in Berlin without a direct invasion, thanks to the strange criss-cross of arrangements for running the divided city. All the Berlin local overland trains (which correspond to the London Underground) are controlled from East Berlin. So are the canals, which are more important as a commercial highway than they are in London. The power stations are also vulnerable.

But still West Berlin goes on, a good posting for the British soldier who is not totally blind to its subtleties and diplomatic requirements. The British Army even has its own social institutions and buildings such as the Edinburgh House Hotel in Theodor Heuss Platz, at the end of the long East-West central road which leads to the Brandenburg Gate several miles up the road: a military hotel where soldiers and their wives from West Germany, or on posting, can stay for a quarter of what the same comfort would cost them in Britain, and also drink French wine at around five pence per glass. Small wonder that in the hotel you will see and hear visiting soldiers and their families drinking or relaxing in the neat suits and dresses they would use for an evening meal on a Clacton holiday. There *is* a holiday atmosphere about West Berlin, for all its almost frantic work and bustle by the 800,000 labour force (including 40,000 Turks) who produce goods and services worth 46,000 *million* Deutschmarks a year (£11,500 million). The city, despite the fact it has a very high proportion of old people, eats and drinks well, drives fast, lives for today. Its ability to do so, as good relations between soldiers and

Berliners show, depends in part on the presence of the three thousand, mostly rather young, British soldiers, and their French and American allies.

What sort of people are they? What sort of people are the British military of the late twentieth century as a whole? How are they chosen, how are they promoted and what do they think about it all?

PART TWO

Who They Are

6

Mother Regiment

'Some regiments used to have a very rigid hierarchy. You certainly knew who you were. I once spent a day in the cells of the Tower of London. I had committed a terrible crime. I was a Corporal and I was accused of 'fraternizing' with a Private. He met me by chance in Regent Street and told me that I had been posted for guard duty, and that he had laid out my uniform. An officer saw us. I was taken before the Colonel the next morning, and reprimanded for fraternizing. I am talking about before the last war. I don't know what things are like today.'

— Retired Grenadier Guards Sergeant.

'It is a good reflection on a regiment that its officers are not turned out with a die-stamp to be all the same; that you have the chap who is interested in Grecian pottery and another officer who is taking a motor bike apart. The regiment itself is still something that officers and men can identify with personally — a family, a very individual thing.'

— Brigadier, Queens Own Hussars.

There is no *one* British Army. There are only a number of *different* specialist corps and individual regiments, each with their separate identity and quirks, their different caps and trousers, their insistence that they stand up or that they sit down for the Loyal Toast to Her Majesty the Queen. Officers and other ranks — more especially the lowly in the hierarchy — are bristlingly sensitive about any attempt to interfere with this very singular, very British arrangement. Ah, Mother Regiment! How she must be defended at all costs by her sons, however eccentric she may sometimes appear to casual callers!

Tell the story of the Queen and the tulip in any British

Army regimental mess and you will make more enemies than friends. You will have suggested that regimental codes and lore *can* be nonsense. The story is that the Queen so liked one particularly magnificent tulip in the garden of her palace one season that she ordered a sentry of the Palace Guard to be posted there to guard it. Summer turned to autumn and then to winter. Winter turned to spring and then to summer again. Fresh tulips grew, and the favoured one was long forgotten. First the years, then the decades and, after that, the centuries went by; and still a Palace Guard stood at the same spot, defending precisely nothing. But, because no one could remember why the sentry had been put there in the first place, and because the sentry had become part of the lore of the Palace Guard, no one cared or dared to change the order. No doubt if anyone had suggested his removal to more useful work he would have been accused of a subversive wish to tamper with the traditional fabric of the soldiery concerned. The Queen, it will have been inferred with relief, was not the present Queen of England. She was a Scandinavian lady of a different age — as British soldiers who spin the yarn will be the first to tell you.

In the much depleted British Army of today, the little intricacies of regimental life tend not to be — though not invariably — the sort that waste available manpower. But it does remain highly unusual in giving any credence at all to regimental custom, basing its whole structure on the concept of 'The Regiment' and not of the 'British Army' as a monolithic entity. 'No young man joins the Army,' seasoned officers will say proudly. 'He joins his Regiment,' and you can *hear* the capital R in the word Regiment.

Justified or an anachronism? After seeing many and diverse regiments in barracks and in the field, the mind remains surprisingly open. The regimental idea is not logical; but neither are human beings. There is little doubt that some regiments foster team spirit by fostering a miniature version of a semi-feudal system, with officers in the role of squires and men in the role of protected or patronized peasantry; and in so doing they set like concrete the social attitudes and assumptions that have largely disappeared, whether spontaneously or through positive political and social action, outside the Army. The question is: is the Army a more comfortable institution to work for, and a more effective instrument in action, because of it? Many who see regiments in action for themselves as distinct from contemplating protocol at long range (as they might look at African tribal customs on a television screen in Ascot), would be extremely reluctant to say the answer was a definite no.

Often differences in regimental practice and protocol are minor, the sort of rules and rituals used in public schools to bewilder newcomers, put them in their place, and then, as the practice becomes more familiar, make them feel part of the team. The niceties of personal address would call for a handbook in itself: whether brother officers call themselves by their Christian names in the presence of the men; whether they call all senior officers Sir at all times, or only the CO Sir; and whether the CO is saluted only once in the day, the first time he is seen, or on every occasion. It varies from regiment to regiment. It is not written down, but woe betide any newcomer who does not know the form.

In one Household Cavalry regiment, The Blues and Royals, with their history of physical proximity to the monarchy, officers salute even when they have not got their hats on. Other regiments would put a man on charge for doing so, suspecting a derisive gesture towards those in authority. The Foot Guards, such as the Coldstream Guards, can wear Sam Browne leather belts in the mess, whereas in other regiments it might well be tantamount to going into the club bar wearing window cleaner's overalls. The Coldstream Guards will wear their Sam Brownes when in another *Guards* mess, but *never* when in the mess of a regiment with a quite different protocol. In Regiments of the Line, it is not unusual for the Orderly Officer, alone, to wear his Sam Browne, even in the mess, to show he is the duty man to be approached in the case of any difficulty — a measure with an obvious utilitarian value.

'It has all just evolved,' said a Major with thirty years' experience of the Army. 'If you asked for a clear-cut rule about anything when you came into the British Army, you wouldn't get a clear-cut answer. It is a rational absurdity. But in fact it promotes a feeling of fellowship within regiments.'

The days when brother officers would try to lure an officer into the mess wearing a Sam Browne when he shouldn't be, or *not* wearing one when he should be — knowing that either happening would mean drinks all round — may have gone. Private incomes still exist, but they are usually greatly depleted, and large unpaid mess bills are no longer quite the joke they were in, say, 1909, when *Punch* published a cartoon of a Major slumped in the armchair of a mess saying to the Subaltern: 'It's pretty certain we shall have to fight 'em in the course of the next few years.' To which the Subaltern replies: 'Well, let's hope it'll come between the polo and the huntin'.'

Even though such attitudes are now so distant that they are beyond the reach of satirists, regimental ritual of little operational value persists. It can be regarded as merely juvenile or merely picturesque, according to taste. National individuality is encouraged to the point of idiosyncracy, rather than the reverse. The Irish Guards invariably have a wolfhound as their mascot. The Royal Regiment of Wales has a Welsh goat and has done since the Crimean War. Do such traditions foster a sense of national independence within the troops, thereby making the Welsh and Scots feel less dominated by Big Brother England? Do they thus contribute to the solidarity of the assaulted Union? Possibly.

On their first St David's Day, the day of the Welsh patron saint, Junior Subalterns of the Royal Regiment of Wales are required to eat a raw leek — the largest obtainable — while standing with one foot on the mess table. It is brought to them on a silver tray by the Mess Sergeant.

Everyone beats the table and a drummer gives rolls on his drum to help the process along. To facilitate digestion, the newcomer is then required to drink a pint of beer, from a silver goblet, in a single gulp. He is also required to sing a national song. If he doesn't sing loudly enough, a not entirely unusual inadequacy by this point, he is what is called 'referred back'. This means he has to wait another year and then go through the whole thing again. 'The majority *do* pass the singing test,' said one officer who had seen it happen on many memorable occasions. One could readily see that there was a powerful incentive to do so.

Some regimental practices stem back to touchy points in far, far distant history. Often they entail virtual rewriting (or at least reinterpretation) of history itself. The Scots Guards are (from their own point of view) the oldest of all the Guards Regiments: older than the Grenadiers or the Coldstream Guards. Unfortunately, they made the mistake of supporting the wrong side in the last British civil war — they supported Cromwell against the King — and were defeated at the Battle of Dunbar. The result was that they were disbanded, to reappear in a slightly different form when memories had cooled — and when the Grenadiers (on the King's side) and the Coldstream Guards (on Cromwell's) were already in existence. These events, centuries before America even became a nation, have left a rich legacy of regimental niceties. For a start, the Grenadiers and the Coldstream Guards (together with the Welsh Guards) never rise to drink the Loyal Toast to the Queen, an omission which, if it happened in other regiments, would cause the court martial machinery of the British Army to be choked for as many years forwards as these events date backwards. This is because, a bit like schoolboy creeps and other absolute rotters, they want to make the point that *their* loyalty is not in question. Perhaps it is a way of keeping the Scots Guards in their place, reminding them of the fact that one error of loyalty cost them their seniority as the oldest Guards Regiment.

Similarly, to this day, the Grenadiers and Coldstream

Guards will not (except for the Queen's Birthday Parade, when they form the escort) go on parade side by side. They are always grouped so that the Scots Guards go in the middle. The Coldstream Guards will not stand next to the Grenadiers: their motto is 'Second to None'; and, as the Grenadiers *claim* to be the first and best Guards Regiment, the Coldstream Guards will simply not be in any juxtaposition to them which could be interpreted as being in second place. The rule applies to the Queen's Review of the Guards Division, harmlessly, but I was assured it would not apply to battle. There is little practical price to be paid for such niceties.

Only one regiment, the Royal Gloucesters, are allowed to wear *two* badges on their caps, a large one at the front and a smaller one at the back. This dates back to the days of the British Raj in India, when the regiment was mercilessly squeezed both in the van and in the rear, an experience it survived with valour. Queen Victoria sanctioned one badge per fighting front in commemoration. Bearing in mind that all the men involved in this action are long departed, as is the British Empire, can the two buttons constitute more than a childish affectation today? An officer with knowledge of the regiment over a long period of time said: 'It is much more than that. There is a high pride and morale in that regiment. It has a value in the modern field. During the Korean war, 600 Gloucesters were taken prisoner by the Chinese. They kept their morale. Almost all came back eventually. Whereas the Americans, with no comparable tradition ... well, enormous numbers died of acute melancholia. They just gave up. That is the difference between the way we endeavour to build self-pride into a chap, and their way. We tell everyone wanting to join the British Army that a soldier must do his best when conditions are worst. Regimental pride helps that.'

Even in establishments which are not part of a regiment and cannot by definition be part of a regiment, there is an attempt to create the regimental atmosphere. At the Recruit Selection Centre at Sutton Coldfield in the West Midlands, regimental silver borrowed from regiments is scattered about the Officers Mess to make the officers feel regimental, perhaps the more so because their job, by its very nature, takes them away from purely regimental considerations and atmospheres. In such a way might a missionary, at the height of Empire a century ago, proof himself against the possibility of failing faith by having a Bible always at his bedside in the middle of the jungle.

I referred earlier to reinterpretation of history as a means to regimental pride. It is a reasonable *academic* criticism that, especially among other ranks, the 'tradition' which the soldier is expected to identify himself with may be chopped and changed in his own mind without apparently losing credibility. Some officers have noticed that, when a man is switched from one battalion to another, or when battalions are split up and regrouped, the men soon start relating just as well to their new 'history of the battalion' as they did to the original one, rather as a man moving from one town to another would embrace 'his' new local football team.

One Major, who had witnessed at close quarters the adaptability of the serving soldier in this respect said: 'The men will switch their "historical" loyalties in a moment. You can rename a battery, from Niagara to Le Cateaux or something, and then programme them into a completely different history to be proud of. This sometimes makes me think that the whole business of regimental traditions is a bit of a farce.' His Commanding Officer smartly trod on the sentiment: 'I don't agree at all. If you had seen what a regiment can be like when it has regimental pride instilled into it compared with when it hasn't, you wouldn't say that.' A Captain who was present at the same discussion came in on the side of the Major: 'You can ask the Guards *why* they think they are the best, and you get a conditioned response. They stop discussing the point, if indeed they have ever started discussing it, take one step backwards, bang their feet down and say, "Because we *are* the best, that's why." They think they don't have to give a reason.' At least this discussion proved that the modern soldier is not frightened to express an unorthodox view, even in the presence of his Commanding Officer, provided it is within the four walls of the mess and not in the presence of Other Ranks.

Officers who prefer reasoned argument to mere assertion of regimental superiority still support the idea of the regiment because they say it gives a man a 'home' within the vast and inevitably impersonal institution of the whole Army, with which no man could hope to identify himself. 'I go back to my old regiment,' said a Brigadier, 'and there I will find some of the same men as when I was there, though in different ranks. And immediately you feel at home. You see the same regimental silver. In a way it is like looking at your own mantelpiece.'

The point here is that 'home' does not need to be the birthplace of the soldier concerned. 'They will cling to their adopted home. You will even find Welshmen in the Royal Hampshires now and again.'

Do the Officers, the NCOs or the men really believe in the superiority of their own regiment over all others? One particular Sergeant Major from the Household Division admitted cheerfully enough, and under no pressure from me, that the other Guards Regiments would *each* think they were superior to the others. Could all of them be right? A knowing twinkle crept into the Sergeant Major's eyes, showing he took the point well enough, as befitted a man whose ambition was to get his own children into university. Then, quite straight-faced again, he said: 'I seriously believe it. We are best.' He believed it as one might 'believe' a stirring passage from Shakespeare's *Henry V*; and who is to say that a man who may have to fire a gun in anger does not need a harmless piece of self-dramatization to help him on his way?

But can the regimental concept ever be actively harmful to efficiency in the post-Empire British Army? It can certainly provide corners in which can exist master-and-man relationships which would not exist in civilian life. Officers say that to be comfortable in a regiment, you must 'share similar interests'. This, in practice, means the same sports and pastimes, the same attitude to life and manners. I met many officers of the Household Division in my military travels and practically all, if they were not public schoolboys in fact, would have passed as such. In some of the specialist corps — the Medical Corps, the Ordnance Corps, the Royal Engineers, the Royal Electrical and Mechanical Engineers, the Royal Corps of Transport, the Intelligence Corps — officers and men were indistinguishable from their counterparts in civilian life, except for their uniform and the fact that it was rather better cared for than the equivalent civilian clothes would have been. No one can say that the whole of the British Army thinks in terms of Above Stairs, Below Stairs, master and servant. But in the Guards and some of the Infantry Regiments, shades of these attitudes, especially on ceremonial duties, persist, and it would be resented by officers and men if any attempt were to be made to undermine them. 'People who wouldn't fit in tend to join parts of the Army where they can,' argue officers. 'There are plenty to choose from.'

It is the concept of the regiment which makes these differences in atmosphere and social usage possible. There is no such thing in the British Army (as there is in the German Army, for instance) as an Officer Corps. The absence seems healthy rather than not. British officers point out that where there is an Officer Corps which spans an entire Army, there is an elite which may end up owing its major loyalty to itself. In the British Army, officers and other ranks have their separate messes, but they both come together as members of one regiment, and share a common history. 'It is the difference,' one officer argued, 'between a boss who mixes only with his cronies and a boss who mixes with his family, some younger, some older, some richer, some poorer.' The concept of the family is a powerful ingredient in the continued life of the regiment as a central idea in the British Army. Families are messy, inconsistent, easily derided; but people, it has been decided, are nevertheless more likely to fight and, if need be, die for the family than they are for the 'organization' — too abstract a concept for the secretly emotional and poetic British, Above or Below Stairs.

As the 1980s began, one of the regiments who were doing extremely well were The Royal Green Jackets, the regiment that grew out of the crack anti-guerrilla riflemen used against the locals in the American War of Independence. Wherever I went, I seemed to see Royal Green Jackets. More, I seemed to be made intensely *aware* of them. They are very good at self-projection. Their jealous rivals say they are very good at public relations, and that we will all know that the Day of Judgement has come when we meet a sincere Green Jacket. They are very good at grabbing the best recruits from Sandhurst, and at getting themselves into the upper hierarchy of the Army (especially in the devious corridors of Whitehall, where many excellent military men are hopelessly lost). Even the newest 2nd Lieutenant, barely in his twenties, will address you with the assurance of an intellectual equal, whereas a Guards Officer of the same age will tend to project an air of social superiority, but leave you wondering just how clever he is.

In messes of the Guards, I was entertained with considerable social skill and courtesy, and left with a strong impression that, whether or not I would gravitate towards them in the bar, they would be the sort of men I would want to go tiger shooting with. In messes of The Royal Green Jackets, I was in the company of men who wished to match wits with anyone they encountered, men who were as intellectually fascinated with the problems of their job as they were impeccably determined to overcome them. It was as if, even hundreds of years after the American War of Independence, they *still* realized that *any* shaft of perception might be useful in the essential job of overcoming the enemy, and that they would be happy to look anew at anything, whereas in slower regiments new ideas can be seen as a threat.

The Infantry Regiments tend to be the Cinderellas of the British Army. Their heritage is one of foot-slogging; and foot-slogging has little glamour to the West of today. They often have trouble in attracting the quota of officers and men allocated to them. Does this suggest that the atmosphere of encrusted tradition is bad for some vintage parts of the British Army? There is a case for saying that precisely the reverse is true. Regiments which have a strong *atmosphere* (social certainty in the case of the Guards, intellectual dexterity in the case of The Royal Green Jackets) tend to attract men and become buoyant. Infantry Regiments, which depend on a strong link with a geographical *locality* and its history, have fared less well. The reason, argue some officers and men, could be that these regiments were amalgamated into larger, more regional regiments in the military shake-up of the 1960s and 1970s; and the larger the unit, the less men can associate themselves with it personally. A man may wish to defend his native county rather more than he may wish to defend the area encompassed by the Royal Anglian Regiment, for instance, which covers part of industrial Leicestershire, parts of rural Lincolnshire and a jumble of other areas which are alike only in that they do *not* include parts of East Anglia proper (despite the title). Such amalgamations took place when it was thought that Big was Beautiful. What has happened to one or two British industrial firms who followed this maxim is beginning to be noted by some soldiers. It has not (yet) persuaded the Ministry of Defence to have a rethink about the area-based Infantry Regiments, but there is nothing sacred about organizational patterns. It is quite possible that one day we will see a real Suffolk Regiment again, with a history that is closely defined and manageable in the human mind.

It is in the messes that the flavour and morale of a regiment conveys itself. The general tone — more egalitarian in terms of social nicety, more functional and less fussy — conveys the flavour of the British Army of today.

In an Officers Mess at Colchester Garrison, I found more commercial travellers entertaining clients, more local businessmen talking business, than I did soldiers. The mess has been thrown open to public membership, and the menu carries items appropriate to this status, from Beef Stroganoff to Chicken Maryland. Such flirting with the outside world partly on *its* terms (only partly, because one reason businessmen like to entertain at the mess is its military atmosphere) would have horrified officers at the time of the British Raj. It does not please all of them today — even if they profit by it financially, to the extent that more money can be spent on the mess upkeep than otherwise.

Even the corps still strive for exclusivity in their messes wherever possible, often buttressed by a retired Major with a flowing grey moustache called the Mess Secretary, who is damned if the young 'uns are going to walk all over him. One such, a former infantryman who was, when I met him, the Mess Secretary for the Royal Engineers in Kent, claimed he had the finest mess in the British Army and that he would 'in no circumstances' allow a queue-up cafeteria system. 'But then, I am terribly pompous about these things,' he added, obviously not meaning it for a moment, 'and I am fully supported by the other officers. There have been occasions when young officers have wanted to lower standards and suggested it at general mess meetings. They have never got very far. If they come to me, they don't get further than me. I would say, "Not in any circumstances. If the standards are going to be lowered, I am off." Some of them want to wear jeans and roll-neck sweaters. I say, "Certainly not." They want microwave ovens and slot machines, so they can rush off and play tennis. Can you imagine it?'

He spoke with some envy of the building of the Royal Artillery Mess at Woolwich: 'I have been doing this job for eighteen years. My mess dates back to 1812. I think, if anything, we have more pomp and circumstance than the average mess. On Guest Nights we have trumpeters and feed by candlelight. The waiters wear white clothes. I must have gone into thousands of messes, and I consider we are more formal and more like what *I* would call an Officers

Mess than the average. But the Gunners Mess at Woolwich is slightly more ornate because they are what I would call a *Regimental* Regiment. But,' added the Major with scarcely concealed gratification, 'one is absolutely *horrified* to find one has to queue up on the cafeteria system.'

It was quite clear what the Major meant by the mess of 'a regimental regiment' — one which conveyed, by its atmosphere, that its use was reserved for a body of men who thought themselves unique; that it was not a nosherie at the top of a chain store. The fact that more and more officers now live out of mess appears to make them more determined, not less, to stand by the idea of the regiment. The Major said that in his mess he could sleep eighty, but the average number of living-in officers was now only thirty. But that didn't mean they didn't respect the regimental idea, just that, in peacetime, they expected to live some of their lives independently as well.

The truth seems to be that the modern British Army officer wants to be conscious of the regiment when he is at work, wants to use its history as a working tool, but wants it to be more of a brother and less of a mother. A high degree of toughness, mental and physical, is now expected from him from the start. Mental toughness can feel respect, more easily than it can feel thoughtless reverence, for things past — including the story of how Buffy Fanshawe, in the year of the Crimea, could down fourteen gins in the regimental mess and next day fight like a hero.

Could Buffy do it in a modern and complicated rocket-launcher? Doubtful. He would need, as we shall now see, to be a rather different type of man, one who could pass muster by the standards of meritocracy, even if he himself were as well connected as a Duke.

7

Officers or Gentlemen?

'Officers in the 1920s, when I was in the Guards, could be stupid. I remember a man was once put on a charge for having greasy buttons. He was taken before an officer. "The bacon we had for breakfast was greasy and I breathed on them," he claimed. He was let off. The others who were on charges laughed out loud at that. They were all charged with the additional charge of insubordination.'

— Retired NCO of the Brigade of Guards (now known as the Household Division).

'It is virtually impossible for even the most well-connected man to become an officer in the British Army today unless he also has brains and ability.'

— Officer at the Regular Commissions Board in 1980.

Rowbotham was perhaps a little out of his element. He threw the rope over the bar without holding the end of it, and lost it in the lake. When his taller colleagues stood in front of him, as they tended to, he didn't push his way through them and speak up. Determination, yes — in other areas. He had gone back to school after leaving to get his 'A' levels. He had spent time in an Israeli kibbutz. But here, sweating in the grounds of a Wiltshire country house, his spectacles tended to mist up in perplexity. Alas, thumbs down to Rowbotham.

Marchbanks was different. He had the fair locks and sensuous mouth of the archetypal poet. He started giving orders about what to do with the planks and ropes from the word go. Increasingly, as planks failed to fit and ropes came undone, his colleagues failed to share his good opinion of his worth. They came to ignore him. Thumbs down to Marchbanks.

Then there was Grimm. He was not easy to notice. A dour angular young man, he stayed on the fringes of the group, on his own, until he had something to suggest, and then he suggested it in a tense voice. He did not smile once, not even when asked in what country baked beans were grown. He started off quietly and stayed quiet until the end. The authorities said thumbs up to Grimm and so, I discovered, rather to my surprise, when I did a little research of my own, did the contemporaries he was working alongside.

It was all very strange at first to a civilian eye — strange, remarkably demanding and ultimately revealing.

In the grounds of Leighton House, at Westbury in Wiltshire, seven young men, with foot-high numbers on their chests and backs, were trying to carry a pole painted green past poles painted red without touching either the red poles or the ground. Some painted motor tyres swinging from lengths of rope were there to help them, and a steely-eyed Major with a clipboard and scribbling pencil was there to judge them. Soon they were busy trying to span an imposingly fetid pond with the aid of planks too short to go over it, to the accompaniment of agonized or energizing cries: 'Get some more weight on the end of that plank!' 'Keep your weight the other side!' 'Stop arguing, we've only got another minute to go!' Splash. Groans. Laughter.

The seven young men (the youngest eighteen, the oldest twenty-four, although they could have been a bit younger and much older) were discovering whether they were fit to follow in the footsteps of Wellington, Kitchener and Montgomery by being accepted for training as officers in the British Army. Diving head-first through a window came into it, too.

A satirist, taking the quickest of looks, could have seen it as self-parody. Was it? Did it play into a satirist's view of what a British Army officer should be: a young man with a tweed suit as thick as his huntin' accent; eyes like a dull brute's, softening fawningly only at the sight of Higher Rank; a skin as sensitive as a dead rhinoceros's; a head strongly armour-plated from ear to ear and an awareness of contemporary conditions at least three years ahead of Marie-Antoinette's?

To the planks and the ponds must be added the fact that the present system for picking men suitable for officer training at Sandhurst was devised thirty-eight years ago by psychologists, who then largely abdicated from participation because 'only the Army itself really knew what was wanted from a practical point of view'. When it comes to selecting its own officers, the Army is very firmly master in its own house, and must stand or fall by the results, with no excuses. The vital question is whether the method works for the best, even in the nuclear age, or whether the satirist is right: that the Army is most happy under the command of socially well-connected burly dolts and conducts its screening processes accordingly.

Leighton House, for centuries previously the home of the Phipps family, is not immediately suggestive of a new democratic spirit. Even its converted stables, in which the officers of the Regular Commissions Board meet to thrash out final judgements, are more elegant than many a country mansion. The main building houses the Officers Mess, and includes an ante-room with a leather-topped and gold RCB-monogrammed fender the size of a table tennis table. The dining-room has silver candelabra. All RCB officers are expected to dine there with their visitors (careers masters from schools, headmasters and other influential teachers, officers from other units) on the second night of a board session, paying for their own dinner (often Boeuf Wellington, two choices of wine, fruit in season, choice of savoury, with port or madeira passed round the table, always to the left, of course) and wearing their own dinner jackets for which, unlike many civilians who require them for professional purposes, they get no expense allowances or income tax concessions. An officer with a black eyepatch

134

and a brightly-coloured cummerbund may suggest a complete break with timid civilian values; it is the endearingly venerable state of some of the dinner jackets that most readily suggests that here, after all, is no ivory tower. When there are no guests, there are no dinner jackets for what was, I was assured, a 'very ordinary' supper.

Many subjects are virtually taboo at these candlelit soirées — especially sex, religion and the candidates. There is no such inhibition about money. 'Damned worrying, this money business,' an officer will say as he grabs the rotating port. 'I've got two boys at boarding school now and one who will be shortly going up to university. Where I'll get the money from I don't know. We only get tax concessions on our boarding allowances if we're overseas. I believe in putting my children first, which is as it should be, so how can I save much to get a house for when I retire in five years' time?' The proceedings are never allowed to reach the maudlin stage, because there is an early start with the would-be officers on the morrow. But such sentiments are assured of general sympathy. 'It's not a snobbish matter to send one's children to a public school,' says another officer. 'It is not really a question of public schools or state schools at all. Frankly, boarding school, where you *have* to be self-reliant and do your homework, is a better grounding for someone who wants to be an officer in the British Army. Whether it's private or state is really not the point. I think that's what we've found in practice.'

The candidates themselves are hardly aware of these compromised grandeurs. They spend most of their spare time in their own block, since the little town of Westbury has one or two nice pubs, a bingo hall and not much else. Their own quarters are made of brick, single-storeyed, and with a mess that houses a billiards table, a table tennis table and electronic equipment to summon them for interview or other activities. Older candidates may sleep in single rooms, most of the others sleep two to a room, a few three to a room.

It is often assumed, sometimes by candidates themselves,

that their social deportment is under scrutiny at Westbury, and that bad marks will be given for eating peas with a knife, or referring to table napkins as serviettes, or drinking the contents of finger bowls. Wrong. I saw no finger bowls in the Officers Mess; and the candidates do not *see* the inside of the Officers Mess, let alone any finger bowls. 'Social class has nothing to do with what we are looking for,' said the Group Leader of the seven candidates I joined. He was a young Major whose legs twitched exuberantly as he sat on the mess table after dinner — as well they might, for he had just driven nearly two hundred miles back from Yorkshire at a claimed time which Concorde would find it hard to beat. 'I can't tell you in one neat phrase what we are looking for, but it isn't a certain sort of social behaviour. The candidates are not under scrutiny in their spare time at all. We make a special point of that. My job as Group Leader, the one working most closely with them on their practical tasks, is to judge them only on their performance *here* and *now*.'

The Regular Commissions Board psychologists devised a scheme in which so many individual attributes have to be assessed separately, and so many people have to go on the record separately with their views, that an individual penchant for Eton boys with fair hair, or state school boys with monotonous voices, could not be an overriding factor, even if it existed in the Major General who heads the Board as its President.

The structure of the Board which, at a stretch, is capable of processing about one hundred would-be officers a week, has its built-in checks and balances. Under the Major General are three Vice-Presidents, who are Brigadiers. Each Brigadier has under him two Lieutenant Colonels who are Deputy Presidents, each controlling a group of seven or eight boys. A smaller number than that and the interaction of personalities is restricted, a larger one and the picture becomes diffuse. Under each Lieutenant Colonel is a Group Leader who is a Major. An Education Advisor, a Lieutenant Colonel in the Royal Army Education Corps, is aptly named. He *is* merely an adviser. He stands to one side in all deliberations and he speaks, but does not vote, at the final 'boarding' process at which the Vice-President, the Deputy President and the Group Leader thrash out in detail the fate of the would-be leaders of tomorrow's Army. The Group Leader, who actually puts the cadidates through their practical tasks, knows practically nothing about the boys — except what he sees for himself as the candidates go through their complicated paces. He is wilfully kept in ignorance. The Lieutenant Colonel who is Deputy President knows a bit more about their background, the Brigadier who is Vice-President a bit more still. The Major General is the nearest to God. He usually interviews a boy personally only if there is likely to be a clash of opinion about him, though he sometimes merely takes a 'sample' of any particular board entry. He knows almost all about them — or is soon able to find out. 'It is amazing how candid these chaps are prepared to be,' said the Major General, drawing hard on a comfortable pipe. 'I sometimes think they tell me more than they tell their mothers. Things they wouldn't tell young officers, who are closer to them, they will tell a harmless old Major General.'

Fine. So there are checks and balances in the system, and there is some psychological subtlety. Adjudicating officers are not only encouraged but obliged to stand by their views if they are not swayed by discussion, even if the views go against those of senior officers. (Try that in many civilian organizations who pay lip-service to democratic structures.) But the planks, windows, ropes and ponds may still seem slightly manic until the central point of it all is firmly grasped. This is that the whole system is designed to test candidates *not* in the atmosphere of the dreaming spires of a university, nor at the desk of an ICI or a Unilever, but in the sort of vexatious stress they may have to face in battle. 'I've seen them cry on some of the ropes,' said the Group Leader of the group I joined. 'Their minds just seize up.'

The testing of each group of the Army's future officers lasts three and a half days. Some weeks (as on my visit) there are two Boards. The strain does not fall only on the candidates. Six groups of seven or eight candidates take their tests at any one time in the grounds of Leighton House, and sometimes a group of female candidates replaces a male group, which causes further administrative problems. At the time of my visit, the proportion of candidates who were succeeding had fallen to thirty-five per cent from the fifty-five per cent of the same period in the previous year; but the officers of all the Boards were adamant that in no circumstances whatever, short of Armageddon, and perhaps not even then, would the Army's standards be lowered.

'That would be a very slippery slope!' argued a Brigadier. 'The first consideration must be given to the men who are going to be put under these would-be officers. If there is any doubt at Westbury, it must be resolved in favour of the soldiers who will be serving under the potential officer, *not* in favour of the candidate. That would be a false kindness.'

There were only seven in the group I watched throughout their entire boarding processes (at the suggestion of the Army itself, which thought — rightly — that a mere day's viewing would give no idea of the underlying rationale). Each of the young men was given a group colour — let us say purple in the case of the group I joined. They were consecutively numbered, fore and aft, on waistcoats of purple and fitted up in track suits. The essays and the intelligence tests had come immediately after their arrival and the young men were now on the really gruelling part of their three and a half days — days which the RCB asked me not to describe *too* exactly because it might unfairly help future candidates.

Under the strains of the course, which might have been judged to be the work of a perverse sadist but for its constructive purpose, each of the seven candidates emerged very clearly (or not clearly at all, according to personality or lack of it) as individuals.

Numerically first in the group, although all names of

candidates will be fictional, was Rowbotham, as 101, the product of a Northern polytechnic. He was seeking a Regular Commission (a long-term one). The key to his character, it struck me, was expressed in a casual sentence in conversation before the hard slog: 'You can go through life without scaling mountains.' A very dogged determination never disguised his modesty: to him, mountain-climbing might seem a bit of an affectation, though in no circumstances whatever could one imagine him chickening out, if he regarded it as necessary by his own standards. When it was a question of walking over precarious planks, he neither pushed himself forward nor hung back. Faced with the free choice of flinging himself bodily through a window or going through it in a less spectacular and dangerous way, he chose the less spectacular alternative, but when asked to do it the other way, he stoically took his glasses off and jumped crabwise through the window — a method neither shrinking nor splendid but effective.

For a time, Rowbotham seemed content to play second fiddle to number 102, Marchbanks, who was equally willing to play Number One in the relationship. Marchbanks was seeking a Short Service Commission. Though he was already in the Army as a private soldier, his stated interests were cultural and solitary. I would, at first meeting in civilian clothes, have thought him more suitable for the graphics department of an advertising agency than the rough-and-tumble of Army life. He was obviously intelligent, though his rating in the intelligence tests was modestly, rather than exceptionally, successful. His solutions to problems in the field were thought by some watching officers to be 'superficial', though expressed with a doggedness that took little note of the fact that the other young men were taking less and less note of them. When weight needed to be put on the end of a plank, he shouted, 'Three pairs of feet on here!' but did not stand on the plank himself. 'Bit selfish, this chap,' said the Lieutenant Colonel. 'He tends to want other people to do the work, so he can be first across.'

What a recipe for success in many walks of civilian life! But not in the Army; which might not, so it seemed to me, be able to make use of the *best* characteristics of Marchbanks, but would only make him conscious of his worst. Marchbanks, in a secret ballot I arranged, was the one the group would *least* like to serve under as leader. Number 103, Summers, was the product of a public school. He was the son of a prosperous and enterprising father who had been failed for the Services himself on medical grounds. Was the son trying for the Army because it was one way he could escape comparison with his father? That would have been my hunch; but the Regular Commissions Board works on evidence and not on hunches, except for cases (like this one) referred to the Major General. Summers was seeking a Short Service Limited Commission, under which he would attend a three-week course at Sandhurst and serve for a minimum of four months as a 2nd Lieutenant on a special rate of pay before going off to university, on leaving which he would return to the Army, if he so wished. Summers had diffident charm, which was especially noticeable in his lecturette, which all candidates have to give. It might have commended him to a civilian audience, but struck his military invigilators as not very British-officerish. In spite of several favourable points made by the Major General ('Essentially honest, I think, and aware of his faults, which is no bad thing') those of junior rank stuck to their view that his mind seized up more than once when he was put in command of the group for a task. Summers was one of those who emerged quite clearly as a positive personality, though not necessarily a military one. His failure to get a Commission might well turn out to be a good thing for him as well as for the Army.

Number 104 was Lake. He had the highest intelligence grade of all the group, he made the most sophisticated joke heard in the group, quite early in discussion, and played chess and bridge in his spare time. He was recommended for a Cadetship by the unanimous vote of all three officers who boarded him. In *personality* terms, he disappeared, for me, quite early in the proceedings, so that I always had to cudgel my brains to remember who number 104 *was*. Perhaps the idea of being amorphous was suggested to him, by his chess-playing mind, as being the most effective one in these proceedings; perhaps he just lost interest in imposing himself in human terms. But the results, from his point of view, were most satisfactory.

Boyce, number 105, was given to grey tweed suits of a superior cut and high white collars — in the moments away from the practical tests. He had a round boyish face. He soon abandoned his earlier technique of shouting derogatory remarks and suggestions at other people — seeing that they simply ignored it, and him. A grammar school boy from the North, he took no pains to eradicate his regional accent, while obviously being very conscious of being watched. His intelligence rating was modestly good, one point ahead of number 106, Dearth, a British boy educated in South Africa, with handsome features hardly noticeable because of his withdrawn attitude. He made several useful suggestions on the gruelling course, many of which weren't acted on, or even *heard*, by his colleagues.

Finally, at 107, there was Grimm, whose grey suits and angular frame and apparent ability to make himself listened to (though he never visibly pushed) were destined to win him the chance of a Regular Commission via Sandhurst, and the respect of his colleagues.

It was only with the continuous battering of the Command tasks that the full potential and limitations of the candidates emerged. First there were the so-called leaderless tasks, in which a group were set a problem they well might find on the battlefield and left to solve it in any way they thought fit. The interest here was to see who emerged as a potential leader. At first, presumably because of their preconceived ideas of what constituted 'leadership', they tended to shout instructions or merely imprecations like 'Hurry Up!' to others. Gradually it began to filter through to them that they were all in the same boat, and that if this was the only contribution they had to make, no one was likely to listen to it. It was odd to observe that number 102, who had defended the principle of petrol-rationing with the words, 'Exhortations in a democracy won't work,' was slow to take this point in leaderless combat tasks. By contrast, staid 107 Grimm was careful to say nothing when he had nothing to say. Gradually the group came to follow his suggestions when given, finding they tended to be sound.

In the Command tasks with a leader, the candidates in pre-ordained leadership positions were sometimes *not* in command of the situation although they *appeared* to be. And vice versa. The quiet and introverted Dearth fell completely into the background of his own Command task, but others seemed to work well around him, which must surely be one of the most important, if most intangible, aspects of leadership.

The board members reported their interim findings to their Brigadier and the Major General at various points of the three and a half days. Very little stress was laid on what the candidates had said would be their alternative choice of employment if they did not get a crack at the Army. 'We are advertising that we will give a man more responsibility and managerial skill than he could get in civvy street, so you can't blame a candidate for coming to us for these things, and making no bones about it,' said the Lieutenant Colonel, a burly officer of the Black Watch with kilt and half-moon spectacles. 'You can't blame him for not saying, "I want to come into the Army for the good of the country and the British Empire." If he had *hinted* ten years ago that he was going to Marconi, or a wine merchants, if he didn't get into the Army, that would have been the end of it. People today will say, "When do I have to decide between the Army and Marconi?" Ten years ago I would have been staggered by that.'

'We are looking for the boy who can plan, be practical and be dominant,' said the Major, and much the same thing could be said by any talent spotter for a large civilian organization. An executive of Marconi, Leyland, Unilever or ICI, however, is unlikely to be faced with the sort of task given to candidates at Westbury as their project (theoretical) exercise. A dam is likely to burst into a valley where marooned sheep and an injured man are trapped. You have such-and-such in the way of alternative equipment, so what do you do, and in what order do you do it? There are no 'right' answers to the project. Whatever way the candidates tackle the job, they must sacrifice a lesser priority for a higher one, and thus give an idea of their notions of priority as well as their practical grasp: no flair for putting subordinates in the wrong will suffice here.

The obstacle course, which members of my group had to tackle on their own, was a pulverizer of any sort of affectation. It consisted of a number of obstacles which could be dealt with in more than one way — some cautious and some dangerous. Each candidate was allowed to inspect the course briefly, on his own, and choose the required number of obstacles he would take in the set time of three minutes. If the designer of the Westbury boarding system had been a sadist, this is where he would have gained most enjoyment. The window test itself was part of the obstacle course. It did not defeat Marchbanks, however 'immature' some of his adjudicators may have regarded him. He hurled himself straight through it, whereas Summers climbed through it by using a plank. The dour Grimm jumped through the window voluntarily, but caught his feet against the ledge and only got through successfully, without touching, at the second attempt. His manner suggested he would have jumped it a hundred times if necessary. The highly rational Lake, the man with the highest IQ, took the cautious way through the window, hit the ledge twice when told to jump through it, and was the *only* candidate to adopt the most cumbersome way of getting a box from one end of a narrow tube to the other. He was shrewd enough not to attempt the most difficult task of the lot, hauling a steel box up a treacherously swinging rope — a task which Grimm took on and determinedly solved, being the only candidate to do so. I had to admit that such an ability on a battlefield would be more relevant than conversational sparkle, and began to see the method in the Westbury madness.

The final decisions on whether the candidates have passed or failed are not taken until the young men themselves have taken part in a last team race, in which difficult cases can be watched carefully; have changed into their civvies; have taken their extrovert farewells and the earliest train home.

Then the Brigadier sits between the Lieutenant Colonel and the Major as the score cards of the candidates, in turn, are projected on to a screen. The Education Adviser (though, as a Lieutenant Colonel, he outranks the Group Leader, who is a Major) sits on a separate table in the corner of the room. He symbolizes the role of academic education in the proceedings: as a yardstick, but a subordinate one. It soon became obvious that a complete bonehead and coward would and could get precisely nowhere in the modern Army's screening procedures, even if he were the son of a Duke, the grandson of a Prime Minister and the nephew of an Archbishop of Canterbury.

Each member of the Board in turn had to give his own assessment of nineteen separate aspects of the candidate's performance, on a one-to-five rating. At each point the Board Officer had to declare himself, and could 'box' his own entry (literally drawing a box round it), if he specifically declined to change it to make the assessment unanimous.

The final boarding of Purple Group took five hours. All three officers — Brigadier, Lieutenant Colonel and Major — agreed that Rowbotham must be a 'Fox' (the Army jargon for Fail), while Lake, despite showing little planning skill on the obstacle course was equally well a 'Dog' (Pass). In Lake's case, the internal politics of Army life surfaced: he was applying for a Cadetship, but the officers round the table thought it more likely he would get only the more limited bursary. 'Well,' said one officer, 'this chap *deserves* a Cadetship, so let's recommend him anyway, whatever he gets in the end. The rest isn't up to us.'

A certain proprietorial interest had already developed in the successful candidates, so that voices changed when discussing them. Only Summers, who in his project thought saving sheep a higher priority than warning people, posed a doubt. 'Perhaps a bit immature, that's all?' suggested the Major General.

In the end, it was agreed that Summers would be told he could not have a Cadetship, but might get into Sandhurst if he liked to do a toughening-up course at Rowallan, the Army College for those who, in the Army's view, need more time and stimulus to develop leadership qualities such as self-confidence, ability to project oneself, bite and drive.

Score: two winners out of seven, Grimm and Lake, and one doubtful.

So how successful is the thirty-eight-year-old system still operated by the British Army for choosing its future elite? Are the low numbers of passes because Wellington's successors don't have his moral strength, or are they because young men have become too intelligent to want to throw themselves bodily through windows?

An officer from one of the other two fighting services expressed a crucial problem when he said, 'I sometimes think the Army's difficulty is that its chaps must be good in a rough and tumble, however brainy they are, while in the other two services what you often want is a highly-trained technocrat, even if he has no chin.'

Certainly a chinless technocrat (or aristocrat) would stand no chance of passing at Westbury. The whole experience is calculated to cool off very considerably any puffed-up young gent obsessed with the idea of getting an easy life for himself by leaving the nasty bits to others. I saw nothing crass in the methods used, and I would quite happily have employed, in a civilian capacity, any of the seven candidates I saw, and expected a competent performance from each of them. But in the light of the possibly gruelling conditions of the field of battle, I saw the reason why the Army gave its Fox for fail to four of them. I would have been tempted to Dog (Pass) the quiet Dearth, on the

145

hunch that his South African experience had caused him to lean over backwards to avoid being thought insensitive and domineering; and that quite another aspect of his character would have been revealed if, say, his mother or sister had been threatened in any way. But I can well understand that a highly structured organization like the Army, which insists (quite properly) on *evidence* of qualities, can give only a limited role to hunches. In toto, Westbury, with all its planks, ponds and candelabra, makes a rough sort of sense. Like much else about the Army, it works.

The Army did not suggest I asked the candidates' views, but put no obstacle in my way when I said I would like to. They were happy, said the candidates, with the tests.

'I would be a little different to the average,' said Rowbotham, who failed, 'because I want to go in the Education Corps, which is more a mental job. But obviously you are expected to do the same physical things as any other officer does, otherwise you won't get the respect.'

Marchbanks had begun to realize, if he had not realized before, why his own leadership was not successful at this stage. 'A leader stands out because he is not worried about what others think of him. I *am* worried about what people think about me.'

Grimm, who at that stage did not know he had passed for a place in Sandhurst, or that he had been selected in my secret ballot as the member of the group the others would most like to serve under, said: 'I am not actually sure that any leaders exist nowadays. Perhaps it is our whole lifestyle these days.' Typically, he offered no opinion on the tests themselves, contenting himself with saying that there were too many application forms which had to be filled out too many times. Grimm's success indicated to me that an officer in the British Army today may survive without sparkle, but not without practical grip, not without competence. That is the central point, and it tends to prove that the satirists' view of the Army is more out of date than the Army itself. Nevertheless, one or two niggling doubts

— no more than that — remained for me as I drove away through the rolling hills of Wiltshire.

Going to the right school — a public school — may not be necessary to pass at Westbury, but the two who passed unequivocally in my particular group did, in fact, both come from public schools. And, more importantly, every officer judging them knew in advance that they did. It is true that the Group Leader did not know of the content of their *reports* at these schools, but he knew from the outset the *name* of the schools. The stated object is to keep the Group Leader entirely ignorant of everything but the young man's actual performance. In that light I saw, and see, no reason why he should know in advance the name of the candidate's school.

The second niggling doubt, or at least regret, is that intuitive hunches have a limited place in deciding who will go to Sandhurst for training and who will not. 'We do not like hunches because we do not like favouritism,' said an officer on the Board. A fair point. But when an unsuitable officer can be failed at Sandhurst in any case, and when the recruiting of officers is lagging behind the needs of even the modest British Army of the post-Suez era, it seems perverse not to take a chance sometimes. 'Think of this man in Northern Ireland,' is not an adequate answer: Sandhurst could be the necessary filter to see an unsuitable man never gets there. 'We will never lower our standards,' is not a complete answer either, because if a 'doubtful' candidate was in fact successful at Sandhurst (the hunch in his favour vindicated) the standard would not *be* lowered.

What except a hunch could today get to Sandhurst a candidate who was 'a loner, an ugly duckling, a child who wet his bed at night'? Would today's rigorous tests have weeded out the Duke of Wellington himself — to whom that description was applied? Perhaps not. The Army's self-awareness helps. It was, after all, an officer at Westbury who reminded me about that description of the historic Duke.

In any case, though it may be applied with a harsh and

no doubt occasionally mistaken rigour, the Army's passion for keeping up standards is laudable enough in itself, and it does not stop at the Regular Commissions Board. After the gruelling and often humiliating demands there, with their strong flavour of initiation ritual, the would-be officer goes, for the start of his military education proper, to a place that does much to heal the wounds and put him at ease in an atmosphere of British country house life.

8

Dear Old Sanders

'They really break you down here at Sandhurst at first. They rush
you around the barrack square and shout at you until you are
rendered down into the proverbial rasher of crispy bacon. Then
they build you up again.'

> — Young Guards Officer, recalling his first six
> months at the Royal Military Academy, Sand-
> hurst.

'The whole way of life is not twentieth century. But that is not a
bad thing. My wife came to Sovereign's Parade and when she was
introduced to a group of friends of mine here, they actually stood
up. She had not come across this before. You may say it is quaint,
but it is good to know standards are being preserved somewhere.'

> — Ex-teacher educated at Training College in
> the North and later an Officer Student at
> Sandhurst.

Setting fire to an Officer Cadet's shirt was a mere bagatelle
to the Sandhurst of the 1920s. A Cadet soon to become
famous as one of Britain's most feted Second World War
heroes assisted in one of these skittish enterprises. Today
at Sandhurst, the world's best-known military academy,
the boyish pranks still go on, but tend to involve water or
clocks rather than the more dangerous fire.

'You couldn't get away now with the sort of horseplay
they got away with then,' today's young officers at
Sandhurst will insist, in tones of high propriety which do
not quite conceal their impish regret.

Couldn't they? One night, or early morning, in 1980 a
group of Officer Students at the ancient and palatial

military academy, near the Berkshire-Surrey border in Southern England, decided on some formation bicycling — the bicycle being the respectable way often-impecunious young officers get themselves around Sandhurst's two hundred and fifty green acres — their evening having been an *extremely* social one. The formation was rather like a tank advance.

They were actually advanced students at Old College, the handsomest building of the Sandhurst complex, which houses students going on a Regular Commission Course as distinct from the more basic one for the Short Service Commission. The Sergeant on guard duty that night found some difficulty in believing it. Since students at the more elementary level are fair game for hard-nosed Sergeants if they step too far out of line, he requested them to desist, dismount and identify themselves. They escaped with a caution. Apparently the students who indulged in 'submarine bicycling', by cycling into one side of a deep duck pond and pedalling through it until they came out of it on the other, escaped altogether. Even the most vigilant Sergeants are not trained to keep an eye out for underwater cyclists.

Other high-spirited events, as the academy entered the last two decades of the twentieth century, included The Affair of The Missing Clock. The clock had been high in one of the clocktowers, but now there stood merely an empty hole. Perhaps strangely, the students had *not* pinched it. It had been sent away for repair, a matter of some irritation, since the Commander of the day's parade was in the habit of starting parade when, and only when, it struck.

Ingenious students decided to assist him. One student dressed up as a bird and emerged from the hole in the clock tower, bang on the hour, crying, 'Cuckoo! Cuckoo!' Noting that the Commander of the parade was not entirely pleased by this intervention, another student appeared with a gun and let fly at the bird, which hastily retreated into the clock-tower and poured out a bagful of feathers as a tribute to his fellow jester's aim.

150

'I think that at Sandhurst, they have too many jokes, if anything,' said an Officer Student from Kenya — one of the usual ten per cent of overseas students. 'In the Kenyan Army, such things would not be thought funny.'

It was notable, however, and perhaps a tribute to the strange magic of Sandhurst, that he laughed no less than anyone else, and in Sandhurst intonation, at the story of the students who dressed up as a visiting General, his Adjutant, and an Arab guest in full Middle Eastern dress. They announced by telephone they were coming to inspect a parade. It is possible that, had a suspicious Regimental Sergeant Major not noticed Army boots under the Arab's robe, or some such detail, this official visit from the Middle East would still stand today in Sandhurst's records as one of its contributions to international diplomacy — of which it has many genuine ones to its credit.

The fact is that Sandhurst, keeper of the traditional values of the British Army since it opened in 1812, home for six months or a year to many soldiers of other countries (not all of which are still friendly to us), is *not* what it appears.

It appears to be a languid piece of Old England in the rolling English Home Counties, a dreaming sequel to the Regular Commissions Board's country house in Wiltshire. Old College, facing magnificent lawns and with a four-columned entrance arch with steps up which the Adjutant traditionally rides at the end of every Sovereign's Parade (Passing Out), makes Buckingham Palace look meagre by comparison. The New College building, for Regular and Short Service Commission students, is a red brick reminder of the First World War. It is true that Victory College, for graduate students, who take a shorter course (twenty weeks against twenty-eight), is post-war, but it is within sight of ornamental duck ponds. A collection of ancient cannon is littered about the grounds, together with the Karnaul Mortar. This is probably the largest in the world, with a weight of nearly nine tons and a bore of twenty-seven inches. It was found in India at the height of Britain's glory in 1839, two years after Queen Victoria ascended the throne, and has been lovingly preserved. One shudders to think what the more rakish Sandhurst students of the past were tempted to do in its open barrel, but it does serve as a reminder that it could kill or maim you for life, and that a nuclear bomb can do no more.

That is the *appearance* of the place today: a marvellous country house relic quite out of step with the A30 road which now runs close by, bringing the benefits of modern living in diesel fumes by the ton. But the appearance lies. Sandhurst is, in fact, a place of highly compressed and demanding activity in which traditional values are challengeable and challenged, sometimes by the strong civilian academic establishment within the academy and sometimes by the Officer Students, especially those who have come from a university or an outside job rather than straight from school.

It is also a place where the Officer Students, university swots or dashing rich young blades, are sworn at most horribly by the non-commissioned officers who are among the instructors. The French do not affront the snootiness of their young officers by allowing mere NCOs to order them about at all. But the NCOs at Sandhurst can use, and indeed develop, their full vocabulary at the expense of someone who next month may well be telling them what to do, provided they always address the Officer Student as 'Sir' while doing it. 'If brains were chocolate, you wouldn't have enough to fill a Smartie — Sir!'

The results are weird, but they do contain a serious message: that today's Army officer is respected not because of himself, not even because of his uniform, but because, and ultimately only because, of his *skill*. When he is skilled he goes out into the real world, where the NCOs will call him Sir, without adding, 'You useless bundle of arthritis!' or some such endearment.

The occasional break-outs from strict discipline, always referred to as high spirits and not vandalism or inanity, are looked upon with actual approval by the powers-that-be, who insist that students are rigorously expected to follow the Sandhurst motto — Serve to Lead — and are therefore entitled to let off steam sometimes.

'Yes, pranks do still go on and in my view it is a good thing that they do,' said the Commandant, a Major General of The Blues and Royals with much experience of Army training. 'The Army's great appeal, apart from its professionalism and adventure, is this sense of fun and this sense of individuality. It must not be stifled.'

But, added the Commandant firmly, that did not apply to setting fire to shirts nor to things that got in the way of work. He himself was a tall, silver-haired man with a greyly benevolent face that could have passed under a mortar board as easily as under a peaked cap with gold braid. He plainly thought that the 1980s were ushering in a social wind that would blow in the Army's favour, as far as its dealings with Officer Students were concerned.

'The whole essence,' he said, 'is service, not self. I think that the Cynical Sixties could be said to have been succeeded by the Self-seeking Seventies and that, in turn, there is now evidence that they will be superseded by the Establishment Eighties. I am not *sure* it is right — they could be called the Agonizing Eighties, but at any rate there is a swing to the Establishment. But it is the human product of the Self-seeking Seventies that we are trying to train now, and this means that the service-not-self theme has to be carefully put across. It has to be put across not as jingoism, but as service to the soldier, to the led. The idea is to detach them from the material awards ethic of modern life and to replace it by the stimulus and motivation and fulfilment which true service can give.'

Quite a long speech for a soldier, even a soldier in charge of modern Sandhurst, where Communication is one of the most important recent additions to the curriculum — prodded on, perhaps, by the public relations needs of Northern Ireland. What the Major General meant — he soon put it in so many words — was that, in appealing to the young soldier of the British Army in the twilight of the

British Empire and the twentieth century, patriotism is not enough.

A certain scepticism is apparent in many Sandhurst students, and the Army does not try to hide it away from visitors. On my first visit to Sandhurst, I was met by a 2nd Lieutenant student who was in charge of the Guardroom, and who was as unlike the Poona-and-pig-sticking Victorian image of the British Army as could be. For a start, he had an accent which he was kind enough to delineate himself as a 'blend of Geordie and North Yorkshire'. He was twenty-one, the grandson of a Durham miner and the son of a professor of a particularly esoteric brand of chemistry: a mixed ancestry that admirably reflected the social transitions of Britain in the 1980s, but which might have disconcerted former students of Sandhurst such as Churchill, Haig and Montgomery; and even perhaps David Niven, the film actor and smooth raconteur, also in a strictly upper-class mould.

This student had been at Sandhurst four months, and claimed it had made a new man of him. 'I can wear paisley neckties now,' he instanced by way of proof. This remark was not so elliptical as it sounded at first. I took it to mean that his grandfather — the miner — had worn paisley ties; that he himself had shunned them, possibly as his ambitious father had done, but that now Sandhurst had given him enough confidence to wear what he liked.

Freedom in dress for Sandhurst students is only relative. The Army will accept you as an Officer and Gentleman if you wear a very old tweed jacket, or a dinner jacket with a greenish tinge from age, but it may turn a stonily forbidding face on you if you take the most obvious and fashionable way of preventing your necktie from slipping — tieing a triangular Windsor knot in it. It is simply not done. The Duke of Windsor may have done it, and given his name to it, but what is good enough for abdicated kings circa 1936 is still not good enough for British Army officers. Indeed the fact the contentious Monarch abdicated to marry a divorced woman may possibly have hardened the hearts of the Army establishment so much against the Windsor knot that not even the presence of NCOs studying to be commissioned officers at Sandhurst, and other signs of the times, have made them relent.

'The Canadian Army is just the reverse,' said one Officer Student. 'In that, if you *don't* wear a Windsor knot, you don't wear a tie. It is true that I have seen three or four people here who still wear Windsor knots, but they are mainly people from the *ranks* who have always worn Windsor knots.' I did not feel quite comfortable with my own Windsor knot until I had driven well clear of Sandhurst, and was back on the M3, where I could feel a certain kinship with commercial travellers driving homewards. (That, on reflection, only made it *worse*. So who are we, with our own brands of snobbery, to deride the snobberies of others?)

'Even in a London street,' said one Officer Student, 'you can spot a Sandhurst cadet. I was in London with a group and we bumped into two guys with short hair, jackets and grey flannels, and plain wrap-around ties. They were in a gang, looking for a drink. I said, "Are you Sandhurst?" They said, "Yes, how did you know?"'

But even if the etiquette of dress bears equally on all the thousand students who may be passing through Sandhurst at any given time, there are subtle and not-so-subtle social (or professional) differences which the system does enforce. They are, the Army argues, based on notions of meritocracy rather than of aristocracy.

When students enter New College, either for their Short Service Commission Course or for the first part of their Regular Commission Course, they are treated more like rookies at an Army camp than as gentlemen destined to lead the British Army. There is little wonder one student called the place Alice's Wonderland. The young officers may be excused for thinking their surroundings somewhat surrealistic: inside the academy they are called Sir and sworn at; they have to fetch their own food, within sight of the ornamental duck ponds, and they have to mix on a quite equal basis with other officers whose parents may have been their butlers. The hooting and tooting of the traffic in Camberley, and along the A30, merely buttresses the sense of unreality, but the surrealism is an essential part of the British Army itself, which no longer insists in the least that you are a gentleman by birth, but rigidly insists that you are a gentleman by behaviour.

After their six months or so in the red brick of New College, the students going on for a Regular Commission pass into Old College and a rather different world. Here are incredibly high-arched ceilings, venerable stucco, oils of military heroes the size of billiard tables and private rooms with time-honoured heating radiators, art deco furniture and solid brass locks which would tempt any antique collector, let alone kleptomaniac. Here in the grand Mess Hall, young officers still have to collect their own main dish, but servants bring the vegetable tureens: a subtle difference with enormous implications psychologically for the developing young officer. If he is a gentleman already, he realizes the Army will allow him to keep the title; if he is not, then the Army will enable him to feel like one and present himself as one.

If there is something about Old College which says 'First Class Only', and something which says 'Second Class Only' about New College, then students at Rowallan College in the Sandhurst complex must at times feel they are occupying a third-class carriage on the British Army Officer Express. The Army might dispute this interpretation, but students of Rowallan have their ear penetrated by the subliminal message that they are definitely there to earn their corn and prove themselves.

Rowallan occupies a building which is not only red brick, but which physically resembles a council house terrace. No delusions of grandeur for any student walking into this part of Sandhurst. It is for young men whom the Regular Commissions Board at Westbury have diagnosed as having officer potential but lacking maturity. The regime at Rowallan both recognizes this immaturity and insinuates

156

into the mind of the immature student a strong desire to remedy the situation quickly. Rowallan will give him, in fact, only three months to convert his potentiality into actuality. Just over a quarter of candidates don't manage it. One in ten of them throw in their hand voluntarily, and the rest of them are invited to try some other occupation.

It is a tribute to the stoicism of the students of Rowallan, and to the acumen of the adjudicators at Westbury, that the proportion of failures is not higher. Students live in barracks, eight to a room, an arrangement which the average humble Infantry Private in the 1980s would turn his nose up at, except in field conditions. They have to clean their own rooms, stay on campus and have no contact with young officers elsewhere in Sandhurst. They are also invited to criticize one another in public.

'It could seem a rather Soviet way of carrying on, but it isn't,' said the Company Commander of Rowallan, a Sapper Major. 'We are trying to look at a man from as many points of view as possible, to help him. None of them minds, and I find it helpful.'

Perhaps surprisingly, in view of all the social limitations and humiliations it heaps on him, Rowallan tries not to make the Officer Student feel a failure — which is what being sent to Rowallan in the first place *could* make him feel. 'Lack of self-confidence is the single most important factor,' said the Commander. 'We work on the assumption that most people have more potential than they ever fully realize. We develop his self-reliance, particularly in the field of personal communication, and give practical experience in simple command tasks. We introduce turbulence through stress, so that the student develops his character.'

Sometimes it doesn't work, and the Rowallan student retires hurt, perhaps to deride the whole system. One grammar school pupil with no 'A' levels and a limited experience of outdoor life discovered that though he talked quite a lot he had 'slight influence' on those around him, because they didn't listen. He lacked confidence when it

157

came to specific tasks. 'He learned a certain amount but could never think well under pressure,' said the Commander. 'And he always had a rather irritating aspect to his personality. When he was tired and wet, others in his group found him a difficult person to live with. After nine weeks we were unable to see any significant change in him. He was asked to leave. He was disappointed, but it didn't come out of the blue.'

Rowallan's make-or-break atmosphere might, in the eyes of some of the disaffected, make Borstal seem a rest cure. But the young men who submit themselves to it *are* very young, tending to look even younger, some almost like junior schoolboys; and the post-Afghanistan British Army does not want schoolboys. However, the system does enjoy a three-to-one success rate, even if 'enjoy' is not a word that would spring naturally to the minds of a quarter of the students — those who fail. A case more typical than that of the failed grammar school boy was that of the son of the retired Regimental Sergeant Major who had a job in a Civil Service department and became very bored with it. Perhaps as a reaction against his RSM father, he was quiet and rather retiring. He would give an opinion only when asked, at least when he arrived at Rowallan, but by the end of the course, he was far more happy to express his views. The pinpricks and social humiliations of Rowallan *do* seem to have the effect of waking sleeping tigers.

At the other end of the social, or at least intellectual, scale are the students in Victory College, which enjoys the prestige of newness and modernity rather than of tradition and cast-iron radiators. Here it tends to be the students, rather than the pictures, which are old. They are from universities, either direct or via intervening jobs in civilian life; they have to contend with a nineteen-week course instead of a twenty-three-week one; and they face comparitively minor restrictions on their personal freedom and are not afraid to talk about it.

A Cambridge graduate who worked for an estate agent and with a property agency, with a view to becoming a surveyor, abandoned this idea because it did not seem 'relevant in real life terms'. He was twenty-five and had spent fifteen weeks at Sandhurst when I talked to him. 'I had been making vast sums of money for somebody else and a lot for myself, but it didn't seem to be leading anywhere. Sandhurst struck me as very different from what I had been doing. It is different in that you have a large number of people with the same interests put together at the same time, which is good. It is not a situation that repeats itself very often in life. Obviously there are a lot of restrictions on what one can and cannot do. For example, timings here are strict where before in civvy street they are lax, even at work. But there is an awful lot to be crammed in here, so I suppose there have to be restrictions. If I had more time on the course I would be more efficient, once I got to my unit, than if I had to learn a lot of it when I had already joined it.'

The older the student, the more the restrictions of Sandhurst strike a jarring note. A twenty-nine-year-old product of a teacher training college who worked in a bank, and as a teacher, before going to Victory College said that Sandhurst could be 'a medieval, mindless place in some respects. You are standing in a trench in the most insanitary conditions, and at the same time you are being required to brush your boots every morning. When you have been in the trench forty-eight hours and are cold and miserable you don't feel like having to brush boots.'

Instructors at Sandhurst make short shrift of such civilian reasoning; and, indeed, the value of spit and polish in keeping up morale in the most primitive conditions has been well proven in battle. Even this particular student at Victory College, whose intellectual candour was refreshing and not frowned upon greatly by the Establishment, admitted quite readily that the drill-and-parade side of Sandhurst, which he had expected to find boring, had in fact left him feeling 'excited and stirred'. 'So perhaps,' he said, 'I am wrong in thinking that Sandhurst has killed off

159

the glamorous side of the job of soldiering for me. Perhaps there is some of the magic left.'

A group of his fellow students thought that Sandhurst was 'not really' mindless, that washing and shaving properly and cleaning your boots made you feel fresher and in better fettle, and that the good social life of the academy compensated for many irritating restrictions. Perhaps the lure of underwater bicycling was not sufficient to compensate such graduates at Sandhurst for not being able to leave campus just when they wanted to; but the university men there are a distinct breed who have decided on the Army for their own reasons, and will follow through deliberately and patiently even if they have limited interest in spit and polish.

'What *encouraged* me to join the Army,' said one, 'was meeting so many anti-Establishment anarchists at university.' Such sentiments, for the men of Victory College, often amount to a New Patriotism, possibly less vulnerable to the shocks of the modern world than the older jingoistic variety.

But most students of Sandhurst go to neither of the extreme poles, Rowallan and Victory. They go to New College and perhaps on to Old College: middle-of-the-way young men intellectually and perhaps socially. They learn military techniques and how to be at ease with themselves and their fellows. The latter is of great importance in the highly professional and compact British Army — almost as important as learning, on the electronically controlled rifle ranges, how to fire the heavy high velocity self-loading rifle, or, on the thousand acres of pitted ground and woods adjoining Sandhurst, staging standard attack and defence command tasks under an instructor who lost a leg in Northern Ireland but who walks over the squelchy and pot-holed ground as well as the next man.

Old hands at Sandhurst say that the atmosphere of the place is less cohesive since the methods of training were changed in the early 1970s, and life fragmented between the four separate colleges. But the corporate air of the place does have an emotional pull that will last officers all their lives, whether they be white and well-connected, white and plebeian, or black overseas guests. The latter may sometimes be baffled by its rules; but these rules will permeate other Armies and strengthen, if only at an emotional level, the British connection.

The pull of history is great. George III built Sandhurst. It was bought by William Pitt the Younger, who sold it to his own War Department at a handsome profit. A hint of raffishness still pervades the place, even in the (academic) War Studies and International Affairs Department, the Military Department, and in the Library, which has eighty thousand books of a very sophisticated range. Instructors here may have dons' swollen midriffs, but they are also apt to be in the Territorial Army Voluntary Reserve and to be in the habit of playing a few brisk games of squash before dinner, if not before breakfast.

Men who may have to make life-and-death decisions in battle — the students — are glad to draw on this atmosphere and exploit the lighter side of Sandhurst life. One officer of the Military Police recently greatly endeared himself to the students in a revealing way, though it did not start too well.

After a Christmas party, he booked one of the students for speeding. The student's friends ganged up, stripped the Royal Military Police man (who bore a hyphenated name) down to his underpants, and rowed him across to the island in the middle of a large duck pond, where they were confident he would have to stay until they rescued him in the morning. Instead, he swam back through the ice-cold water, dried himself off, dressed in his rooms and appeared at the same party, half an hour after he had precipitately left it. His manner was studiously casual.

'He took it with panache. Everyone thought it was marvellous,' said one of the observers. 'A training at Sandhurst welds you firmly into a sense of humour and a better relationship with your betters and subordinates than I saw at university or in civilian jobs.'

Such lessons are part of a young officer's education — administered when he is young and frisky enough to enjoy it. Later on, he will have to buckle down much more seriously; but there is hearty fun and good fellowship for the emergent young officer. What is it like, on the other side of the fence, for the humbler, non-commissioned, ranks?

9

First Acquaintance

'When a lad disappears after the first day, saying he has family problems, you can assume it is his own problems. "Grannie is dying," may mean "Grandson is dying — of loneliness".'

> — Officer at Recruit Selection Centre, Sutton Coldfield.

Choosing Britain's private soldiers for the unpredictable 1980s and beyond is becoming a subtler process. The safety and certainty of Empire and its standards is no longer there. Technical skills are more diffuse and complicated. Even loyalties are less automatic, less capable of being taken on trust one hundred per cent. Colonel Blimp, the comfortably pot-bellied Pukka Sahib Indian Colonel, created by the iconoclastic Australian cartoonist, David Low, and later the hero of a prestigious British film of the 1940s, is dead — or almost. His heirs, and those who serve under him, must now live on their skills and wits in an increasingly professional, challenging and dangerous world.

In a small, tidy office in almost the dead centre of England, a candidate for the other ranks of the British Army faces one of the nineteen Personnel Selection Officers of the Army's Recruit Selection Centre. It is at St George's Barracks, a converted airfield at Sutton Coldfield, in the stockbroker belt of Birmingham, deep in the industrial West Midlands.

Here, about a month after they have been selected through one of the Army Careers Information Offices in England, Wales and Northern Ireland, the Army looks at its latest batch of recruits who are about to sign the oath of loyalty to the Queen; and the recruits look at the Army, to see if they will like one another. At the end of three days at Sutton Coldfield, either party can change its mind. In practice, the man changes his mind far more often than the Army does — although the Selection Officers of Sutton Coldfield say that many of the men who back out of their own accord have thereby saved the Army the trouble of giving the shove.

The particular new recruit facing his Selection Officer at the time I started to explore the procedure was seventeen and a half, and from a Midlands town. He had a chiselled, rather sensitive face, young even for its age; a high Grecian forehead; and large grey eyes that looked into his own lap more often than at the Selection Officer.

In theory, he should have been an easy case to deal with, one of the easiest of over fifteen thousand young men who pass through the centre every year. His preliminary tests at Sutton Coldfield had gone well, and he had been rated at level one out of a possible five. 'With a one rating,' the Selection Officer, a Major, remarked before letting the young man into his office, 'all the corps are open to him. He could have his pick of the bunch.' The fact that the young man's parents were still together was also in his favour — he was less likely to be a disturbed personality, of which the centre saw its fair share. The candidate, on arrival, had said he wanted to go into the Royal Corps of Transport — a corps with one of the lower sets of requirements.

Obviously there should have been no trouble here in pleasing both the candidate and the Army. But the obvious, in choosing the modern soldier, does not always happen. This was proved by the only two remaining questions. They were: was his choice of corps acceptable to the Army? Did he still wish to follow his original choice of career in the Army? The answers were to be established at a half-hour interview which ended the stay at Sutton Coldfield for all candidates.

The interview started simply enough. Was he still happy

about the prospect of joining the Army itself? — Yes, he was.

Was his home life happy? — Yes, he had a very good home life. His father gave him a fair amount of freedom because he himself was an immigrant to Britain. 'He doesn't mind the family being split up, if we know what we are doing.'

The Major was conducting the interview in the tones of a sympathetic bank manager, interpolating the conversation with, 'Do lean back in your chair and relax,' from time to time. He now asked, 'Are your parents worried about your joining the Army?'

'Yes, my mother was worried a bit at first, because two of her brothers were in the Army. She thought it might be as bad today, and I would not be able to get out of it.'

Well, he could have a three-year contract, so that disposed of that. Any other reasons why his people were worried?

Here became visible one of the two tripwires of the interview. 'I have always been brought up to admire my grandfather,' said the young man, 'and he was in the Easter Uprising in Dublin. He was a member of the IRA, I believe, in the Irish Republic ... But I think the IRA are doing it wrongly.'

The Selection Officer passed lightly over this. Perhaps, if anything, he had put the candour of the candidate down as a positive factor in his favour; and in any case the Royal Corps of Transport is not an especially sensitive trade. He established that the candidate's father was from Eire, though he had lived in Britain for some years. Had he any other relatives still in the Republic of Ireland? — Yes, two aunts and two uncles.

'Do you have any other relatives in the Forces?' — 'Yes, my brother was in the Navy. He was an aircraft handler and he was nearly killed twice.'

School. Why did he decide to leave and not take his maths up to 'A' level, as suggested by the school? — 'I didn't want to stay on and then find I could not get a job because of the way the economy is going.'

Which subjects had interested him? — 'I went to a company doing civil engineering tests in the laboratory, in shear strengths of soil for exploration purposes. I asked myself what the prospects were if I stuck there until I was twenty-one. I had got stuck in a rut, really. I was getting up at the same time every morning, and nothing seemed to change the routine.'

Why the Army? — 'A few of my friends had gone there from school. My girl friend joined.'

Clubs? — Yes, night clubs and the rugby club.

Other hobbies? — 'Crosswords. Once I got halfway through the *Daily Telegraph* book.'

Martial arts, such as boxing or wrestling? — No.

Then the Selection Officer said, quite suddenly: 'Do you drink?' — Yes. He knew it was against the law if you were under eighteen, but if you walked into a pub looking relaxed and not uptight, they tended to serve you.

'Hmmm. . .' said the Major, as if not able to decide whether to chastise the youth for a technical breach of the law or to applaud him for psychological ingenuity. 'How much do you drink?' — 'I don't drink much. Five or six pints. I used to do it at weekends and sometimes in the week.'

The Major laughed a little uneasily. Drugs? — 'No, sir. A boy offered me some drugs once, but I didn't try them. I didn't fancy them. He was getting the children to try it, and then sell it to them regularly.'

No trouble with the police? Even a caution? — Well, he was once cautioned in a hayfield about the possibility of starting a fire. Such candour about a nit-picking point, which need not have been mentioned at all, was obviously standing the recruit in good stead with his Selection Officer. But the Major tried one more question on the delicate matter of Northern Ireland.

'You may be asked to fire in anger, at some stage or other. Have you any qualms?' — 'Not really, sir.'

The Major did not ask what 'not *really*' meant. He let the point go. He asked, almost with a note of finality, whether the candidate still wanted to join the Royal Corps of Transport. The second tripwire was beginning to emerge.

No, said the recruit; now that more possibilities seemed to be open to him, he would like to become an Intelligence Corps Operator.

The Major became noticeably more attentive. Why the Intelligence Corps? — Travel.

How often did his father visit Ireland? — Not much. Once when his grandmother died.

'We,' said the Major, 'have to be very careful who we send to the Intelligence Corps.' What would his other choices be? — The Royal Corps of Transport, as he had first thought.

'I think,' said the Major, 'that you had better wait while I take up a point with my colleagues.'

The young man went out of the office. 'If he went into the Intelligence Corps, he would not be sent to Ireland,' said the Selection Officer. 'He might be sent to Ireland in the Royal Corps of Transport. But we only send people to the various corps as being *possibly* useful to them. It would be up to the Intelligence Corps to say they didn't want him, if they didn't.'

The Major consulted his checklist of personal qualities an Intelligence Corps Operator needed. 'You must be self-reliant and usually NCO material. I would not have said that of him. But if they are short of men in the Intelligence Corps ... I will have to go into this one more deeply.' And he went off to consult a superior.

Usually applications are simpler, with absolute priority given to revealing whatever qualities the would-be professional soldier has, and meeting his own wishes wherever humanly possible, while taking into account the Army's particular needs at any one time.

The verdict in this particular case? The Major returned after ten minutes and said, 'I don't think the Intelligence Corps. Nothing to do with his nationality, just because I don't feel he has got the stature for the job. I will bring him back in, and let him down gently. He *would* have got in, if it was just a question of his background; they would have vetted him pretty severely down at the Intelligence Corps.'

The lad was brought back and told, 'The Intelligence Corps is not for you.'

'How do you account for that?' said the candidate, going red in the face and meeting the eyes of the Selection Officer with something like manly aggression for the first time. Perhaps if he had displayed, sooner, how to look people in the eye, he would have made the Intelligence Corps? But the matter had now got past that point. The Major explained, quietly and kindly, that in the Intelligence Corps he would be struggling to keep up, whereas in the Royal Corps of Transport he would have a better career, with more chances of promotion. Also (to meet the mother's point about the possibility of being trapped in the Army) he could sign on for three years in the Royal Corps of Transport, whereas in the Intelligence Corps it would be for six.

'Now,' said the Major, 'what is your reaction to that? Are you still happy about the Royal Corps of Transport?' — 'I'm a bit disappointed, but I'm still willing to go to the Royal Corps of Transport.'

So ended a more or less successful encounter between a soldier of the future and the selection machine at Sutton Coldfield — a machine which had a target of 7,000 candidates every six months when I visited it, but which, at that time, was dealing with only 5,600, largely owing to lack of applicants.

It is a smooth machine, nevertheless; in which the Army puts itself out to delve deeply into each candidate's feelings, wishes and qualities in a way that would have seemed effete at the time of the Charge of the Light Brigade. It is still not, I would judge, a machine that suits everybody, especially the young and bewildered recruit who has joined precisely because he actively wants to be *told* what to do. This type

168

of young man may be beyond the capacity of many sophisticated intellectuals to understand; but he does tend to show his lost and inattentive face at Sutton Coldfield, coming alive only when hearing a barked and simple instruction. The modern British Army, wisely not adjusting its style only to this sort of youth ('The very basic Brit,' as one officer put it) is quite happy to expect soldiers to make the *attempt* to think for themselves, and to watch how they get on.

The Centre was set up as a new idea in 1971. It did not make instant friends with everyone in the British Army, much of which is geared to the virtual autonomy of regiments. The regiments used to choosing their own men had some initial suspicions. Would Sutton Coldfield channel the best candidates away from them and towards its own favourite regiments? It would be impossible for any individual regiment to know, for they would see only the candidates filtered through to them, not the whole of the available intake.

A rather delicate balance had to be struck to appease regimental pride and sensitivities. It entailed individual corps and regiments drafting their own requirements, to some extent framing their own criteria; and then sending them to Sutton Coldfield as the basis on which the Recruit Selection Centre would operate. Individual corps and regiments were also permitted to ask for a certain number of recruits which, after general discussion within the Army, would be expressed as a percentage of Sutton Coldfield's total output.

The percentage figures (if not the totals in absolute terms) are more or less met. The more skilled jobs are the most difficult to fill: the Royal Army Medical Corps, the Royal Army Dental Corps and the Royal Army Pay Corps were under-served in percentage terms when I visited the centre. The Infantry was only very slightly under-served (35.1 per cent as against the target of 36.3 per cent).

'Your basic Brit,' said an officer with long experience of the school, 'can be an ideal combat soldier, though intellectually not bright. You do not need to be clever, you need to be dependable, loyal and with integrity. Above all that, you need to be able to accept motivation.'

Accept motivation? Surely this was something that could only come from inside the individual? Officers to whom I put this point reacted with the tolerance of a professional being kind to a layman. It may be against all so-called liberal notions, they said; but, in fact, the transformation of a personality from the first diffident brushes with the Army Careers Office, through Sutton Coldfield to the regiment or corps, could be remarkable.

In some cases, it would *need* to be remarkable. A new intake is not inevitably impressive; there are too many straggly hairs, uncleaned teeth, bad complexions and eyes which wander inattentively during group discussions. Young men with a bright academic future will still be at school or university; 'officer material' will be at Sandhurst; here at Sutton Coldfield there are many bright recruits, but many who have to haul themselves out of some sort of private fugue whenever they are addressed; who are simply not used to controlling their own lives; who perhaps come from families which are themselves without the discipline to shape their own lives effectively, and who will have passed on some of the resulting insecurity to their children. Faces at this stage tend not to be memorable. Very little registers on them, except a look of vague panic. Modern society has leaned over backwards to make such young people feel they are not 'inferior', almost to the extent of being prepared to dismantle all standards of excellence; it may have deceived itself, but it has not deceived some of the young men who come to Sutton Coldfield, saying, in effect: '*Tell* me please, what I can do?'

One officer who himself came from a working-class background tried to make his spoken introduction to the intake as informal and as broadly philosophical as possible, setting out all the Army could offer in professional and human terms, and then asking for responses. He got few. 'They were waiting for short, sharp instructions. Then they

On foot patrol in County Londonderry and other troubled parts of Northern Ireland soldiers cannot rest without taking any available cover.

The contrast between ordinary domesticity and the possibility of bloody encounter in Northern Ireland can be macabre. Here a foot patrol makes friends with local children.

Gurkhas training by moving a modern girder bridge into place in the New Territories, Hong Kong.

above The East-West German border. A regular patrol of the East German army inspects the raked-over earth for signs of vehicles or footprints.

left Royal Engineers help both in a civilian and a military capacity. Here in Cyprus they supervise the rescue of one of three stone coffins dating from the 5th century B C.

above Members of the WRAC practise the use of automatic weapons in Germany.

right Territorial Army soldiers like living a life as tough, or tougher, than the regular soldier's. Here during a territorial exercise near Salisbury Plain, temporary field kitchens are set up in a deserted house, which is under mock attack.

Ceremonial outside Buckingham Palace is one of the most esoteric Army activities. Here the day guard in their Bearskins (left) are about to come off duty and the night guard in their more ordinary peaked caps (right) about to go on.

Photographs are reproduced with the kind permission of the Ministry of Defence, the British Army Headquarters London District, the Territorial Army and the author could carry them out and get a sense of achievement,' he was advised by an older officer. He revised his introduction accordingly, and got better results.

Soldiers at Sutton Coldfield may have toyed with the loyal oath to the Queen, but they have not yet entered the Army beyond recall. They have not been issued with uniform. At Sutton Coldfield they are issued with standard khaki trousers, khaki shirt and sweater, and their hair is cut. This does two things. It gives them their first real taste of Army life and it removes any class identity, good or bad, that their own clothes may have suggested. The poorest recruit is now on terms of sartorial equality, at least, with the most well-off.

Many of the recruits are visibly immature, looking even younger than their age, still highly self-conscious, and often much sadder to be away from home than a university student of the same age propelled spontaneously by his own academic prowess. Some try to disappear after the first day, saying that they have 'family problems'. In nine cases out of ten, the family problem is their own homesickness. 'Mother is ill,' usually means, 'Son is pining for the home which has put no precise demands on him and therefore not prepared him for the fact that the world will do so.'

It is easy for a highly-educated, middle-class person to forget that a restricted intellectual range slows up the possibilities of friendship and heartening human exchange. Often the recruits have already spent two days with their own group, and finished their stay in Sutton Coldfield, before they are at ease with one another. At any time, even if they are happy as a group, they are vulnerable to the intrusion of an alien personality. I stood, as invisibly as possible, in a corner of one of the twin rooms in which the possibilities open to them in view of their test rating were explained by means of words written in large letters on the walls; but immediately I entered the room, the recruits who had been talking stopped as if my presence were some sort of device to catch them out. The routine is stylized: each group is given a briefing and a film in one room about the careers possible in the Army, and then shepherded through to the twinned room to see the possibilities written up on the wall, and explained by a Sergeant with a billiard cue or other convenient pointer. This can also be stilted, especially when visitors are present. Humour can be a risky business. One Sergeant Instructor was describing the Army Catering Corps. 'The only legal assassination squad in the British Army,' he said, and waited for the laugh. Only one of the group of twelve gave as much as a titter. 'Any questions?' said the Sergeant, to cover the silence. Still silence. 'Don't forget, lads, it's your future. *I* don't mind. But if you don't ask, I can't answer, and that's what I'm here for.'

One recruit thought he might be interested in a part of the Catering Corps that entailed writing reports, and was worried about his bad English. 'British education has spent £50,000 educating you, son. If you haven't qualified in English in all those years, what can we do about it in a few days? Apart from being a well-built lad like you, a soldier in the Catering Corps has got to be able to write reports. When it comes to writing reports, you would be struggling. You don't play a goalie at wing half, lad. Think again.'

The Sergeant pointed out to me that the lads were all from levels three and four (the combat rather than the technical grades), and that normally they asked more questions, even from these grades. 'Someone strange comes in, and they just clam up. I make sure they get a straight answer to a straight question. You will get the bright boys, who start talking about their personal experiences, or ask me about my particular corps. They are trying to draw you off the line you are trying for. They are trying to dominate you, trying to take over *your* particular job. You can normally pick out the good soldiers. The bad ones will go because they are shouted at. Some of them look half asleep. Some of them have never got up at six-thirty in the morning in their lives.'

The imposition of the 'line' and a rather rule-of-thumb method of initial selection for one of the five grades may be inevitable in an establishment like Sutton Coldfield, always working at slightly more than a fair pressure. I could see that this would be most attractive to a large number of recruits. I did not always feel (and it was part of a general unease about the 'middle' strata of the Army) that the more thoughtful recruit was being actively encouraged, or that officers, having to be somewhat impersonal evaluators on a long assembly line, could take into sufficient account the impact their *own* personalities might have on the more intelligent recruit. The young man who flirted with the idea of the Intelligence Corps before being guided back to the Royal Corps of Transport was told by the major interviewing him, 'I think you will be happy there. *It is my own corps.*' He was visibly reassured by this personal piece of information. An Oxbridge tutor is well aware of his power to influence simply by being himself. Unfortunately, the Army NCO or officer will tend to regard a personal question from a recruit as an impertinence or as a diversionary tactic, while it may be only a request for the lifeline of human guidance. If there is room for such a lifeline, the place for it is obviously at Sutton Coldfield rather than in the corps or regiment. It may be more possible to take this point into consideration in the future, given the changes to the system introduced late in 1980, which meant young men went to Sutton Coldfield as civilians, not already-enlisted men.

The method of grading from one to five is of necessity arbitrary, though adequate in finding the particular sort of recruit the Army is looking for (which only in exceptional circumstances will be officer material). After being streamed into one of the four or five companies that will be passing through the centre at any one time (company merely means a batch who arrive at the same time, and are at the same stage of the procedure), the recruits will do tests and be told about 150 jobs in the Army, by means of slides and presentations. This takes the first morning.

Then the recruits each have a five-minute interview with their Selection Officer about the range of Army jobs open to them in the light of their rating. These are relatively sophisticated. Few men (about seven per cent) are rated in the top one grade (though more than in the five grade). Officers went out of their way to point out that, though a grade five was bad on paper, such a man might nevertheless make a good combat soldier. 'You can get a chap who is very bright and an absolute menace in a battalion in somewhere like Northern Ireland,' said one officer. 'Wet. Lacking in stamina. Falling out on an assault course. That sort of thing. You can get a chap who is bulging with brains who has not got the robustness or the guts to be good at combat.' Most of the men end up at grade three, in which they can be either three-plus or three-minus. There is the further refinement that, apart from the 'objective' results of the tests, each man is also graded according to the 'subjective' view of the Selection Officer after their longer, final talk. Officers at Sutton Coldfield tend to be older than average, perhaps not 'high fliers' themselves in strict Army terms, but men with enough humanity and experience to make a good human judgement. I was assured that the subjective rating would have a 'distinct bearing' on the sort of position a recruit could hold.

This is just as well. Some of the 'objective' tests appeared to be calculated to discover which recruits were best trained at answering tests. The three heave-ups to the beam, the three dips on parallel bars and the seven sit-ups in the gymnasium may be immaculate tests for physical fitness (and only one man in a thousand fails for reasons of ill-health), but in the mental domain the tests are more controversial.

Perhaps I am pleading this as an extenuating circumstance. Two of the tests were an intelligence test and a test in applied physics. I asked to take both. The first concerned putting domino-shapes into logical order, and the second answering problems of practical physics, like which dam would collapse first and which cogwheel would turn in which direction in a complicated series. The intelligence test showed that, by fiddling a mark in my favour, the Army could just about offer me a job. This conclusion would cause consternation to my friends. The other test showed that I was brilliant at applied physics, which would cause even more consternation to my old physics master. It is perfectly true that I came to the tests quite unprepared, and many years away from my own schooling (I had tried to find some subtle mathematical logic in the dominoes, when all they had wanted was pretty patterns), but it is just as well the Army has built the 'subjective' judgement factor — grading A to C — well into its procedures at Sutton Coldfield, where decisions are made by which recruits may have to live for several years. Young lads were told, when I was there, that though they could sometimes transfer from one corps or regiment to another, chopping and changing was not looked upon with favour.

There is also an emphasis on honesty in forming the subjective opinion. All recruits are asked to declare any crimes, or other offences of any kind, when they are still at the local Army Careers Office. Many don't. When they arrive at Sutton Coldfield, they are told that such offences must be revealed at once, if need be to a member of the staff in private. Small offences are overlooked; serious crime, especially involving violence, will almost certainly mean being shown the door (or facing a later perjury charge if the crime is not then declared).

Less than two men in a hundred go at this point because the Army doesn't want them — and in the case of the two, it is often for not disclosing a crime. One in ten men decide voluntarily to break with the Army after Sutton Coldfield, which on the face of it is a relative slap in the face to the Army. 'But quite a lot of these we would not have wanted anyway,' said a high-ranking officer. 'Some come back to us for a second try, and we may take them. If a man were to come back for a third try, I think we would have to look rather closely at him. Some come here just to qualify for the dole.'

I asked to speak to one of the current intake who had decided, of his own accord, that the Army was *not* for him. No difficulties were put in my way. Paul, from the North of England (a fictitious name), was aged just under eighteen, and had asked to go into the Royal Armoured Corps. Asked why he didn't want to do it after all, he said: 'I have been in the Army before, in the Royal Artillery. It didn't work out. I started thinking, "Will it happen again?"'

It appeared to be a man he had not got on with while he was doing his training at Woolwich Barracks. He had bought himself out with £20. He had always wanted to go into tanks, but though his examination results were high enough, it wasn't a success. 'I got lonely. Some lads wouldn't talk to you and some lads take it out of you. They would just ignore you.' What it boiled down to was that the man he couldn't get on with had obviously tried to get everyone on his side, and to make life unpleasant for a potential rival who didn't want to be a member of his court. Eighteen was perhaps too young an age to indulge in this sort of analysis. 'My father is disappointed, but he says it is my own life,' said Paul.

Eventually in the Royal Artillery, he had got into a fight with the man he couldn't get on with, who had pushed him while he was looking in his locker. 'I turned round and hit him. It made things even worse. I had made friends only with a Scottish lad, and when he went, I went.' Paul was a large young man, but with very little mental or physical presence. He sat listlessly on the chair as he answered my questions. Yes, he was going to feel cowardly, passing up another chance to join the Army. Yes, he supposed he would have to go back to his old job as a labourer in the North of England. Could he live with that decision? Well, he'd have to, wouldn't he? Wasn't he going to find one difficult bastard wherever he worked — and find he had to survive him? Well, he hadn't thought as far as that. 'I have got nothing against the Army,' he said with his loose mouth twitching. 'It is the finest thing for a young lad. But I just can't face the same thing happening again.'

Plainly Sutton Coldfield, short of becoming a prison, cannot adapt itself to the emotional needs of such indecisive young men. Selection Officers may decide to face recruits across their desks 'because that is what they expect — me in my place here and him in his place there' — but they can hardly apply handcuffs; and in today's professional army, would never dream of trying to do so.

One of the people they do look out for at Sutton Coldfield is the Walter Mitty, the dreamer of premature gold braid. One officer with a broader experience said that perhaps one recruit in fifty put down on his application form that one day he wanted to be an officer. 'Some want to be surgeons, when they have been bloody indifferent stretcher bearers! They will say they want to be engineers, when their examination results show that they could not get a shifting spanner on to a nut. They want to be military policemen, and they spell "policemen" incorrectly.' If a man was academically clever, with perhaps two 'A' levels, said the officer, and if he had done all sorts of active things in his spare time, then he would probably recommend the man to 'try elsewhere' — in other words try the Regular Commissions Board. Some civilians who have seen Sutton Coldfield might think this a sensible and realistic separation. Others might be disturbed that the Officer Material and the Other Material is so formally segregated at such an early stage, the men going to Sutton Coldfield and the officers to Westbury, miles apart physically and many more miles apart morally, socially and intellectually.

It must be admitted that at Sutton Coldfield one sees some intelligent faces and some confident manners — though relatively seldom in the same man. This may be used as a defence of the present system. It has been a fashionable liberal view that all men could be raised to more ideal forms (i.e. more like fashionable liberals) if artificial class constraints were removed. The experience of Sutton Coldfield, in its first decade, suggests that the men coming forward for the lower ranks of the British Army are content with the system as it is; indeed, might even welcome a more paternalistic grip on their lives. It was the men, rather than the officers, who talked a lot about the good effects of discipline. Should people be given what they want, even when it is not the intellectually respectable thing? This argument, as the Army achieves more importance and prominence in the 1980s, is likely to be almost as long-running as the history of regimental protocol, though not, perhaps, as entertaining.

It is certainly just as well that, in practice, most soldiers in the British Army who are not commissioned officers *are* satisfied with their lot. The man who starts in the other ranks *may* jump the high fence between officers and others, but he must have exceptional persistence and he is unlikely ever to lead men in combat.

10

Who Gets Promoted?

'A public school accent is absolutely no advantage now, I think, no advantage at all in becoming an officer. The whole thing is almost classless now. It depends on ability. We have got a boy in The Life Guards with a very strong Midlands accent.'

— Officer in The Life Guards.

'Every officer should be in the ranks himself for at least two years before he is put in charge of men. Then he would know the effect on the men of the orders he casually gives out. Ranker officers are always the best. Perhaps the powers that be think that an officer wouldn't give an order to clean up the latrines if he'd had to do the job himself, but personally I don't buy that. I'd give whatever order I had to give if *I* were an officer.'

— Sergeant in the Army Technical Corps.

'Not as many officers have their own horses now. I have very few.'

— Officer in Guards Regiment.

The two principal characters in this chapter will be the Council House Captain and the Lost Lance Sergeant, neither of whom were much at ease. Or perhaps they will be the Satisfied Regimental Sergeant Major and the Mandarin Major, both of whom were very much in their element, thank you very much.

I got the feeling that the first two might not have gone gladly to the stake in defence of the Army's promotion system, whereas the second two might well have done. The first two may, to some extent, have been square pegs in round holes, the second two were as firmly slotted into their jobs as a mortice and tenon joint. Which was the more typical? If it were statistically possible to get an answer to that question, the Army would know in statistical terms whether its modern promotion procedures are efficient enough in tapping available potential. As it is, one can only judge by claim, counter-claim and inference. Though the picture may have blemishes, it is not a generally discouraging one.

The young Mandarin Major was visibly going places. He was well-tailored, tall and not too handsome for the comfort of those likely to have to decide on his future career. He came from a minor public school, but would have done credit to a major one. Conversationally, he obviously believed in the right word in the right place. He was quite willing to discuss his background and his interests in front of both me and the Colonel.

'Before I was married, I used to ride in steeple chases,' he said, 'and I did have some horses. I probably had four polo ponies and a couple of racehorses. Now I have no polo ponies, and I am breeding very few horses. Ten years ago, a polo pony cost £300. Now it would cost you £3,000. It is out of all proportion to inflation.'

The young Major was — of course — a Cavalry Officer. He had his commission in the Household Cavalry, where horses can be thought of almost as a sideline to the trade. They might also be thought of as an indication that the Cavalry Regiments are still the forte of the well-connected young man, lips turned down (into a receding chin) who has been for so long the epitome of the privileged Officer Class. Is it still so?

This particular young officer did not have a receding chin. He had a quite effective face, both strong and mobile, and a manner — both firm and ingratiating — to go with it. 'There is a mass of difference between hunters, which are comparatively cheap, and polo ponies and racehorses,' he said, shrugging off any suggestion of being especially privileged. 'In the old days of soldiers' races at Sandown, lots of officers entered. There are probably no more than six officers in the whole Army who actually own racehorses now. Occasionally, six or seven officers get together, and the Regiment owns a horse. One of the Cavalry Regiments' Sergeants Mess and Officers Mess combined have a horse.'

Those six who still have horses in their own names, so to speak, are in the King's Troop of the Royal Horse Artillery. Usually it is Cavalry Regiments, or Gunners, or the Household Division who have communal horses. They can pass them off as tools of the trade. And, officers point out, there *are* grammar school officers in the Household Division — the soldiers closest to the Throne. One officer who had just spent some months teaching at Sandhurst said that, of the eighty boys he had taught, between twelve and fifteen per cent would be from overseas. Another forty to fifty per cent would be public school boys. But the majority of these would be from minor public schools, not the top twenty. 'I would say that the top public schools would be responsible for only about twenty per cent of the total intake.'

The Colonel present at the discussion between the Major and myself supported this point of view. 'From time to time some left-wing Member of Parliament gets up and asks what schools our officers come from. When I was commanding a battalion, I was asked to provide a list of where my officers went to school, so that an answer could be given. When I looked it up, the results were quite extraordinary. Half the fee-paying schools I had never heard of. When I joined in the early 1950s it seemed to make an enormous difference where you went to school, but now, as a CO, I was able to answer this rather damning question about where my men had gone to school.'

'But,' said the Major, 'you have got to be able to mix in with your other officers. If you can't get on with other people, even if you are a brilliant officer, you will have trouble.' One could see that in a regiment whose officers were mostly made up of young men with wealthy fathers, such a man as the Major might have less trouble than an officer from the background of, say, a council house.

I met one of the latter, by accident — the Council House

Captain. He was standing on his own at the bar of his mess, not excluded from other conversations but not being enthusiastically invited in, either. Part of the difficulty might have been that he happened to be considerably younger than most of the other officers present; but there was something about his face, sallow and pitted, which would have stood out even more if the mess had been that of, say, a Guards Regiment.

He had, he said, come by promotion slowly. It was not really the Army's fault. In civilian life he had been a plumber. Then he was called up, and found himself living on twenty-eight shillings a week (about 140 pence or 300 cents) instead of the £20 he had been earning as a plumber. He couldn't live on the money; but found, to his surprise, that he quite enjoyed soldiering. This posed a problem.

There was another. He had really wanted to be a commercial artist or something to do with forestry. 'But,' he said, 'these were not things for secondary modern school boys.' He was brought up on a council estate in the Midlands, first an old one and then a new one which actually had hot and cold water. Before that, to have a hot bath, the family had to stoke up the boiler in the kitchen and then pump the hot water up into the bathroom — if the pump worked. His father was a hotel porter, then moved into an industrial job from which he was sacked for being a blackleg. His mother had been a millinery apprentice and then a hotel maid. His own life did not seem to offer much except the prospect of plumbing again once he got out of the Army. He signed on for a three-year engagement, more of less solely for the three guineas (£3.15) a week he would get under the three-year contract.

He had been in the Army only six months when he was promoted Lance Corporal. Within the next six months he was *offered* promotion to full Corporal, but then didn't get it. 'Somebody found out I could read and write, and so they put my name down for a clerk's course. But if I was going to be a clerk, they didn't want me to go on the clerk's course as a full Corporal, though they were quite happy for me to go as Lance Corporal. So my promotion was held back and I didn't get promoted to full Corporal until I had been in the Army nearly two and a half years,' he said. He thought his eventual promotion to officer had been 'most unlikely' at that stage: 'One can never see much further than the next rank along.'

When he was promoted Sergeant, it was only Acting Sergeant, because most of his contemporaries in age had ten or so years' service whereas he had only five. The Army system of promotion, as I was to discover later, takes into account both experience and ability — not necessarily in that order. His substantive promotion was delayed, but eventually he became a Colour Sergeant, then Warrant Officer Two and then Warrant Officer One.

After that, he said, it was very much in the lap of the gods whether he actually picked up a commission or not. 'It depends on how long one has been in the Army going through the ranks. On a twenty-two-year engagement, if you have picked up Warrant Officer One promotion after twenty-one years, then you have only one more year to prove yourself, by which time you have come to the end of your twenty-two-year engagement and are on your way out. I was fortunate in that I had been in only sixteen years by the time I was a Warrant Officer One.'

It had, of course, taken him a quite frightening time to get to the *starting point where he might become an officer* — when it is remembered that some young men who come into the Army at the *right* angle are officers (very junior officers, but officers nevertheless) after *seven months* at Sandhurst.

He was commissioned into the General List, the list of officers in the Army who can be switched around to do any specialized jobs available. 'I found it difficult at the start,' he admitted. 'One had been in the position where you had been respecting the senior officers — the Majors and upwards — and it was difficult to adjust to addressing one of these as Larry or Bill. I had been giving them the yes-sir-no-sir treatment for the past ten or twenty years. But I found that after about six months it came fairly easily. I

183

remember they were all very helpful, and certainly didn't make it difficult for me to get on with them as proper associates. I think every effort is made to bring the Short Service Commission ex-Warrant Officer or the Quartermaster type into the Officers Mess. There is always a great deal of effort to make him feel at home, and to make his wife feel at home. Functions are arranged. You are invited to a lot of people's homes for dinners and supper parties. It is very much first-name terms. Everybody does really bend over backwards.'

Even if the wife was rather tense, and drank rather too much or talked too much, it did not nowadays necessarily mean that the man would be ruled out for further promotion, though it just might tip the balance against him if things got too out of hand. 'It is very liberal now. They go for the man rather than the wife,' said the Captain.

I wondered how this polite and amiable officer, who confessed he still would be more likely to enjoy himself in the Sergeants Mess than in the Officers Mess, would fit into the mess of some of the Guards Regiments; and I recalled what the horse-owning Major had said about chaps having to get on with their brother officers.

'The type of evening one has in the Officers Mess is rather different from the Sergeants Mess, where you can let your hair down,' said the Council House Captain. 'It follows stricter rules. I feel so, anyway. Although one can relax and have a damn good time, I am aware all the time that I am in the Officers Mess and that there is a limit to the sort of daft things I could get up to. I am always aware that I come from a council estate in the Midlands. It is the Mark of Cain. It is always with you, just as someone who is aware that he is a public schoolboy is aware that *that* is always with him. He doesn't go around saying it all the time, but he knows it.'

Obviously this officer found the conversation of the Officers Mess rather intellectually unsatisfying. 'The type of officer who puts my back up is the one who is always talking about old Pongo Waring or Jamie Smithers. These

184

are all Generals they have met at some time in their service. They must spend a lot of time reading up on these guys, checking up where they have gone. Their bedside reading must be the Army List. Their sole topic of conversation is which General is doing which job. It gives them something to talk about, whereas I am perhaps a bit short of something to talk about in those situations. One makes small talk. I find ordinary small talk very quickly bores me. It doesn't mean anything. Mind you, there is also a lot of this "Old Pongo Waring" talk going on in the Sergeants Mess.'

Fairly said. This particular officer, though he said he sometimes felt he was not introduced to visitors to the mess as other Captains were 'because I am not someone of influence', also said he might be mistaken: it might be just a feeling on his part. He left *me*, nonetheless, with the feeling that extreme patience with small talk might well help a man become officer material but that, of course, precisely the same thing applied in civilian occupations, especially hierarchical ones in which greasing the right people was not precisely a substitute for ability but a *part* of the necessary ability.

Would the Council House Captain stay in and hope for more promotion? He thought probably not. He might get to be made up to Major if there was a job suited to his special skills which needed a Major; but the chances were against it. He thought that at the end of his engagement he might try something completely different. But his reservations about Army life were 'minor matters'. 'It may be that I am a little too sensitive,' he reflected. 'I think the Army has given me a chance to educate myself by allowing me to go to evening classes and to attend educational courses. I have managed to get myself four or five 'O' levels and an 'A' level, which I would never have had the opportunity to do at school. I am very grateful for everything the Army has done for me. And I think that, even though the British Empire has shrunk, the Army is still a worthwhile job and offers a lot more than a lot of jobs in civvy street offer at the moment, with the union conflicts and everything else.

I have thoroughly enjoyed every minute of it. But I shall be glad, possibly, when the time comes to go, because you can have too much of a good thing.'

That point of view seemed to me significantly ambivalent, though the chief element was undoubtedly in favour of Army life. But it is that dividing line, between being a non-commissioned officer and being a commissioned officer, which is still the broadest chasm to cross in the British Army.

Those who have crossed it, or merely looked at it from the wrong side and *not* crossed it, though they might have liked to, tended to be amongst the most personally complex and least socially easy people I encountered in my dealings with the Army over a two-year period.

There was, for instance, the Lance Corporal in the Scots Guards. In Chelsea Barracks at the time I visited them, the Scots Guards superficially presented a picture of a semifeudal Squirearchy which somehow worked. It was quite easy to tell, from faces alone, who were the Squires (Officers) and who were the happy peasants (Other Ranks and NCOs), with the exception of this particular Lance Sergeant. His face didn't belong — it fitted into neither convenient stereotype. It was that of an intelligent technician or junior executive in some technical field — keen and accommodating, but neither regal nor subservient. He was the man who, without in any way suggesting he didn't like the Army *as such,* gave the impression of being a fish out of water — and rather wasted. The Army is a house of many mansions, and perhaps he should merely have been in another in which he would have been happier. Perhaps.

It would not have surprised me to see him as an officer — had he been in one of the technical corps. Instead he was my Lost Lance Sergeant, and was talking about leaving the Army, after fifteen years' service, the following year — a fact which he gave me by way of answer when I asked him if he would like to become a commissioned officer. 'In this regiment,' he said, 'you have to have money to become an officer, you have to have something backing you. They are all well-to-do people, the officers in this regiment. I have seen other regiments, and the officers have started off with nothing at all and they have become great officers. I am thinking of the Royal Engineers in particular. To me the officers seem to come into this regiment as nineteen-year-olds who think they know it all. It is just like class distinction.'

The Lance Sergeant's father, also in the Army, had advised him to join the Royal Engineers, but he had joined the Scots Guards because he thought that he was bettering himself that way. It is arguable that this was his *own* snobbery in action, and that it unhorsed him, preventing his chances of promotion.

'It is the little niggling things that get on your nerves,' he said. 'They think they know best from the start. When someone has had fifteen years' experience as a Platoon Sergeant they try to tell the officers, but some of them don't want to know. I have seen only one or two decent ones come in during the last year or so. Of the five who have come in the past year, there are only one or two you can really speak to. Some of them are really snobs. A lot of them are big landowners — squires and that sort of thing. I would never fit into their Officers Mess. I saw, out in Belize, that officers of the Royal Engineers would speak to their own blokes. They would go away camping at the weekend. They used to go with their men downtown to parties. It would not happen in the Scots Guards, at least not very often.'

The Lieutenant Colonel who commanded one company of the Scots Guards, the amiable son of a well-known politician usually regarded as well to the right of British politics, said it was nonsense to suggest that there was less informality in the Guards Regiments than in others. It might be the other way about — where all ranks were expected meticulously to remember their hierarchical place while on public parade, they could afford to be *more* informal while off parade. I sensed, in the Officers Mess, where everyone used Christian names except when talking to the Commanding Officer, that what he said might be true among officers themselves and even, at times, among officers and other ranks who knew how to keep their place; but I could also sense a truth in what the Lance Sergeant had said: the genuine geniality of the atmosphere rested on the assumption that one was 'the right sort of chap'. I could imagine a grammar school boy fitting in quite easily — but only if he *spoke* with a public school accent and acquired the 'right' mannerisms. In this light, his chances of promotion would be prejudiced if he didn't 'fit in with the other chaps', because his *not* fitting in would tell against his actual performance, on which he would be judged fit or unfit for promotion.

'I think it is all a wee bit out of date,' said the Lance Sergeant. 'I can't see, for instance, why they can't have patent leather boots. We still have leather and we have to burn them down to polish them. We use the head of a spoon or irons. It takes two days really to get them down. To really get them up to full standard it would take a week or a fortnight. For that fortnight, you would spend two or three hours a day, and then one hour every day to keep them clean. And belts. They brought out a plastic belt on trial, but all the rest are blancoed. To get it up to standard would need two hours a day, and to keep it up to standard needs half an hour a day.'

It was easy to see that such a questioner of time-honoured and almost mystical rites would not be best suited to a Guards Regiment and would tend to do worse in promotion than a man more wedded to the role prescribed for him.

On the other hand, the Regimental Sergeant Major of one battalion of the Scots Guards, a man of roughly the same age as both the Lance Sergeant and the Commanding Officer, was very happy with the system which prevented him going on to become an ordinary Regular Officer (though he might be eligible for a Quartermaster Commission, a Special Regular Commission or a Short Service Commission).

'I would never become a Regular Officer, no, no,' he insisted. 'There is no way possible this could happen. You see this years in advance. It is a wonderful system we have got. It *is* a class structure we have got, and long may it reign. There is an Officer's Structure and there is a Warrant Officer's structure. Let's put it this way. There are some who are born to lead. You look at the officer system — these are the people who perhaps in years gone by have got where they are through hard work and enterprise. I remember one young officer told me that his grandfather had, at the age of fourteen, to start work as a clerk, because the family wealth had gone and he got the family back on its feet again. Most of it has been bloodshed and fighting for what they have. I cannot decry that system. If I myself have moved up only one notch, I have achieved something, and if I can get my children to university, I will have achieved something.'

The Scots Guards had been a wonderful place for the satisfied Regimental Sergeant Major, who at thirty-six had got most of the promotion he ever visualized, as well as being made part of 'a family': 'I am not very close to either of my parents, to be honest. I had a very disrupted childhood. This regiment is very much a family. That was not the fascination for me when I joined — I was a farm labourer and decided I wanted to see a bit of the world — but it is something I have since learned and appreciated.'

It had also been a wonderful place for the Commanding Officer of the company I saw, a well-connected man who maintained that he would be richer in the City of London but not half as interested, and who would almost certainly rise higher than Lieutenant Colonel unless he removed his trousers in the Officers Mess and danced on the table — perhaps even if he *did*.

But had it been a wonderful place for the Lance Sergeant, a thinking man with no liking for spit and polish, who in civilian life would almost certainly have been categorized as 'staff' rather than 'labour force', and worn a white collar in an executive office? Not so wonderful, perhaps, as for the other two of roughly his own age. And almost certainly containing less chance of promotion.

It is quite possible to argue that the Lance Sergeant's mild misfortunes were caused by the simple fact that he joined a Guards Regiment when he should have joined the Royal Engineers, Royal Corps of Transport or similar corps. And even he did not suggest that he had gained nothing from his Army experience: 'It will have left its impression on me when I go into civilian life. I won't be one of those layabouts. I will be a smart civilian. I would not have known discipline but for the Army. I might have been hanging round a street corner like everyone else. The Army definitely makes a better man of you.'

But does the Army, being inevitably bureaucratic and hierarchical, allow too many square pegs in round holes, and thus prejudice the promotion chances of the square pegs? It could well be that joining the wrong sort of regiment or corps could prejudice the way a man thought and felt about the Army, and therefore his actual performance and chances of promotion.

In an age in which divisions by social class are breaking down in civilian life, some might argue that the Guards should fall more into line. At the moment they do not, though they play down the upper-class atmosphere. A twenty-year-old Etonian officer with aristocratically drooping eyelids diligently insisted that he knew what it was to be poor — because his father had sent him off to tour America on £100, a definition of social hardship which was far from convincing.

The British Army of the 1980s may still permit some square pegs in round holes, and men may resent it more than they would have done in Kipling's time. But, since the power of promotion has been taken away from individual regiments and been assumed by the Army as a whole, the system is undoubtedly more fair than it used to be — perhaps more fair *because* of its very complexity, its intricate system of checks and balances.

The man responsible for administering the promotions procedure is the Deputy Director of Manning (Army) at the

Ministry of Defence. He has his office not in Whitehall itself but in the West End of London, next door to an exclusive gaming casino. He firmly rejected any suggestion that the Army's promotion system also rested on the rules of chance — the right school, the right father . . .

'Elitism is not rife in the British Army today, in promotion or anything else,' said the Deputy Director of Manning, a Brigadier with the bespectacled thoughtfulness of a good headmaster. 'I will tell you the only sense in which we are elitist. Our Army cooks are the best in the world. Our helicopter pilots are the best in the world. So are our doctors and dentists. *That* is where there is elitism — in professionalism. Otherwise, no.'

Whatever some civilians might think, said the Brigadier, even Guards Officers were not chosen for their socially decorative qualities. They were expected to do ordinary jobs in Northern Ireland, like any other infantry soldier, and they did them. Even their ceremonial functions were useful to the tourist trade. Guards Officers had to be good professionally, as in any other regiments.

But surely there were *some* upper-class twits in the Guards Regiments? 'Oh yes,' agreed the Brigadier, 'and you could find pretty young nits in civilian occupations, too — banks, for instance. Nothing very unusual about the Army from that point of view. We are civilians as well as soldiers, you know. A lot of these people are play-acting a bit. That goes on. They are putting on a pose.'

I quoted the Brigadier a story (possibly apocryphal) told me by an RAF man who had been in a barracks in Northern Ireland when a Guards Battalion had arrived with their polo ponies. A young officer was allegedly heard to say in public school accent so thick it could have been used to curdle cream. 'Ah saiy! Is this *ah* barracks?' 'No, it's *our* bloody barracks,' was the reply from the residents.

'I think that sounds very healthy,' said the Brigadier emphatically. 'I like the use of the word "our" barracks, even if it was said as "ah", because everyone is proud of their own organization, and that Guards Officer meant, by "our" barracks, *everyone* in his battalion — officers and men. It may irritate the men who have regarded it as "their" barracks, but it is only a display of the competitive spirit. They said in Suez that the first thing that came off was the polo ponies of The Life Guards. I have got nothing against polo ponies particularly — better than hot air balloons, wouldn't you say? I am proud, in fact, because they are looking at the sporting interest side of life, and keeping fit. I would much rather men played on polo ponies than sat all night in discos or playing black-jack.'

After this spirited defence of the status quo, we got down to details. A 2nd Lieutenant of nineteen, having spent his seven months at Sandhurst, is almost bound to be made up to 1st Lieutenant and then Captain if he keeps his nose clean and is not manifestly incompetent. This will happen broadly according to a time scale. From Captain to Major is by selection. The Deputy Director of Manning will chair a committee consisting of another Brigadier and two Colonels, who will know what quota of Majors is required. They will work their way through the various 'teeth' Arms and Services one by one, considering the case of every man of thirty-two and over. This takes place once a year, around January and February, for ten days. In the course of this period four hundred men are considered in detail, on the findings of three officers who will have reported, independently, on about twenty separate characteristics of their performance.

'You mustn't try to do too much in one day or you get punch-drunk,' said the Brigadier. 'It is damned hard work. We decide them at the age of thirty-two, thirty-three or thirty-four. Those who are promoted at thirty-two are not necessarily the Field Marshalls of the future. It is not automatic at all.'

If any of the Senior Reporting Officers have made *adverse* comments on a candidate for promotion, the candidate must be shown it — a process which might with benefit be followed by many civilian organizations who regard the Army as autocratic. Most of the report on a candidate is written by an Initiating Officer (lower in seniority than the Senior Reporting Officers) and candidates see *all* of this.

'From the age of thirty-two,' said the Brigadier, 'a man who started harum-scarum, who has rushed round the world, and done quite badly in some things, and annoyed people intensely, may find that it dawns on him that the Army is a bit more of a career than he thought. You can then *see* him settling down and getting noticeably better. He is probably just getting married. We don't go too far back in their reports when we are reading them, because in some ways it would be unfair. If you go back as far as Sandhurst, you may find he poured water over the Regimental Sergeant Major or something.'

It is an irony that the Army, which is a hierarchical organization, lets personality bygones be bygones at a time when many civilian organizations, and the people in them, never forgive or forget that Bloggs or Jones, at the age of twenty-two, got tight at the office party, called the Assistant-to-the-Deputy a boring old twit and stood on the table to sing 'Annie Laurie' five times over. But the Brigadier was emphatic that — though he couldn't prove it statistically — the Army today was continually reassessing its people in quite radical ways.

Officers were graded, he said, in one of five grades: Excellent, Very Good, Good, Adequate and Weak. Dead certainties for promotion were rarely reviewed by the boards under his chairmanship. Nor were the men who weren't recommended. It was the ones in the middle that they spent most time considering.

Was it possible for a senior officer to block a man's promotion because of personal jealousy and pique? The Brigadier produced a one inch thick volume of loose sheets of paper bearing the name of one young officer, with two fact sheets pinned on the top of it. It was the young officer's file from the moment he joined the Army, periodically up-dated. One of the papers on top was like a football pools coupon — which is, in fact, its nickname in the Army, because all the Reporting Officers have to fill in what

' amounts to 'lose', 'win' or 'draw' on a list of human qualities they think the officer possesses — things like energy, intelligence, reliability, tactical ability and zeal.

'Someone once said,' commented the Brigadier drily, 'that there should be another box at the bottom of the form for sense of humour — that that was what was lacking in the Army. Well, the form is reviewed every five years, so it might be changed. It is not reviewed more often than five years. You have got, after all, to get the Army educated in the use of this form. If you make a change you could distort the picture.'

The 'pools results' on the young officer's form did give a balanced picture. Indeed, it would not be easy for any senior officer with a down on a man to put his knife into him about *everything* without revealing his own personal prejudice. One thing that appeared on this particular man's pools coupon was: 'Innate shyness makes him look at the ceiling instead of who he is talking to.' But another read: 'Dogged, determined.'

Any senior officer wanting to knife a subordinate in the back by a series of vague nods and winks would find himself more frustrated in the Army than he might in some civilian organizations with more liberal and progressive pretensions. 'The chance of an officer having all three Reporting Officers saying, "No, no, no," to him — if he is good — is not great,' insisted the Brigadier.

The three Reporting Officers are the Initiating Officer (usually his Commanding Officer); his 1st Superior Reporting Officer, who is a Brigadier; and his 2nd Superior Reporting Officer, who is usually a Major General.

The Deputy Director of Manning admitted that if he took against a man he *could* give him a bad report. 'But — oh yes! — the examiners are on trial as well as the men. The General might write that the Brigadier who had made comments was a hard taskmaster, so you would get the thing in perspective. You build up a picture of the people who are doing the judging. You don't get any major blocking of candidates. In any case, I will do my job here for three years and then someone else will take over.'

An officer will have been made a Major almost certainly at thirty-four if not thirty-two, and if he has not, he will be out at the end of sixteen years' service, the earliest pensionable point. But he may well find that his promotion to Major is his last; for the rank is the sticking point for many, many officers who are then known as 'Passed-Over Majors'.

Curiously, I found that of all the people in the Army I met, it was the Passed-Over Majors who were the *most* like the traditional idea of the Army officer. They were the most ready with the 'Old boy' and the 'My dear chap', and the most likely to fire remarks like bullets, to grow moustaches like barbed wire entanglements. Does this say something about the effectiveness of the Army's screening system for advancement? That it must be good if such men are not allowed into the top positions? Perhaps. I certainly tended to find that when I came across a Passed-Over Major who was a self-caricature, his own colleagues tended to view him in the same light as I did. This was encouraging.

Many of these Majors are, of course, men of great experience, who bring to the job valuable skills. The Army would be the poorer without them. Their personal misfortune is the Army's good fortune, just as it is good for a civilian firm to have some mature people at every rung of the ladder.

'I would not belittle the Passed-Over Majors,' said the Brigadier. 'They are needed by the Army very much. We have got jobs for them. The vast majority of them are very good officers indeed and have a lot of expertise. Perhaps they have missed promotion by half a mark. The line has to be drawn somewhere. I sometimes say to my chums who are Generals, "It may be only one mark that has put you where you are today, compared with some Major who just didn't get it — who just consistently missed."'

The age at which a Major is considered for the critical promotion to Lieutenant Colonel is between thirty-seven and forty-seven. In the old days, the man who became a Lieutenant Colonel tended to be a man who the head of the regiment *wanted* to be Lieutenant Colonel. There might be a vacancy in the regiment, and six men in it said, in effect, 'Appoint me.' Even those in the Army today who think that the old system worked out fairly well admit it was based on a lot of personal and social prejudice.

Now, as it is the Army as a whole which decides whether a Major is to become a Lieutenant Colonel or not, he will find himself chopped and changed from one job to another sometimes with his regiment and sometimes on the General Staff list doing a bureaucratic job, so that any personal prejudices about his personal antecedents cannot loom very large. Regiments now have an incentive to produce really good officers — as distinct from officers who happen to please a particular Commanding Officer. If a regiment cannot produce a Major who, in the opinion of the Army in general, is good enough to be made a Lieutenant Colonel in that regiment, then one will have to be drafted in from elsewhere.

On the whole, the Army has found that officers are more diligent about their examinations and promotion chances now than they were even ten years ago; more professional in their attitude. As the Brigadier put it: 'They are passing their examinations today. People were much more cavalier in their attitude to the Army in the old days. They said, "We are in the Army to get a certain way of life and enjoy it — nuts to all these bureaucrats producing all these exams!" Now it is exceptional to find people who fall by the wayside. People are much more career conscious. Officers' attitudes have changed considerably. We will find that more people will get promoted at the *average* age, because the standard is raised.'

Even if an historic old regiment is virtually awash with good breeding and polo ponies, it will not alter the fact that, in having to call in a Lieutenant Colonel from another regiment, it will have suffered a reverse — possibly at the hands of a regiment less pretentious. 'At one stage,' said the

Brigadier, 'my own regiment provided five Commanding Officers for other regiments. Since then we have had one outsider come to command us, because we couldn't provide one. This is the way things fluctuate. And this was within the space of eight years.'

The Army has four selection boards, each handling a different range of ranks. The Number Two selection board chooses Colonels at age forty-one to fifty and Brigadiers at age forty-three to fifty-two. Number One selection board consists of six senior Generals, and selects Major Generals (at age forty-six to fifty-two). Lieutenant Generals are chosen to fill the few very senior specialized appointments, by a less formalized system, based on the judgement of the existing top echelon of the Army.

Those who may have missed top promotion in the Army may comfort themselves with the knowledge that the higher an officer goes, the more rigorous the demands he has to meet and the more likely he is to be thrown on the scrapheap. A man may be delighted to get promotion to Major General at forty-nine (the earliest age). His delight may turn to disappointment when (as may happen) he gets compulsorily retired after only two years, because there is no job available for him to do as a Major General. In such a case, his pension is adjusted to cushion the blow but at fifty-one he may have twenty years left to brood on the fact that his skills are not necessarily very easy to transfer to civilian life.

'What happens a bit more as you go on and up,' explained the Brigadier, 'is that it is a bit more a matter of horses for courses. There are certain jobs where you do want a chap to have the right background for it. Take some Brigadier chaps — well, if you are going to be a Brigadier commanding Gunners, then you want a Gunner. There may be a better full Colonel in another Arm, but he won't get the job. That is unavoidable. This job I am doing now can be done by any officer of any corps whatever. But there are some jobs which require an officer from the right corps. There may be some chaps who will miss promotion because they haven't got the correct specialization for a situation which must be unforeseen.'

What makes a really top Commander? A variety of experience, said the Brigadier, between Command and Staff duties — between, in other words, 'teeth' and 'desk' duties. And if it was sometimes said that a man could be passed over for a really top position because he was too old for a Command role, 'you must remember the Army is made to fight. It is not Whitehall. The chap who gets the top job is a good Commander. He will have been an *outstanding* Commander — with perhaps not quite as much Staff experience as some politicians would wish. We should be identifying the next Chief of General Staff *now*, very privately, and making sure he has the right training.'

In the end, the professional head of the Army is appointed in Whitehall, meeting Whitehall's standards. It is bound to be so as long as the Army is the subordinate and the politicians the boss. The Brigadier agreed: 'And that is another battle altogether! That takes some expertise of its own. But the personality and character of the man who actually reaches that position can vary enormously, from what some people would call a striving little shit to a big, expansive, openhearted, generous chap. They are as various as people are various.'

There is one very clear indicator of the men the Army regards as having future merit. It is called the British Army Staff College and stands in the same grounds as Sandhurst, at Camberley. It gives a year's course to the top third of the Army's high-fliers — a course which certainly does not flatten out individuality and assertive self-expression. The Staff College is no device for the brainwashing of ciphers. Dash and flair are looked for and used, and egotism survives as long as its owner is also a survivor — and can think.

Field Marshal Montgomery, *the* military success story of World War Two, was there as a student, as an instructor and, later still, as the opener of the new wing bearing his name. Even as a student he was not cowed in his personal manner. In one 1920s' issue of *Owl Pie*, the students' magazine, a list of elliptical questions of the hour contained the following: 'If and where Monty spent two silent minutes on Armistice Day?' What was required, asked another item, to stop Monty 'babbling at breakfast'?

Entrance, as a Captain or Major between the ages of thirty-one and thirty-three, is on the basis of both examination and reports by Commanding Officers. The Commandant insisted to me that it was 'not absolute death' to miss coming to the college; that it was possible to recover and climb without having done so.

Literally, this is true, but young men who want to get on in the Army still practically burst themselves trying to get to Camberley, thrust themselves forward with the right answers when they get there, and do not let any lax behaviour by their competitors pass by in Christian silence. You *may* rise to the top of the British Army if you have not been to Camberley, just as you may become Prime Minister of Great Britain if you left school at fourteen; but in neither case do the names of people who have actually done it flood into the mind.

Two young officers drinking a pre-lunch gin in the Officers Mess told me insistently that the social background of officers there was as broad as that of officers in the Army as a whole. 'But in all honesty,' said one, 'that is not very broad.' He was a public school boy, son of a civil engineer. The other, an officer in the Guards, described himself as, 'Son of a doctor, public school, no money'. He may have had no money (in the sense of the personal fortune of a financial manipulator) but he was so plainly in the right mould (as a Guards Officer from a major public school) that it was reflected in the confidence of his manner. When I asked a question, he usually answered first, and when he interrupted others *they* tended to stop talking. He would do well at Camberley; but in fairness so might quite different types of officers from the corps: men with necks too squat, faces too sallow and chins too swarthy to be upper class, but men capable of coldly assessing how and when a certain bridge must be blown up in the course of a retreat.

White-jacketed waiters brought the food to the dining-tables — no self-service here. But the Commandant would not agree that the atmosphere was that of a country house. 'It is hard work here,' he said.

It certainly is. During his first month, a student will be given a practical test in the form of an actual battle test, with as much realism as possible in the classroom. The course starts with a fortnight's briefing, followed by eight weeks of groundwork: industrial, legal and political consider-ations. The second term involves tactics, including training in a real terrain. The third term is devoted to the most controversial and perhaps most potentially important subject of the course — counter-revolutionary warfare. There are lessons in techniques in the jungle, in the mountains and in Northern Ireland. Sometimes there have been exercises in counter-revolutionary warfare on the United Kingdom mainland, using a hypothetical city created by turning the map of Aberdeen upside down and putting it in the middle of Wales.

'But we don't use any real organizations or real people for the purposes of these exercises,' said one of the Directing Staff. 'And the object, anyway, is not to look at the political aspects, but to study the military environment and do what would be required in support of the police.'

The sort of fictional situation which the course assumes is a breakdown of law and order on lines which the students are asked to envisage for themselves. The students are quite sophisticated, in private conversation, about the sort of things that might happen, even if their political impartiality is rigidly asserted. 'It would not surprise me,' said one instructor, 'to see someone reading Mao's Red Book.'

At every stage, students are subject to the most ruthless intellectual cross-examination, both by the instructors and their fellow students. Camberley may be a country house, but its students are scarcely encouraged to relax in it like country gentlemen. If a man reaches the very top echelon of the British Army, merit as well as pure chance will be decisive, whether he emerges through the Staff College or not.

The Army is proud of its claim that nearly a third of its officers now come up through the ranks. These men often have a Short Service Commission in the Army; the man who tells the fighting man to fight still tends to be the product of Sandhurst, which sets him apart, from the age of eighteen or nineteen, from the men he will command. Here he is told his maxim must be 'serve to lead' and that he must consider his men and look after them and, as far as circumstances will allow, their comfort at all times. But the separation is much more final than it would be in a civilian occupation, where it is possible for a man to pass from shop floor to top management, however few men do it in practice.

It would be condescendingly artificial nonsense to suggest that the ordinary soldier ('Your actual basic Brit,' as one seasoned Major put it) is much aggrieved because of this. Though he is certainly more intelligent, or at least more television-worldly, than his predecessors of a generation or so ago, his purely intellectual dexterity may be limited, and focused entirely on his own chances of promotion within the quite different career structure of the other ranks.

The Deputy Director of Manning (Army) is also responsible for the promotion of other ranks.

'With soldiers,' said the Colonel under him dealing with soldier policy, 'their promotion depends, more than with officers, on their actual trade. If you are talking about the promotion potential of a Pay Corps Corporal, you are looking for different qualities and expertise than you would look for in a Corporal in the Royal Artillery or Royal Armoured Corps. Obviously you are looking for technical expertise to a much greater extent in the corps and leadership and man-management qualities in the teeth arms.'

The marking system for soldiers is more specific than that of officers. 'More pedantic, if you like,' said the Colonel. 'The exact number of marks determines the assessment of the man, though there is a pen picture of him at the bottom of the form.'

Soldiers broadly have a ladder of seven ranks on a twenty-two-year engagement, ending up — if they are lucky — as Warrant Officer Class One. There is no assumption that the man even *may* cross the sacred line, and become a commissioned officer rather than a non-commissioned officer. This state of affairs is rather different from that in large and bureaucratic civilian organizations like Unilever or Shell, which pride themselves on the fact that (though most of their top executives may be graduates) a considerable proportion, even at board level, have come up through the ranks.

Who is right — the big civilian corporations or the British Army? Some soldiers who have seen the Army in action in Northern Ireland argue that its considerable successes can be set against a rather uncertain performance by much of British industry. The reasons for this relative success and relative failure may be far broader than mere promotion systems. But many officers point out that, as yet, there seems to be no solid evidence that businesses run *without* a firm hierarchical system thrive any better than those *with* them; that, in any case, in time of war, success depends on the automatic carrying out of orders; and that men are more likely to carry out orders, and not argue, if there is a certain distance between officer and man.

Whatever the truth of this argument, the fact remains that the career structure of other ranks is quite separate from that of the officer. But, argue top Army officers, at least it is clearly visible to the recruit.

'The thing is based firstly on the confidential report by the man's Reporting Officer,' said the Colonel in charge of manning for other ranks. 'They themselves see this report, unlike the Navy and the Royal Air Force system, in which reports are unseen. In the Army reports are seen for two reasons. The Reporting Officer has to make sure in his own mind that he is writing an objective report. And, more importantly, the man can see and correct his own faults.'

Putting the best interpretation on the Army's psychology, this can also be seen as part of the unwritten Army code of facing out a man on any issue and not going behind his back: a system which, while repudiating egalitarianism absolutely, believes in mutual reponsibility and brotherly candour. It may not be a fashionable concept, but in relation to the Army's particular requirements it seems to work.

As the man gets to the rank of Sergeant (via Lance Corporal and Corporal) promotion boards are held. 'The principle,' said the Colonel 'is merit tempered by seniority. The flyer can go much faster than the average stream. But this is tempered by seniority. If you err on the side of merit you come unstuck, because you find the chap is not as good as the man who is more experienced.'

If Major is the main sticking point for officers, the men have several. If a soldier doesn't make Lance Corporal by the age of twenty-five, he may just continue as a senior Private soldier, with no particular problems. He may be promoted later. At least one in five Privates in infantry battalions are said to be quite satisfied to remain Privates. Most of them leave the Army after six years of their engagement, though a few carry on till the end of their full term. In fact, half the Army comes in initially on a three-year engagement, and of these, half leave after three years, with no special trauma on either side; they are just young men who have tried one career and not settled to its demands and rewards.

When I asked the Colonel what sort of man was likely to gain promotion fastest in the ranks, he said, 'Firstly he has got to be intelligent. The chaps who are going up fast are. Whether they come in with a good *academic* record I don't think is the point, but it is difficult to gain fast promotion if you are not intelligent. Secondly, they have to demonstrate, rather more than in civilian life, strength of personality and leadership qualities. But there is no room for the bull-headed Sergeant Major type. Whereas in the old days you could become a Regimental Sergeant Major on the infantry drill square with very little nous, you couldn't do that now, because you would not pass the exams.'

I was glad to hear this assurance, which came at roughly the same time as allegations in Sunday newspapers that one NCO had gone down on all fours and bitten a Private in the bottom and another had hit a recruit over the head with a bit of copper pipe as he put his head out of his tent, saying, 'That will teach you to wear your helmet next time!' There were also allegations that an NCO had forced a recruit to kiss the shoes of a young officer. It is fair to say that all these alleged abuses by soldiers who had achieved promotion were the subject of disciplinary proceedings, and were so *un*common that they made the front pages of mass circulation newspapers in a way they would never have done if they had not been so unusual. An Army man, reading about the allegations and the military court proceedings, said at the time, 'If these things are proved true, it will not be the NCOs who will get into real trouble — they will find their stripes gone, that's all — it will be the officers. You are always taught that you are supposed to look after your soldiers, which are the most valuable pieces of Army equipment there are. I would not like to be the officers in these cases.'

Mistakes are visibly made in promoting people, as is inevitable in any occupation. Some officers believe, too, that Northern Ireland can make some young NCOs callous because of the things they see done to their own men by the enemy; and that some of this callousness comes out when they are dealing with young greenhorns who have, irritatingly, only the vaguest idea that doing the right thing at the right time may save a man's life.

But, as with officers, NCO material is reported on by more than one person. 'You can't fool all the people all the time,' said the Colonel. 'If there is a major personality defect in a man it will show. With soldiers, if a man is graded 'A' at the time he is made Corporal, you find that nearly *all* his reports are 'A'. In a way, it is easier to judge. With an officer, you can well find the majority of reports are 'A', but you suddenly find one hiccough of a 'C'. I think it is the fact that when we are talking about an officer, we are talking about a closer relationship of policy and ideas. In these areas you can have a clash of views, which might be reflected in the reports on the officer. But this doesn't appertain to soldiers. In any case, those doing the reporting can be objective, because distant. Reporting Officers are always commissioned officers, *not* Warrant Officers.'

Bearing in mind the mistakes that sometimes, evidently, do occur in the appointment of NCOs, perhaps their own colleagues *should* be among those sitting in judgement on them? But the Army has an ingrained reluctance to have other than commissioned officers reporting on men. 'The Reporting Officer,' said the Colonel, when I asked what influence NCOs did have on the appointment of other NCOs, 'should take an informal view of senior ranks as to the man's capabilities.' There is, however, no rule that requires this to be done.

The major sticking-point in the promotion scale, even for some without great character defects, is Corporal. Becoming a Sergeant is a big jump, in non-commissioned ranks. The man uses a different mess, and he is often left to do a quite responsible job on his own. It is not unusual for a Sergeant to be left in sole charge of all private travel by all ranks in his division's area in Germany, including Berlin, for instance.

Supposing a man became Warrant Officer Class One by the age of thirty-three, which showed he had been good at his job, could he then go on to become a commissioned officer? I put this question to the Colonel.

'I hesitate,' was the reply. 'There are a mass of things he *can* do. He can get a Quartermaster Commission, a Short Service Commission or a Special Regular Commission.' Any of these commissions does make an NCO into an officer. Whether he will ever *feel* fully on a par with an officer who has never been anything else is rather doubtful. The only way he could do that would be to hold a high combat post. And the Army points out that you really need to have been trained for that from the word go, and to have had experience of it throughout your career.

But whether or not NCOs who have become officers will ever feel *absolutely* at home in the Officers Mess, there is no doubt the Army has substantially increased the number of ranker officers since the last war. In 1951, fewer than one in fifty of that year's intake of officers came up via the ranks. The following year, the ratio had more than doubled. By 1960, one officer in ten was an ex-ranker. The ratio crept steadily up throughout the 1960s when National Service was abolished. It hit the peak of one in three in 1975, and continued more or less at that figure for the rest of the 1970s, ending up fractionally below one in three in 1979. This is encouraging, but it remains true that the Army is something in which you need to make progress early for best results later — one of the few things it has in common with the ballet.

The Colonel's second-in-command, a Major, admitted: 'Over the age of thirty, outlets are somewhat limited. There could be a Special Regular Commission or a Short Service Commission. Opportunity is restricted within the Combat Arms, because of the age of the man. He is too old and senior to be a Platoon Commander. If he does more administrative duties — for example as an Infantry Motor Transport Officer — he could well become a commissioned soldier. At Warrant Officer Second Class, he could be recommended for these different types of commission.'

Is such an officer a 'real' one in the sense that those are who have gone through Sandhurst when they hardly knew how to shave properly? 'He is a proper officer in all respects,' said the Colonel. 'But his pay may well not go up.'

This is no doubt an accidental circumstance, but it certainly is not likely to persuade non-commissioned officers to cross over the line. A Warrant Officer First Class cannot be expected to fight to become a Captain, when his salary is already at the level of a Major's — around £7,000 to £8,000 a year after the last major pay increase. He may get a 'special' rate as Captain in these circumstances but, in money terms, it could still be only a move sideways, rather than a marked financial improvement.

Perhaps the Army cannot be blamed for making it none too easy (though easier than in the past) to cross over the non-commissioned/commissioned boundary. As a commander in action, a man needs to be both physically in his prime and to have a background of experience in tactical concepts. He is at a disadvantage if he has arrived at the age of thirty-three without having had this experience.

There is a second reason why the Army is prepared to live with the constraints that prevent men crossing the boundary. Many Sergeants and Warrant Officers will tell you that *they* are more important to a corps or regiment than an officer; and the Army has taken them at their word.

'The Sergeants Mess,' said the Colonel, 'is at least *as* important as the Junior Officers' structure. Therefore we have got to be very careful not to take the cream off the Sergeants Mess, and commission it. I would prefer a first-class Sergeant Major to a first-class Second-in-Command of a company, if I had to make the choice.'

The British Army, you will be told at all levels, works on a hierarchical system; and that system works. There is a difference between Corporals and Private soldiers. Sergeants are different from both and divorced socially from the junior ranks, having their own mess, and similarly the Officers Mess is divorced from the Sergeants Mess. But officers will also maintain, and men will tend to agree, that perfectly good professional relationships are possible within the system — and that, in comparison with other armies of the world, they are *especially* possible within the almost unique British regimental system.

Those who talk of egalitarianism will get short shrift from the Director of Manning. 'I think you will find,' he said drily, 'that there is no egalitarianism in the Russian Army.

I think it is impossible to get a commission in the Russian Army unless you have been through the Academy. I suspect another way in which they are very non-egalitarian is in their pay scales. A Major in the Russian Army, for instance, gets about twenty to thirty times the pay of the soldier, when ours get only three or four times. Field Marshals get three hundred times more than a soldier. It is quite astonishing.' End of talk about egalitarianism.

In any case, a man's chances of jumping the officer/other ranks fence are perhaps better in *some* parts of the complex and individual British Army than in others. They are probably better if he is in one of the specialist corps rather than in an infantry regiment, including the Household Division, though on paper they are the same.

At least one specialist corps has done remarkably well in promoting through the ranks — and in using the expertise thus gained, with other know-how, in fields broader than the strictly military.

11

The Better Ambassador

'. . .and Colonel Bulder, in full military uniform, on horseback, galloping first to one place and then to another, and backing his horse among the people, and prancing, and curvetting, and shouting in a most alarming manner, and making himself very hoarse in the voice, and very red in the face, without any assignable cause or reason whatever.'

> — Charles Dickens, describing a display by the forerunners of the Royal Engineers at Chatham, circa 1835.

'Today the British soldier is a good ambassador, and the British Sapper is a *better* ambassador.'

> — Engineer-in-Chief, British Army, at Royal Engineers' display at Chatham, circa 1979.

The British Officer wore a pith helmet too big for his head. His khaki drill shorts just failed to conceal his knobbly knees. He carried an out-of-date rifle and a haversack. A bird, invisible to everyone else in the jungle, rose from the trees. The officer let fly at it with an enormous bang, put the vanquished bird into his haversack with jerky triumph, wiped his white forehead, and moved on relentlessly through the undergrowth, his knock-knees defying the jungle to do its worst.

Thus far — considering the time was not the mid-nineteenth century but the late twentieth — the portrait might have seemed to suggest that the British Army was comically out of date. In fact it suggested more nearly the exact reverse: that the British Army is as much at home (perhaps even *more* at home) in the technological age as much of British industry; and that it can move as an ambassador where pin-striped trousers and old Etonian ties might close more doors than they would open.

There was, it is true, considerable laughter at this anachronistic figure of Empire as he strutted his way through the imaginary jungle thickets of Chatham, England: territory not best known for its attap trees and swamps. The date, being 1979, well past Queen Victoria's Jubilee, was a bit incongruous, too. Surely the coming 1980s were no place for the British Army's pioneering and missionary role in less developed countries?

The knock-kneed officer was a paradoxical reminder that the role was still possible. He was part of a demonstration that showed the British Army's grip on technology was good enough both to defend the realm and make friends abroad.

He was, of course, a spoof; a spoof who showed that the Royal Engineers — a fairly representative technical corps in a British Army which includes many exportable skills useful in peace as well as war — can laugh at themselves while taking their job seriously. His jungle undergrowth, purely imaginary, was near Chattenden Barracks at Chatham in Kent — the home of the Royal Engineers and the venue for the three-yearly Royal Engineer Demonstrations, which show off the work of one of the best remaining ambassadors in the Third World and other countries.

The audience for this display is always a very mixed one. There are local schoolboys who may well be interested in joining the Army. There are influential industrialists, some of them ex-Army. There are local citizens, and local and national newspapermen.

Romantics given to easy nostalgia may see the heyday of the Royal Engineers as the day of the Indian Raj. Certainly railways, bridges, water schemes and other engineering feats remain in India as reminders of British influence. But the continued eager presence of the schoolboys and others at Chattenden Barracks is a sign that the Royal Engineers can still be lively innovators. Every display is enlivened by new devices they have originated or developed.

The British Army is a very broad church, not a narrow one. The Sappers, as a body, are almost as unlike the Guards Division as a computer technician is unlike a gentleman farmer. It is ironical that a group of individualists described by one historian as 'mad, married or Methodist', which can laugh at itself with evident relish and can obtain Corporals good enough to advise Colonels, has probably done more for the continuity of British influence and tradition abroad than many other parts of the Army who might be temperamentally more eager to make the claim.

I attended the 1979 Sapper demonstration as a guest of the Engineer-in-Chief of the moment, a very large Major General who could have passed as the chairman of a large engineering firm or the principal of a large polytechnic. 'See us in action,' he counselled, with a proselytizing glint in the eye. 'You'll probably be surprised at the sheer range of the things we get up to.'

The proceedings were certainly not dull. Nor were the Royal Engineers I met predictable, in accent, social background or appearance — they could have slid into civilian life, one felt, with scarcely a ripple. And the way they presented themselves to the public, knock-kneed Empire builder and all, appealed to technical and intellectual curiosity, not to portentuous solemnity. No doubt this would have pleased the Duke of Wellington. He was the man who first urged the employment of military engineers in a combat support role. He did it in a letter to Lord Liverpool in 1812, the year a more flamboyant but ultimately less successful military reformer, Napoleon, was retreating from Moscow. The previous year many 'carpenters and miners' from the infantry regiments of the British Army had been pressed into Sappers' jobs for which they were not properly and professionally trained and had helped storm Badajoz. Too many of them died. The Duke, addicted to a plain grey uniform and a verbal brevity sometimes verging on the brutal, was offended by such wanton wastage of lives, and thought that only technical expertise could prevent a repetition. He was against the romanticism of the times in believing that a live expert was better than a dead hero, and he was the sort of conservative who was intelligent enough to discard conventions when they got in the way.

Whether the first Commandant of the Royal Engineers Establishment (as it was then called) would have appealed to the Duke is not recorded. He was Major C.W. Pasley, later Sir Charles Pasley, KCB, and he was a great showman. He organized the first of the seige operations in which some of the garrison took part. These were the forerunners of the present-day demonstrations, and could be just as rich in tongue-in-cheek humour. Charles Dickens, who lived in Chatham for a time, gave an account, in *Pickwick Papers*, of one such demonstration under a certain 'Colonel Bulder', a rather obvious *nom de guerre* of Pasley.

'The appearance of everything on the lines,' he wrote, 'denoted that the approaching ceremony was one of the utmost grandeur and importance. There were sentries posted to keep the ground for the troops, and servants on the batteries keeping places for the ladies, and sergeants running to and fro, with vellum-covered books under their arms. . .' Then came the reference to Colonel Bulder, in full military uniform, on horseback, galloping first to one place and then to another, and backing his horse among the people, and prancing, and curvetting, and shouting in a most alarming manner, and making himself very hoarse in the voice, and very red in the face, without any assignable cause or reason whatever. Dickens may have laid it on with a trowel, but the picture is fairly clear.

The tradition of showmanship, if not of prancing and curvetting, lingers on. So does the tradition of flexibility and self-mockery. The demonstration I saw began with military excavation equipment, huge bulldozers with fierce-toothed grabs. They proceeded to take the place of players in a football game, using a three-foot diameter ball.

Then another excavator appeared, with its grab painted as a face with enormous teeth. It proceeded to pick up and crush to a pulp a 'Staff Car' which had just been driven into its path and abandoned. It was only when the audience had realized that the whole thing was a joke, and that no General had been deprived of his transport, that the serious business of the day began.

'Even if an enemy had a three-to-one tank advantage and started to pour his tanks through into Western Europe,' explained an officer in the spectator stands, tactfully not naming the possible enemy, 'it does not follow that he has won. He still has a supply problem and his tanks could, very probably, be dealt with.'

How they could be dealt with was the basis of the displays. With, for example, a range of cratering kits — one of which, in the hands of only two men, can produce in ten minutes a single crater big enough to stop a tank, and, in the hands of more men, a complex of craters in a quarter of an hour. With an anti-personnel minelaying system which can fire 1,296 rounds in a minute, each one becoming a primed anti-personnel mine that will knock out tank crews trying to escape, or other enemy soldiers moving in to assist the ditched tank. With charges which can quickly blow up the bridges which would have given the enemy access. And with devices still in the Think-Tank stage — devices which at Chatham gave more delight to the schoolboys than the more conventional displays.

One of the new ideas — not likely to see military action for at least four years, even if approved — was a sort of Gulliver version of a bubble pipe. A prototype was on display. It produced huge clouds of foam, more suggestive of a detergent factory than a military installation. And what was the object of all this foam? To tackle tanks. The idea of tackling sixty tons of tank with foam is so bizarre that it would be easy to assume that only a romantic innovator like Sir Winston Churchill, goaded by wartime pressures, would be likely to give it credence. In fact the Royal Engineers take foam quite seriously (if not solemnly).

While schoolboys jumped up and down bursting as many bubbles as they could, one RE officer explained the very practical rationale.

The procedure would be to find a narrow place where the enemy tanks would have to pass — a built-up street, an underpass, or better still a tunnel — and fill it up with foam. Tanks are imposing, frightening things. But they are driven by human beings, who have to steer them, and have to be able to *see* in order to steer them. A tank driver driving into an underpass blocked with foam would almost immediately lose all visibility and, with it, his sense of position and direction. In a few seconds he would be as disorientated as a man inside a black box. In this state, he could well run his tank heavily into the underpass walls, where other tanks would in turn ram it, eventually blocking the route completely. The foam could be made so that it persisted for a long time. It might even be made in a form which solidified once ejected from the foam-thrower, so that the enemy motor vehicles would face a solid wall of either buildings or foam, which would stop both visibility and access. This arrangement would certainly be more politically acceptable, in a highly built-up area like West Germany, than trying to block the enemy's path by wholesale demolition of buildings. Foam remained a bright idea rather than an immediately practical possibility — but it showed the imagination of the Royal Engineers.

Another skill they demonstrated was the ability to build a medium girder bridge strong enough to take tanks in just fourteen minutes. They even had time to laugh when a United States Army helicopter bringing in component parts set up such a down-blast that spectators were splashed by the spray and deluged with grit from the simulated battlefield. 'Trust the Yanks to overdo it,' said an industrialist and ex-RE officer, dusting himself down with a mischievous grin.

Countering the enemy's mobility is, of course, only one aspect of the Royal Engineers' technical expertise. It also deals with ways of *achieving* mobility. It is in this sphere, drawing on expertise comparable with the highest civilian engineering qualifications, that the Royal Engineers produce some of the ideas which are of use to other countries in peacetime.

Bridges are an obvious example, and they were well in evidence at Chatham. They have popped up in all sorts of countries. For the past few years, the Sudan has been opening up parts of its southern region with Royal Engineer bridges and Britain was actually asked back, long after her Imperial glories were over, to carry out the bridge-building. 'We don't advertise these things, you understand,' said a senior Royal Engineer officer. 'What appears is a modest little statement of what we have done — if anything appears at all.'

The inconspicuousness of the Royal Engineers, as they help overseas governments, is their singular quality. It is not possessed by technicians of many other nations. The job may be putting right damage done in the autumn NATO exercises in Germany. It may be exercising quality control over two hospitals being built in Saudi Arabia by Korean and Belgian contractors, where the Royal Engineers were asked to do the job because of their reputation for technical expertise and professional integrity. It may be bridge-building in Canada or Bangla Desh, or making garages for tanks in Kenya. Whatever the job, the aim of the Royal Engineers is to blend the maximum possible help with the minimum possible self-exposure and self-assertion. The strategy worked well in Bangla Desh when, after the punishing war of the early 1970s, Royal Engineer officers and men built Bailey Bridges to replace bridges destroyed in the fighting. They did it with two hundred local workers under their direction and, according to eye-witnesses, on a shoulder-to-shoulder basis that made them welcome visitors, and avoided any political opposition.

'The Americans in these sort of situations,' said a high-ranking Royal Engineer, 'tend to send in a lot of equipment, and that's it. I have seen them operate in the Far East, and they don't *relate* to the local people like we do. They haven't the knack of getting the best out of people in these sort of circumstances. I suppose it is the hangover from our Imperial days. The Russians don't understand the local people or their sensibilities. If you know the local people are religiously against drink, then you don't flaunt drink in their faces. We are particularly good at *not* doing this sort of thing.'

The Royal Engineers' involvement in overseas help has declined somewhat since the early 1970s, in spite of the willingness of the Sappers abroad to provide a bit of extra help on their own initiative, if necessary. This willingness has often been a most acceptable ambassador for Britain. In what was then North Borneo, British and Australian soldiers together built a cantonment for tuberculosis patients, in their own time. Senior officers say they found out about it only when the work was well on the way to completion. In Ethiopia, Royal Engineers improved a local Cheshire Home as their own contribution to the community.

Such willingness may indicate strong goodwill. It cannot remove political considerations — the main one being the need for economies in the modern British Army. There is some feeling among officers and men of the Royal Engineers that the slowing down of official Royal Engineer help is a pity, both for the countries which could benefit and for the Army itself.

'We try to get as many peacetime projects as possible, at home or overseas,' said a senior officer. He made it clear the reason was hard-headed as well as altruistic: 'We can afford to do it now for only three months at a time. But these projects are good value to us because the unit Commander gets his unit away from his Commanding Officer and is able to run his own show. When they get back to Chatham, the wives get at them a bit, that's the trouble, but the soldiers generally enjoy these visits.'

One of the major problems faced by the Royal Engineers, at a time when Britain's international influence and range is declining, is that men have fewer chances to practise their artisan skills. Overseas commitments help. So do loans of personnel to industrial firms in Britain for working on specific contracts. Men return with their skills refreshed. They have also made contacts with firms who may be able to employ their skills when they retire from the Army.

'Not *just* a soldier' is the maxim of the Sappers. But suggest that they are any less fighting men than the Infantry, and you will get a strong denial. It may be true that Royal Engineer officers who are brilliant in engineering skills are often steered away from purely regimental duties and chores and allowed to study for, and take, civilian professional qualifications. This obviously gives the Royal Engineer officer a notion of his worth, independent of the Army, that an Infantryman cannot have so easily until hand-to-hand fighting becomes a marketable technique in civvy street. But, though the Royal Engineer may be a boffin, may be able to laugh at himself, may be saddled with a host of subsidiary tasks such as dealing with unexploded bombs, he finally has to justify himself as an efficient fighting man.

How efficient is he? The consensus of opinion is that he stands very high in the world league. Yes, but how efficient are the mechanical devices at his disposal as he faces, in Europe, the Warsaw Pact's advantage where it most matters?

'We are the most misunderstood corps in the British Army,' said a senior officer. 'People don't understand the whole range and extent of our commitment and our capability. If they have met a Sapper personally, it has probably been in very limited circumstances, and that creates a limited idea of our role.'

Just so. But the range of capability of the British Sapper is more and more linked to the internal politics of NATO. Will tanks be standardized? If so will the result be based on the British Chieftan or the German Leopard? Will there be a standard bridge? Where the innovatory British Royal Engineer was once master in his own house (or at least answerable only to his own politicians) he now depends on the diplomatic skill of his government, and the clout it carries in the world, to decide what weapons he will ultimately use.

A German self-drive bridge is now widely used in Europe. The British Army is committed to it until the late 1980s. Its virtue is that it is self-propelling, whereas the Americans and the Russians use a bridge that has to be towed into place by tugs. Its disadvantage is that it is more complicated, and therefore more vulnerable, than the American or Russian bridges. There is a school of thought among Major Pasley's heirs that Britain would be better advised to move towards the Russian and American approach in the 1980s but the issue will have to go through a political labyrinth to be resolved.

The medium girder bridge, which replaced the old Bailey Bridge (used with great effect in the Second World War and for peacetime purposes thereafter) can be built by hand at the rate of about sixty feet in twenty minutes. To build a reinforced double-decker version one hundred feet long would take about an hour. No one in NATO has a better bridge. The Russian version is roughly comparable. But there are some Royal Engineers who believe that the bridge is now on what they call the Acceptable/Unacceptable Line; and that a lighter one that can be built even more speedily would be more useful in a European war in which forces might have to move very quickly indeed to prevent a complete rout.

And the assault bridge, a scissor-shaped device carried on top of a tank and then mechanically unfolded across a river or chasm in very little time? Expensive, but regarded as being as good as the opposition.

So far, as between NATO and the Warsaw Pact countries, the technological honours are about even — as they are between Britain and its allies. The British Sapper, however, has the advantage of having one device which, at the beginning of the 1980s, was unique. This is the combat engineering tractor.

It took ten years to develop, which is a long time, even

by the standards of major weaponry. It is an armoured vehicle with tracks like a tank's. It has buoyancy tanks fore and aft. These, with the air in the hull itself, make the vehicles able to swim rivers with all but the top twelve inches of it invisible under the water. The *pièce de resistance* of this remarkable and self-sufficient machine is a rocket-projected anchor which can be fired if the tractor becomes bogged down in a crater, ditch or lake. It bites into the ground immediately the steel rope is tightened by the winch aboard the tractor. Then the tractor simply winches itself out of its predicament. The crew do not have to show themselves outside the armoured hull during the entire self-rescue procedure.

Armed with such devices, the Royal Engineer seems confident that he will be able to orchestrate the view of Wellington and others that one step towards British soil is a step too many. The East-West German border is considered to be one place where the Sapper could establish superiority in the use of the ground. 'We have been on that piece of ground since 1945,' said one Sapper, 'and a battle on it would be like a home fixture match. With the current idea in defence — everything well forward — it is possible that an enemy could be stopped for long enough for the politicians to search for solutions.'

But with the increasing urbanization of Western Germany, the ground does not get easier to defend. Certainly not from a political point of view. How are efficient operations to be conducted in built-up areas? How would the vast network of motorways be dealt with in the case of invasion? Given that the use of nuclear devices for demolition purposes is most unlikely, the highly selective role of the Sapper becomes more important rather than less. Destabilization of soil and the release of water from reservoirs are two of the possibilities which have been discussed. Both are technical problems and, as such, are the concern of the Sapper.

It is unfortunate that, in exercises in Germany, he may learn false lessons, if he is not careful. In an exercise, for instance, a bridge will be considered 'blown' immediately one side reaches it and *declares* it blown. In real life the job of blowing it may have taken six hours, and the Sapper would have been that much more tired and less effective at the end of it. A modern battle in Europe would be swift, and require swift thinking in engineering terms. Time for preparation of the battlefield would be short. 'It is going to be an engineer's war to start with,' said a senior Sapper officer. 'It will be our job to stop them coming. You can't think in terms of set pieces today. You will have to say, "Christ, this is it!" and then say to your Commander, "You are going to defend *this* piece of ground and, from the engineer's point of view, *this* is the best way to do it." Then you would have to think what modern technology you could utilize. It is very easy to say, "We don't want men to be graduates, we want practical soldiers and good leaders of men." We *do* want that, of course, but they have got to be up with the hunt in technological terms.'

It is a sad fact that the best training ground for the Royal Engineer, as for many other corps and regiments, has been Northern Ireland. 'There,' commented one Royal Engineer, 'he is going to be faced with unpleasant things, and unpleasant risks, which make the adrenalin run faster.' From bombings and mortarings to barricades and checkpoints, the Royal Engineers have been involved in 'real' war conditions.

But the heirs of Wellington and Major Pasley are on the whole a fortunate lot. Privileged? No, that would not be the word for their personal aura. They have the air, rather, of quiet civilian technocrats: self-respecting and free-thinking men who know their worth, and know their worth is known. There is nothing arrogant or defensive about the officers, none of that clubbishness that puts some civilians off officers of 'the Brigade of Guards' (now officially the Household Division). The other ranks have their own expertise too, which means that their officers rely on them for fine judgement far more than would be the case in some other parts of the British Army. In a sense, and not an ephemeral and catchpenny one, the Royal Engineers are the true democrats of the British Army: cosmopolitan when required, knowing that rank is a badge of competence as well as confidence, able to take their stand on their technical expertise.

The British Sapper is perhaps a more respected prophet in his own country than are Sappers of some other countries. The Germans, with their authoritarian tradition, tend to say to their Sappers: 'We will march *this* route, tell us how to do it.' The British Commander is more likely to say, '*Which* route is likely to be the best?'

There is another indication that Britain, which is not always immaculate in relating prestige to actual worth, attaches great importance to the engineering skills of its soldiers. A Sapper doing a given job within NATO is likely to be of a higher rank than a German doing the same sort of job. The British Army does not regard engineering as being a subservient craft.

If I found hints of dissatisfaction in the British Army, it was mainly among some 'middle-management' ranks: the NCOs who would be foremen or supervisors in civilian life. In some regiments a little edginess, in men who might have become technicians outside the Army, was noticeable. What might be loosely termed 'regimental bull' was rather resented, albeit sotto voce. Such men would be least frustrated, or not frustrated at all, if they had gone instead to the Royal Engineers. I asked a senior Royal Engineer officer whether he thought the archetypal Royal Engineer was effectively a different animal from, say, the Guardsman. 'Oh, I think we are,' he said without hesitation. 'You know the old saying about us being mad, married or Methodist. This was said in the days of such characters as General Gordon of Khartoum. He was a Sapper. Married he was *not*. Methodist he certainly was. Mad he perhaps was — well, eccentric. It springs from the nature of the employment. Royal Engineer work tends to be carried out in small groups. You have to be an independent fellow, very much able to stand on your own feet and express your point of view and influence people to take decisions. It used to be the case that the Royal Engineer Corporal would be advising the Lieutenant Colonel on aspects of engineering in the battlefield. The officer-man relationship is therefore very different from some other parts of the Army.'

The officer said he thought the Royal Engineers were probably looking for a much more individual type of man, rather than for one who was likely to want to follow a set pattern. 'The attitude engendered in the Household Division is that of the team rather than that of the individual. Whereas the Sapper officer is going to operate very much as an individual, a Guards officer is going to be conscious of his team position. Horses for courses.'

The Royal Engineers, according to a senior officer, are constrained only by the quota system in recruitment, which limits the number of candidates they are able to recruit as compared with the other corps and regiments of the British Army:'We could take many more men. More are prepared to come to us. We are more popular than the numbers of our quota would suggest, which would not be true, certainly, of some infantry regiments.'

My own observation tended to support the view that the Royal Engineer is a very different man from the Guardsman or The Royal Green Jacket. It is tempting to see in the British Army the three points of a triangle. At one corner would be the Squire and Peasant Alliance (the Household Division); at the second would be the Meritocrats (the urbane and polished regiments, especially The Royal Green Jackets, the crack fighting unit set up as innovatory Riflemen in the attempt to keep the United States Colonies in the face of guerrilla resistance); at the third and last, but not least, corner of the triangle would be the Technocrats. Of these, the Royal Engineers and the Royal Electrical and Mechanical Engineers would have a conspicuous role.

Which of these three points of the triangle fits most happily into modern conditions and Britain's place in the world is a question to keep the port passing happily to the left for many an hour in Officers Messes everywhere. The

Third World, scrutinizing a few of its bridges, railways and water schemes, would doubtless have its own view — a view which might get even Dickens' Colonel Bulder curvetting merrily in his grave.

The good Colonel Bulder might be curvetting the *more* merrily because it is not *only* the Royal Engineers, and their specialist skills, who have enabled the British Army to make and keep friends abroad. Other corps have played their part in this process.

If only the army — or any other institution — could be equally farsighted at every aspect of its diverse life.

12

The Army's Women

'I joined the Women's Royal Army Corps because I wanted to be in charge of a responsible job. I think the Army is even more than I expected in this respect. In civilian life I suppose I would have worked in hotels. I would have had years and years to wait for promotion, whereas in the Army the turnover is so vast you get more chances. I am only twenty-two at the moment and I am in charge of twenty girls in a mess that seats two hundred people. In civilian life, I would possibly be a head waitress.'

— Women's Royal Army Corps Sergeant.

'I think the Army, by the very nature of the fact that we are a ranked structure, does make it difficult sometimes for the wife of a soldier. There is nothing you can do to avoid this, although we make tremendous efforts now to get officers' wives to talk to the wives of other ranks.'

— Unit Families Officer (Major).

The British Army, unconsciously true to its Kiplingesque past, is arguably least comfortable in its dealings with women. Unless, of course, they are strictly part of the Army family and bound to accept the family rules and conventions.

Women are now among the new meritocrats of the modern British Army. On this important score, the Army has perhaps more to boast about than much of civilian industry and commerce. But wives of Army men, who are not themselves in the Army, realize gradually that they have accepted the Army as bridegroom as much as they have accepted the man. Many do not quite like it. Their contentment with their lot is not enhanced by the fact that the Army, as well as featuring as second bridegroom in a sometimes uneasy *ménage à trois*, also features as landlord, interior decorator and perhaps arbiter of private morals.

'If you wanted to have an orgy as a civilian wife in Woking, you could do it,' said one Army wife of a visibly liberated (and theoretical) turn of mind, 'but if you did it as a service wife in Germany, you would be called over the coals.'

'You simply can't have a chap with a loaded rifle walking behind you if you know you are having an affair with his wife,' said a male officer whose mind may, or may not, have been as theoretical as the lady's. 'Anyway, the Army is a *caring* organization, domestic problems included.'

Whichever of the two, the attacking lady or the defending man, is nearest the crux of the matter, is a matter of opinion. What is a matter of observation is that, though the British Army has probably been more 'liberated' than most sections of industry in promoting women to high executive positions, its relations with servicemen's wives are not always a mutual congratulation society. It is an anomaly and a riddle made more irritating to the outside observer by the suspicion that rather minor, and probably inexpensive, reforms on matters concerning service wives could have major psychological benefits.

'We want to feel like women, not like hens in a hen battery,' said one Army wife — rather oblivious, it must be admitted, of the fact that she had previously lived in a high-rise block of council flats, where individuality was perhaps not the commonest commodity.

The two poles of this little anomaly may easily be expressed in directly human terms: first by the Scottish lady who had already risen to Lieutenant Colonel level and was almost certainly destined to blaze further trails; and second by the rather miffed Army wives I met in Hong Kong, who evoked my bilious sympathy by showing me their carpet in regulation pale turquoise, their curtains in regulation sunflower patterns, their regulation furniture upholstered in brown and their regulation walls painted green.

The optimistic side happens to be the more important. It is therefore best considered first, in the person of the Lieutenant Colonel who was the first Women's Royal Army Corps Officer to go to the National Defence College at Latimer and the second Women's Royal Army Corps Officer to be appointed to a Grade 1 Staff position. At the time I met her, she did a Whitehall job *outside* her own corps which could have been occupied by a man.

The lady behind a modest desk in an annexe of the Ministry of Defence did not seem to be the 'Amazon' caricature — of which the Women's Royal Army Corps is by now thoroughly sick. True, she wore a frankly practical frock in grey, blue and white, but a ring with a large amber-coloured stone decorated one finger. Her personality was not as martial as her high office — responsibility for the Army's conditions of service — might have suggested. I had already been told emphatically by the Director of the Women's Royal Army Corps, a Brigadier also given to large-stoned rings, that there was no such thing as the British 'Women's Army', only a Women's Corps of the Army as a whole; and that British women soldiers were not used in Combat Arms of the Army and were not likely to be. The Lieutenant Colonel said frankly that personally she hoped this philosophy would continue, despite other philosophies in other countries that could include women in fighting arms of the Army concerned.

'I don't want a committed combat role, though I recognize that, if circumstances ever took over, you *could* finish up in a place where you were involved in self-defence,' she said. (Her point was officially recognized late in 1980, when it was announced that the WRAC would train in the use of arms for personal defence only.)

This feeling, reflected throughout the WRAC, does credit to the femininity of the ladies concerned. But it does make it more difficult for them to rise in the Army, because many of the highest positions require, not unnaturally, experience of actual combat. The Lieutenant Colonel's progress in the Army was therefore all the more commendable, though not, she herself insisted, remarkable, since other women were following the same trail.

Her personal history is an interesting one and far less 'elitist' than the social background of many who castigate the Army as reactionary. She was born in Dundee in 1938, and therefore never knew Britain's Finest Hour. Her educational background was 'typical Scottish co-educational infants, primary and secondary school', followed by St Andrews University. There she read French and German and joined the Officers Training Corps, where she paid visits to the Regular Army. 'I saw a lot that interested me, in the jobs people did and the places they were going to. I had always been interested in sport and there is a great deal of sporting opportunity in the Army,' she said. Even so, after three years at St Andrews she did a year at Dundee College of Education, taking a teaching diploma, before joining the Army. It seemed sensible to get the qualification straightaway, she said — she might have needed it at some time in the future. There was then the question of whether she was going to become 'totally committed' or not.

At twenty-two she attended the Regular Commissions Board, which was constituted as it would have been for a male candidate, except that it had some WRAC representation on it. She was given initiative tests. These were of the same sort faced by men, if perhaps 'not as physical'.

After that, she went to what was then the WRAC School of Instruction at Hindhead, later to be transferred to the WRAC College at Camberley. She spent sixteen weeks at the school, and at the end was commissioned. Her first posting to a unit was to 12 Battalion, WRAC, in the middle of Richmond Park at Kingston in Surrey; neither the battalion nor the buildings still exist. She became a Platoon Officer in one of the Companies of the Battalion, whose fragmented responsibilities included providing clerks for the Ministry of Defence and workers at the Home Postal Depot of the Royal Engineers at Mill Hill, which happened to be on the diametrically opposite side of London to their

227

camp, though the round-the-clock bus shuttles did not daunt her Scottish tenacity.

The pertinacity paid off after fifteen months. She was sent up to Staffordshire, in the Midlands, to set up a new company for the Central Vehicle depot at Marchington. She was promoted to Acting Captain and enjoyed the duties of an Officer Commanding.

At 12 Battalion she had picked up a reasonable knowledge of administration, because as a Platoon Officer she had had an opportunity to take over from the Company Commander or Adjutant when she was on leave. The new job was well within her powers. Did she see herself as a high-flyer? 'My ambition at the time was really to have an interesting job. Clearly everyone looks forward to promotion. I got both an interesting job *and* promotion out of this one, so I was very content. I didn't get a picture in my mind about how high I would go.' Both men and women officers in the Army tend to protest they never look further than the next promotion; it is a sign either of a stoical character, or a fashion in modesty in the Army which does not apply nearly so widely in civvy street.

'But,' said the Lieutenant Colonel, 'the longer you are in, the more you are likely to look ahead to where you ought next to be going. But it is too young, as a Subaltern, to be imagining what your progress might be. Now I would be foolish not to aim for as high as I can get. That will depend on how my employment in the Services develops. It will depend, naturally, on how I perform in the jobs I am given. I think the scope has been identified. I do not think there are any of the original barriers to the progress of women in the Services now.'

Is this really so? The Lieutenant Colonel's own progress tends to support the claim. The official line is that there is no point in considering women for jobs where infantry or engineering experience are required, even though *in theory* a woman could be considered for an engineering appointment if she had the necessary qualifications. The barrier against a woman Chief of the General Staff would be absolute, because the job would require experience of combat. And this is something which no woman, given the structure of the Army as it is, can possibly have.

'I don't think it is strange that Britain can have a woman Prime Minister and not a woman Chief of the General Staff,' said the Lieutenant Colonel. 'In command of the Army there must obviously be a soldier who has experience — not necessarily of fighting, although at some point this is bound to happen — but experience of the combat side of the Army, and that is something we women will never have, except in a supportive role. And I think that is absolutely right.'

As this view came so openly from a committed and ambitious woman high-ranking officer, it comes as no surprise to find the same view far down the ranks of the WRAC. Those who wish to score points in the sex war could easily claim that the Army is one activity in which women must always be second-class citizens because, in the last analysis, they are not ready to do precisely the equal of the work the men do. It is greatly to the credit of the British Army that it has not trotted out and hidden behind this argument, but rather gone the other way, and tried its very best to promote people like the Director of the WRAC and the Lieutenant Colonel, whose next move after setting up the new company in Staffordshire was to Cyprus for two years. This was just after the 1963 uprising and the establishment of Greek and Turkish areas of influence in Cyprus. The United Nations force was in, and was gradually being built up.

Her appointment — possibly indicative of the way the Army works to develop its bright ones — was a Staff one at headquarters, *not* with the WRAC itself. This gave her experience of working with the Army as a whole, instead of in the narrower and perhaps more psychologically protected atmosphere of the WRAC. Being an instructor in the Officers Wing of the WRAC College at Camberley gave her another facet of experience. In 1967 she was promoted Major to command a WRAC Squadron of the 6th Training

Regiment, Royal Corps of Transport, and under two years later was a student at the Staff College at Camberley for both men and women. It was a one-year course, with qualification by examination, recommendation and selection.

'That was difficult,' recalled the Lieutenant Colonel. 'It is bound to be difficult because of the lack of field experience for women. So many of the exercises are based on knowledge that comes only to men. Questions on how far guns will fire, and what sort of ammunition you need for a particular weapon — that was the difficult area. In other areas I found it much more easy than some of the men — areas concerned with staff work which was not operational.'

The Major, as she then was, had the luck (or strain) to be the only woman of the 180 students on the course — indeed she was only the fourth woman to attend it — a situation designed to inflame the sexual paranoia of the most level-headed lady. She gallantly — and perhaps clear-headedly — did not see her difficulties in sexual terms: 'It was a case of swings and roundabouts for everybody. I got quite a lot from it. My understanding of what a combat soldier is doing was much more developed than it would otherwise have been. It helps you to give what is needed in a supportive role. It is not a question of how a woman becomes involved in the course, it is a matter of how a non-Combat Arm soldier becomes involved. The men in non-Combat Arms were in the same position as the women in this respect.'

Staff jobs at Headquarters West Midlands District, Shrewsbury, and at Headquarters Land Forces Hong Kong followed. The Hong Kong post was concerned with logistic back-up to operations and training, with some equipment management. She handled arrangements for exercise reconnaissances to Australia and for equipment maintenance in Nepal, chiefly for the Gurkhas. She was the Senior WRAC Officer in Hong Kong, acquired a more international perspective and lost much spare time: 'There were no quiet moments at all in that job.' Neither was it especially quiet when she got to Aldershot, where she was given command of the entire womens' barracks. That job lasted fifteen months.

Very few jobs in state or private industry, in trading or even financial manipulation, would have given any man or woman such a variety of jobs while still young. The next challenge also required from any woman a great deal of application and tenacity. In 1976, two females went as students to the National Defence College, Latimer, which is open to all three Services. One was a Women's Royal Navy Officer and the other was the Major, as she still was. They were the only two women among a hundred students.

The WRAC has a quota of seven Lieutenant Colonels more or less within its gift, though others may be promoted to serve outside the corps itself. In July, 1977, the Major was promoted Lieutenant Colonel, to go to the Ministry of Defence in what is termed in the Army a Grade One Staff appointment. She was only the second woman to hold such a position. (The first one later became a full Colonel, with responsibility for officer postings. As the 1980s began, there was no woman full Colonel in a Staff post in the Army as a whole, but the Lieutenant Colonel was one of the three women in Grade One Staff appointments who were eligible.)

'It is up to us,' said the Lieutenant Colonel. The woman who was full Colonel, in the WRAC in Germany, was thought to be 'too far advanced' in her career to make a switch.

But chance, even if chance with an element of stage management, would have a part in deciding who was to become the first woman full Colonel in a Staff job, competing in a straight fight with a man. The Lieutenant Colonel also visualized certain jobs at Brigadier level, outside the WRAC itself, which could be done by women, especially in the field of logistics. 'I think the Army now completely accepts women as an integral part of the structure,' she said. 'They fully recognize the need to continue to have women in the Service.'

The price the Army has paid has been some minor administrative inconvenience. What about the price to women themselves? The fact that they are ruled out from the very highest jobs in the Army seems to bother none of them, since its reversal would involve them in the Combat Arms, and more taunts about 'Amazons' than have even been dreamed of so far. Even after the new Conservative government of 1979 (led for the first time in British history by a woman) greatly increased Army pay, women soldiers got only a five per cent 'X factor' salary weighting, compared with the men's ten per cent. But that doesn't seem to bother them, either. 'Girls still have the right to leave the Service on marriage, which the men don't have,' said the Director, WRAC, and suggested that this levelled things out.

The high-flying Lieutenant Colonel has remained unmarried. Is this, when it comes to the point, the price a woman has to pay if she wants really high rank in the British Army today? The lady would not accept the suggestion: some women could combine being a wife with being a high-ranking Army officer, others chose not to. It was up to the individual. The three officers in Staff appointments at Grade One might *happen* to be single, but there was a Commanding Officer at the college, as a full Colonel, and she was married. The Lieutenant Colonel who was the WRAC Liaison Officer was also married, and large numbers of the Majors were married.

'Whether the majority of married officers would wish to make a full career, I don't know,' said the Lieutenant Colonel. 'My corps does all it can to accommodate women where possible, but when it starts to interfere with a person's mobility, that is where the corps would cease to be accommodating. But if it is an in-Army marriage, with both partners in the Army, the Postings Branches will do all they can.'

No doubt. But the wear and tear imposed on a marriage

when the soldier husband is constantly being reposted must be negligible compared with the strain faced by an officer *wife* trying to hold together a marriage. And the strain on less ambitious women soldiers, who look upon the Army as a job rather than as a career, and are content to stay lower down the ranks, must often be greater still, to the point where leaving the Army on marriage is almost inevitable (though more and more women who have left it are now asking to come back again).

As for intimacies outside marriage, the British Army is still as unamused as Queen Victoria would have been. If a British woman soldier has a sex life, it will be inside wedlock or outside Ministry of Defence property. The Army has spoken, it has not changed its tune with the permissive wave, and it is rather supported by the public reaction against permissivism. The women soldiers conceal any regret with such commendable patience that a cynic might suppose they regarded the restriction as a useful block, not easily obtainable in civilian life, against male pressures to say Yes.

In their professional and social habits, when working with groups of male soldiers, the women of the Women's Royal Army Corps lead lives balanced between the permissive society and the nunnery — with a slight bias, if anything, in favour of the nunnery. The Royal School of Artillery at Larkhill, near Salisbury in Wiltshire, is a microcosm of what does and what *doesn't* happen. There are usually some seventy girls working there as clerks, drivers, stewardesses, cooks, telecommunications technicians, model aircraft targeting systems assistants and physical training instructors. Some I saw were very attractive; some would wish to get married at some stage; but the Army, perhaps because it values them too much to want to lose them, does not fall over itself to assist courting rituals, circa 1980s, though it does not neglect the girl's general comfort.

Most of the single officers live in the mess, which is modern and delightful, with much regimental silver, battle paintings in oils, young female soldier stewardesses and a restaurant with the size and aura of a baronial hall. When I asked one officer if she could have a male guest staying overnight, she said, 'Certainly. There is usually a spare bedroom available somewhere in the mess, where a man could stay.' When I said I supposed that would not meet the requirements of all parties, the officer said, 'I think what many people think are ordinary standards aren't as ordinary as they would think, outside London. The only difficulty is if you want to sleep with men. Certainly in London the majority of people would live in flats, but in the West Country this would be a more *un*usual thing: you would be married from home. London is a small proportion of the country.'

This woman officer thought it 'only a small minority' who would ever want men in their rooms. 'You wouldn't flaunt your promiscuity,' she said. 'Some people *would* call that promiscuity. My brother at university has told me *he* can't have girls in his room after a certain time. We have our Officers Mess Ball next week. That finishes at three-thirty in the morning. After that time we may go up to one of the girls' rooms and have coffee. There is nothing against having a man in a room for coffee.'

It is true that some of the rooms in the mess are small, and that people are living on top of one another — so that any untoward behaviour would be, in effect, unfairly magnified. Officers point out that there are many different personalities of different backgrounds and ages involved, and that, to avoid offence, private lives should be conducted elsewhere. 'In any case,' one officer said, 'I well remember an old saying of my first Sergeant Major. "If he's not worth the price of a hotel room, he isn't worth anything." That's pretty true.'

In the WRAC, tours of different duties, lasting about two years, are usual, as they are with the men. This makes it difficult for the women and officers to buy their own houses or flats, where they might have more personal freedom, because at the end of the two-year period they may have to

234

sell up and buy elsewhere, with heavy removal expenses. Married officers get a moving allowance, unmarried ones do not. The implication may not be deliberate, but it is plain: only married people are entitled to privacy in their private lives.

Could such rules have been constructed and administered by Amazons who dislike the proximity of men — at least until they have been converted into safe amenities as husbands? Some people will suspect so. But in fact the rules cause little trouble in practice, and are certainly *not* a revenge for the fact that some Cavalry Regiments will not allow women into their messes in *any* circumstances — 'living in a world of their own,' as a WRAC officer at Larkhill put it, though Army high-ups 'doubt the accuracy of this statement nowadays'.

But it is none too easy to buy a flat near Salisbury, which is well away from any vast conurbation; and houses are expensive. The twenty-eight-year-old Officer Commanding the WRAC contingent at Larkhill, a Major, told me she had managed it because she had been able to save when serving in Germany. 'I just didn't want to live in the mess at Larkhill,' she said. 'I think I am quite a domestic person. I am not a Women's Libber, I am a great gardener and cook, and I like sewing. But, being near the unit, I still have my own social life. There are four girls living in the mess, with 190 men. It is very much like a hotel. If a girl wanted to *sleep* with a man that would be difficult. It would be an inconvenience to other people as well. You exist in the same way as you might exist in a flat — with other girls, who would not approve of that sort of thing. It is something I have never thought about. If they want to do that sort of thing, people should go elsewhere to do it.'

Kipling might have approved of the Major's clipped pronouncements on such matters; but he might have been unsettled by her appearance off duty, which was extremely feminine: Cartier-tan court shoes, a red and blue pattern dress, elegant stockings, a gold pendant drawing attention to a slimly attractive bosom. Officers and women in their not-quite-nunnery existence at Larkhill are certainly given a very clear idea of what is regarded as slovenly personal behaviour and what is not; but they do not have to be outdoor-and-hearty types straight out of a John Betjeman poem.

Why had she chosen the Army? 'It offers the best scope in jobs, if you want to do a variety of things. We move every two years to do a completely different job. This changing is not an insecure thing, because you are still climbing the ladder and still secure in your job. You are changing your methods of work, but you have always got the same backbone behind you.'

This situation is understandably attractive at a time when many of Kipling's heirs in civvy street are glad to hang on to boring jobs because, in a shrinking labour market, there are dangers in throwing in the towel and trying to move on.

The Major had eight months' training at the WRAC College at Camberley as an Officer Cadet, was then posted to the WRAC at Guildford as a Recruit Training Officer for one year, following which she did two years in Plymouth as Schools Liaison Officer. After that it was back to Camberley, this time as an Instructor of Officer Cadets. She did nearly two years in Germany as a Families Officer, hearing all about problems both men and women face in their military careers. She then came back to Aldershot, with some sense of let-down after Germany, and did two years on administration in a Staff appointment. Then a ten-week course at the Junior Division of the Staff College, followed by her present appointment. It took her nine years to become a Major and it was certainly not done without concentrated hard work.

In fact, women who are keen to join the WRAC at all are usually also keen to put their backs strongly into their work: so much so that the restrictions on private lives do not loom as large as they might. 'When you are working twenty-four hours a day,' said one officer with figurative rather than literal truth, 'you haven't got much time to think about *that*, believe me.'

This stoic resolution comes more easily to officers and senior NCOs — women who are positively determined to regard the Army as a career, not just as a job that will pass the time until they meet Mr Right. So what caused the merest ripple of dissatisfaction I thought I detected in some other ranks at Larkhill? The cooking was high class. The seventy or so women soldiers at Larkhill included the only WRAC Staff Sergeant in the Army, to that date, to get the City and Guilds qualification that made her an A1 cook, the highest qualification in cooking possible in the British Army. Some older women blamed the mood on the lack of the Dunkirk spirit — a lack they were sure would be remedied if the same set of wartime circumstances were to occur again.

'The WRAC doesn't have the same type of spirit today as it used to,' said the WRAC Sergeant Major at Larkhill who was just about to retire. She had been in the Army for twenty-two years, and had been ten years in the Territorial Army before becoming a Regular. 'It was super for a woman when I entered the Territorial Army in 1948. I worked in a factory during the day and I was in heavy Ack-Ack for the Territorial Army. That was wonderful because the spirit was still around — most of the men had been in the war. This super feeling was there and that is what is lost in this Army today. We didn't get the wages we get now, and the girls didn't have motor cars, but it was a great oneness. In getting better for women, it has lost a lot.'

This traditionalist view is certainly not without honour. The women's element of the Army in the post-war years has relied heavily on such doughty figures as the Sergeant Major — educated at a village school in Scotland, able and willing to accept the rough with the smooth when dealing with the not always welcoming male sex, ambitious but putting self-centredness behind her ('If you can look after yourself and one other person, you can promote yourself').

237

And unmarried. It was understandable that this very traditional lady, with a dictatorial father who had stipulated 'no drink and no men', when she wanted to enter the Territorial Army, should see her successors as being of a different breed. Indeed they *are*, though perhaps not quite in the way the Sergeant Major meant. They are professionals like the men. They expect the discipline necessary to do their jobs, and no more.

The girls younger and lower down the ranks at Larkhill (a rather isolated establishment four miles away from the nearest little town, Amesbury, itself no beckoning metropolis) did not, in the main, choose the Army as the only way out of authoritarian homes. Homes have become less authoritarian. A sizeable proportion had joined because other jobs were not available, or to escape the boredom of jobs in examples of mechanized living such as supermarkets. They did not belong to a generation trained to be grateful for a job, *any* job. They had 'expectations', and didn't always relate expectation to personal effort.

One Private, aged twenty-two, who sat knitting and giggling in the restroom, looked about fifteen. 'I've been in nearly three years,' she said, 'and it is different from what I expected. The NCOs are younger than you expect them to be. And a lot of the camps you go to are different from what you expect — you don't expect to be stuck in the middle of nowhere. I don't like it.'

Such girls, with no ambition to rise in the ranks and with limited inner resources, find the separation from civilian social life particularly irksome. If they still had to live in stark barracks of the sort patrolled by Florence Nightingale with the aid of her lamp, they would probably be leaving the Army in droves.

The Army must be aware of this. Indeed, on the evidence of Larkhill, it might even be accused of going overboard in trying to show that the lower ranks of the WRAC are *not* regarded as mere cattle. One twenty-one-year-old Lance Corporal at Larkhill showed me her quarters in a pleasant and manageably small block. She had, to herself, a bedroom better than many university students enjoy. On the bed (which had her own bedcover, not the reasonably pleasant bottle-green standard issue) there was a three foot tall cuddly Teddy Bear, and a large cuddly parrot was perched on the curtain rail. Surely this must be a special privilege for Lance Corporals? Not a bit. I was shown a room housing two Private soldiers, and found a cuddly Sylvester Cat and Tweety-Tweet on one of the beds as well as a Teddy Bear, pictures of David Essex and a plastic peg whose two segments were models of a man and woman who moved in copulatory ecstasy as the peg was opened and closed. One Private's bed was completely covered two-deep in cuddly toys. Field Marshal Lord Kitchener, militant bachelor and hero of an earlier British Army, would have fainted away on the spot.

But it would be a mistake for any enemy to think that the WRAC was a Teddy Bear Army without its own sort of iron discipline. Some forms of it wrankle, and not merely among the grumbling girls with a lesser career drive. A very bustling and active girl, a Lance Corporal of twenty-one who was in charge of all the sporting activities at Larkhill, and well pleased with her Army life, sat down in her track suit for long enough to tell me that she thought that in some respects the Army was behind the times.

First, there was the bureaucratic red tape: 'They seem to go round things an awful long way, whereas you could do something very simply. If you want something, you can't go straight to the person to get it, you have to go through so-and-so all the way up the chain.'

Yes, but that might be unavoidable with an hierarchical organization. What was her other reservation?

'You have got to be in the Army six months before you can get a permanent pass to stay out at night,' she said. 'You get women coming into the Army at thirty, and they have to be in by midnight. It's awful. It isn't made clear to them at the outset. They don't know about it till they come in. They tend to molly-coddle women like children ... I'm going to get thrown out for this!'

But she stuck to her point that it wasn't easy to acquire boy friends, or to keep them. 'There are postings and courses. If you are going out with somebody you can be taken away from him at any minute and you can't do much about it — unless you are married.'

The Lance Corporal may or may not be right in her view that the modern Army still makes it hard on all but institutionalized relationships (platonic or not). She was certainly wrong in her joking observation that she might get thrown out for expressing her views. 'We can tolerate, and in fact welcome, strong expressions of opinion, at the right time and in the right place,' said an officer. 'It is just that all orders must be obeyed at the time, irrespective of what is said afterwards.'

A group of women Private soldiers I met in the rest room at Larkhill were mostly well content with their Service life. But one, a girl with a very firm-boned face, emerged as a very talkative critic of the NCOs. 'The officers are all right,' she said. 'The officers behave as you thought they would behave. You expect to respect NCOs, but you don't. You feel they don't respect *you*, and there should be respect on both sides. They have ways of getting at you through your work rather than shouting at you. I think there is favouritism. Certain ones are picked on, probably because they speak their minds, and people don't like to hear people like Privates speak their minds.'

Afterwards I discussed the girl with an officer who had been present, rather expecting an attempt to discredit her. Instead the officer said, 'She's a very strong-minded girl who will get promotion one day. She has just failed to get promotion she put in for, and another girl got it. The other girl had more experience. This one who spoke up will be all right eventually.' If the WRAC is small enough for occasional bitcheries, it is also small enough for every girl to be known as a person rather than as a caricature.

The British Army has had a long time to get used to the presence of women. If there are still strains, it is arguably because of the contortions of human nature rather than institutional conservatism. The 3,500 women soldiers and 350 WRAC officers of today (the numbers are approximate) walk in the tracks made by wives of soldiers who went with them to battle to feed them and do the laundry. During the Crimean War, Florence Nightingale browbeat the Army into allowing her, and a few other female nurses, to look after the wounded. The First Aid Nursing Yeomanry, which lasted until 1933 (in spite of the bawdy memorability of its name, FANY) was formed in the Boer War to drive the horse-drawn ambulances which ferried the wounded back from the front lines to the field hospitals. FANY continued as a sub-title of the Women's Transport Service, which was formed in 1933. Even today — though it is now a part-time civilian organization — it continues to train volunteers for duties in support of the civil authorities in peace and war. This is not a negligible role in a country, which in the view of many soldiers, has wantonly neglected Civil Defence for a generation, while countries like Russia and China regard it as an integral part of their mode of living.

The inter-war period, 1918 to 1938, was women's low point, as far as the Army was concerned: no women were allowed to serve in the Armed Services. It was only in 1938, with Hitler plainly determined to walk all over Europe and beyond, that the value of the female sex was rediscovered. During the Second World War, the strength of the Auxiliary Territorial Service reached 215,000, and it involved itself in 124 trades. The women had no direct combat tasks, but worked searchlights and radar. Their demonstrable value meant there was no repetition of the 1918 mistake: four years after the war ended the ATS were not disbanded but turned into the WRAC of today, a corps of the British Army with Queen Elizabeth the Queen Mother as Commandant-in-Chief.

This recognition of the continuing value of women in the forces has been amply vindicated throughout the world. In 1980, nearly three hundred service women formed part of the security forces in Northern Ireland. They worked as clerks, drivers, postal and courier operators and policewomen. Some served an emergency tour of eight months, searching women and children at security checkpoints for weapons and explosives. At home and abroad, WRAC officers were being offered jobs as Troop Commanders in the Royal Corps of Transport, where one officer, at least, was commanding men.

With all this experience of dealing with women as employees, the British Army might be expected to know how they tick. But does it? Its dealings with wives of soldiers do not invariably suggest so. Before lending ear to the irritated (rather than disaffected) Army wives in Hong Kong, let a General, no less, speak on the subject: 'It is true that it is a difficult thing to be married to a soldier. Soldiers *do* say, "My wife has got fed up with all this moving about." I suppose the type of girl who marries a soldier is very different now from the one who married the pre-war soldier. Very intelligent girls, the great majority of them.'

One could argue, said the General, that the Army ought to go in for a version of the Royal Navy's home port system. At the home port, the soldier would be able to buy his own house, instead of being given a quarter. 'If a chap could buy his little house,' he added, 'then I think this would help to improve the assimilation of the young wife into military society. I am not decrying the military quarter system, because you have got to have them. I am about to retire, and for the first time in thirty years I have owned my own house. I have been content before to live in a military community. But my wife has been looking forward to this for a long time. Perhaps we don't give enough attention to the question of owning your own house. Perhaps the Army could be a building society.'

Was there a tell-tale phrase in this progressive and sympathetic speech? Was it perhaps the words 'a chap could buy his *little* house?' The words, however sympathetically uttered, suggest a brisk, patronizing scorn of such petty luxuries as one's own house; a scorn which sat easily on a very successful soldier, but which would have rung a little hollowly in the mouth of a less successful one — and even more hollowly on the lips of the less successful soldier's wife. Just as there is an element of the doubting adolescent in every effective artist, so perhaps there is an element of the cocksure schoolboy in every effective soldier; an element which *does* secretly scorn the ordinary domestic comforts — of which women, and what they think and feel, are only one. Perhaps, though he is consciously more sophisticated, and certainly more aware of what is going on in the world than he has ever been, the British Tommy still yearns for the simplicity of monasticism and is unconsciously very determined that his virility and attack should not be smothered by feminine encrustations?

Such psychological speculation may seem fanciful to serving officers and men. But at least it might explain, in terms satisfactory to women, those biliously clashing colours of carpets, furniture and curtains I discovered in the married quarters of Stanley Fort, which guards the southern tip of the colony of Hong Kong from an enemy who would almost certainly not come that way.

There was a general view that the two-bedroomed quarters in Balmoral Block were sub-standard for what each family paid for them (£45 a month). Even wives who had settled down after a while to Army life in a hot and humid climate found their home environment irritating. The wife of a Reconnaissance Platoon Sergeant said that curtains had to be 'dropping to pieces' before the Army would replace them. One of the most articulate of all the wives I spoke to, in Hong Kong or elsewhere, said that on the whole, though the Army had good as well as bad points, she would prefer to be married to a civilian. She thought Army wives ought to have more freedom in arranging the decor of their married quarters, instead of being restricted to a basic range of furnishings, which sometimes did not match.

'It wouldn't be so bad,' she said, 'if they increased the MFO allowance (the allowance of personal belongings

243

which can be shipped from home which has, in fact, more recently, been increased). That's the trouble with family life — you collect things as you go along, and then you can't have your own things around you. If you go abroad you have to put them in storage. We are lucky to have certain things out here, but we go through the same procedure whether we are here, in Germany or anywhere else. Do we stick it up in the attic again for another seven years?' One can almost hear the impatient male soldier saying, in an embarrassed mumble, 'Oh, how the Little Woman does *go on!*'

In fact the wife concerned was a highly personable lady who would have looked equally at home in the Officers Mess as in the Sergeants Mess; who was both definite and diplomatic in putting her views, which weren't greatly out of line with those to be found in civilian life from a woman of her age group (early twenties); and who argued her points very consistently, rationally and politely.

'You aren't an individual really,' she said. 'You can't show your real character in Army quarters. You would be charged if you painted the walls, unless you painted them in Army colours. Men like to paint the house in their spare time. They haven't a garden, after all. If they were able to do a little bit of painting around the place, *they* would be a little happier as well.'

Other wives said that it was high time the system of 'walking in' to a new quarters was stopped. Under this system, the new tenants walk in with a representative of the housing staff, while the old tenants are still there, and inspect the condition of the quarters minutely before signing on the dotted line as official proof that they are now responsible for the quarter. Wives on both sides tend to find this intensely embarrassing: the arriving wife is thrust into the role of inspector and critic, and the departing wife into the role of skivvy whose elementary housework is being questioned.

To put it bluntly, the British Army could aim for much greater civilization of its quartering arrangements without threatening the virility of its fighting men. The point may seem trivial. It is not: a succession of living quarters adds up to a life, especially in the case of those soldiers who are conscientious but perhaps not especially ambitious for promotion. But while not trivial, the point is at least capable of material solution.

Not so the rather more subtle question of how servicemen's and officers' wives conduct themselves and mix with one another. The strains here come about because, though the men of the Army may know their place (they have only to look on their sleeve for their badge of rank to remind them), their wives do not. Do they mentally curtsey to the officer's wife when both are perfectly well aware that in civvy street they would be on Christian name terms? 'I think we get frustrated with the rank-consciousness which is bound to be; the not being treated as individuals,' said one wife. 'I am classed as the "Sergeant's wife" — they probably don't even know my Christian name. I am thinking of the Families Office. And they ask you every time at the Medical Centre, "Rank?" I haven't got a rank! But I am Sergeant Blank's wife, and that annoys me.'

'If I went out and got drunk, it would fall on my *husband's* back,' said the wife of a Private.

'Yes,' said another. 'If I had an affair with someone's husband, I think you would find that either my husband or the other fellow would be shipped out. You are certainly not free to hold an orgy in your front room.'

In civilian life, too, of course, there are constraints put in the way of such goings on. A more material point is that many wives — even those prone to grumble — concede that in the Army a wife's outspokenness is *not* necessarily as lethal to her husband's career as in civilian life.

'In the Army, officers' wives or officers themselves are very probably used to wives coming up to them and protesting,' said one wife. 'It is more the way of life than in civilian occupations.' One officer, a Company Commander, tended to bear this out. He thought that some Company Commanders were glad to be bachelors, like himself. They thought that women might not be so tempted to bring their domestic and other problems to them, thinking they had not had the experience to be helpful.

It is demonstrably true that the British Army takes more of a personal interest in the families of its servants than civilian employers would — the process can be called paternalistic or helpful, depending on the social and political views of the beholder. To some extent the interest is *materialistic*, for the officer's wife, long after she packed away her elbow-length white gloves in India, is still expected to be the officers' antenae, sensing and sorting out personal problems in the ranks whenever possible.

'Our CO's wife used to work without pay as a welfare officer,' said one Major's wife. 'Occasionally she would say to someone else, "I have got a problem with so-and-so. Would you mind popping round?" But only if the woman she was talking to was a friend. Otherwise she practically did it all herself. This was usually when the menfolk were away. Some women do it because it is their duty and because they think it will be good for their husband's career. Although they might do it well, they do it for the wrong reasons. Our CO's wife was not that sort of do-gooder: she was just always there if needed.'

Other CO's wives, equally sincere, will go about things in a different way. One gained the confidence of her husband's driver and batman and heard of any problems through him. 'She used to get to know everything about where problems were arising,' said one admiring observer. 'It was a different technique, but it was successful. She worked from a distance. She was not very popular, in the sense that she did not have great social presence, but she was a very nice person and went about things in her own way. She complemented her husband, who had great drive and knew he was going straight to the top. I don't think she herself was particularly happy with the situation, though.'

The lady would not be entirely alone in her unease. It is arguable that wives of civilian executives who are expected

246

to entertain boring people because it is good for their husbands' careers are no better off. But there is undoubtedly some feeling among many intelligent and articulate officers' wives that they are expected to be 'Lady Bountifuls' without any training for the role, in terms of social class or professional background in welfare work.

'At one stage I stood out against it,' said the wife of an officer who described her social background as working class. 'I feel very strongly about poking my nose into problems I am not qualified to deal with, and treading where angels fear to tread. I think it could do a great deal of harm. I said that if I could act as a messenger and go-between, so that I could refer them to the Families Officer and back out, then I would do it. I would also chat and pass the time of day. I was all ready for a fight on the point, but I found I was *agreed* with, which ruined it all!'

The anecdote is revealing. The British Army is perfectly well aware of the need to change with the times; but where its dealings with women are concerned, it is at its least confident in searching out and applying new solutions. Things like social relationships may take generations to settle into a newer and possibly more relaxed form, because no one in the Army is prepared to be the one who puts his name to the killing of any sacred cow — such as that, broadly, wives still tend to address other wives according to their husband's rank.

While the Army is perhaps waiting for social pressures to force it into line with the times on such matters, a start could be made on apparently more minor matters like regulation married quarters decor. I do not quite accept the Army view that this is 'not a practical suggestion'.

The Army says officially that officers' and soldiers' wives are 'consulted' on types of furniture and colours of decor. In which case, perhaps they have not been consulted quite enough, or not enough attention has been paid to the results of the consultations. One officer's wife had 'a most beautiful' scarlet carpet, royal blue seat covers and mustard and yellow curtains in her Hong Kong married quarters.

They didn't make a good match, but at least each item was fairly distinctive in itself. The wife had no qualms about inviting a businessman and his wife, both ex-British Army, to dinner. As they came through the door of the living room, the first thing the wife said on noticing the decor was, 'Oh, look darling! What a charming example of 1959!' It was then almost 1979.

'The trouble is,' said the hostess a little heavily, in relaying the anecdote to other friends afterwards, 'that it is a permanent way of life, not just for a few years.'

What she didn't say, and didn't need to say, is that wives have a great influence on their husbands when the time comes to decide whether to renew their Army contracts or disappear into civilian life. Is the British Army aware of the fall-out effects of what, in the days of 1880 and the North-West Frontier, might have been derisively dismissed as 'bloody women's talk'?

It is rare for any stiff-upper-lip relic in the British Army today to go unobserved by at least the more intelligent elements. Their influence is becoming more pervasive. Accordingly, they have devised, comparatively recently, an institutional device (because in the Army everything must be institutional) to tackle the potentially insidious problem of the dissatisfied wives.

This is the Unit Families Officer. He is usually an officer, frequently a Major, who has come up through the ranks. He might have been regarded as an insane aberration, an effete dabbler, at the time of the Empire's height, but he is now the nearest thing the Army has to a combined welfare worker, marriage counsellor and housing officer (though it can also call on Soldiers, Sailors and Air Force Association and local authority social workers).

When soldiers go to Northern Ireland or Belize, they are currently unaccompanied by their womenfolk. Apart from Hong Kong and Germany, where whole families are stationed, the Families Officer has his main function back in barracks in the United Kingdom, where left-behind wives are quartered. To these wives he tries to be a sort of universal father figure.

I found one of them, a Major, bingo-calling at a wives' afternoon social session at the Telephone Centre of Colchester Garrison in Essex. He was in civilian clothes — he usually *is* in civilian clothes, 'because otherwise everything would seem like an official inspection.'

'Number nine, visit to the doctor,' sang out the Major, who was Families Officer to one battalion at the 14,000-man garrison, which covers one of the eight districts of the United Kingdom, comprising eleven English counties, from the Thames to Humberside. His was the 1st Battalion, Worcestershire and Sherwood Foresters.

There was something incongruous about the Major — a tall, solidly-built man with a leathery face — calling out bingo numbers to a roomful of very young wives, who were slumped in chairs and sofas at the social centre, some with toddlers dozing on their laps. Fair game for ridicule, surely? A heavy-handed intrusion into the private hours of human beings who were not even themselves in the military employ of the Queen? But conversation with the wives themselves tended to vindicate the worthy Families Officer — certainly this particular one. Even his presence at bingo was welcomed — the more so since he had started the bingo sessions himself.

The wives were married to Privates, Corporals and Sergeants, and they had no doubt that the Major was a better Families Officer for having gone through the ranks himself. If there is a theory in some quarters of the Guards Regiments that a 'gentleman' is better able to get on with the lower ranks than a ranker officer, it has not penetrated to the wives of the Colchester Garrison.

'*This* Families Officer,' said the wife of a Sergeant, 'is a good one. Any wife can meet him here at the centre. You can ring him up at any hour of the day or night. A previous one hadn't any interest in wives. He was not bothered. You always got the impression you were imposing. It was a general attitude — as if he had other things to do. This one started things like the bingo and getting us theatre trips to London. The other was older and *the officer type*.' [My italics.]

One look around the social centre at Colchester Garrison would indicate quite clearly that if the British Army even tried to inflict on wives a sample of the dear old semi-feudal values, they would be playing to a more difficult audience than comedians expected to find at Darlington Hippodrome on a wet Monday. This is partly because the wives, like their husbands, are so young. The average age of the soldier on the streets of Belfast is nineteen and his wife tends to be even younger. Even the wives of Sergeants are often in their late teens, and rarely older than their early twenties. Wives of officers may have an arguable point when they say they resent having the Army as a husband; but the Army *has* to play the father to many wives of servicemen who are scarcely out of school, when they are separated from their parents, when their husbands are away, and when the television set may at any time bring news that a British soldier (whose husband *this* time?) has been shot on the streets of Northern Ireland.

Hence the Families Officer must *not* be an officer who has been shuffled sideways into the job because he has been, or would be, a disaster in some more 'important' activity. The Major at Colchester interrupted his bingo-calling to say he had been in the job for six years — much longer than the average Army tour — and that he thought the job was definitely both a full-time and long-term one. 'It is starting to happen more and more,' he said. 'They have now realized you can't do the job on the basis of two years, and then change. I have learned a hell of a lot from the fact that I have been here in the job as long as I have.'

The major had seen clearly how different sets of conditions created very different sets of problems. When he began the job, the wives of his battalion were with their husbands on an accompanied tour in Northern Ireland. The problems, then, were not so much marital: 'If the men were away, they needed the instant advice they would

250

normally get from a husband — for example the letter from father, saying, "Mother is ill." Did that mean that father was saying, "Mother is *very* ill, so come back at once," or not? We didn't have marital problems so much at this stage, because husbands and wives were together.'

Then the pattern changed. More men were sent to Belize, which could have disintegrated from a border policing to a fighting activity at any moment. Attitudes in Northern Ireland hardened; tensions increased; and it became a difficult place for wives. The marital euphoria of the old Northern Ireland family regime — three weeks with family in quarters, three weeks away — gave way to continuous periods of separation ranging from four to seven months of unaccompanied tours.

'Previously,' said the Families Officer, 'you had repetitions of the honeymoon phase, and this had a marked effect on marriages. They were more tolerant to each other. They were showing more feeling to one another. It finished two marriages, but it cured a lot of dodgy ones.'

The wives at Colchester also felt the beneficial effects of their husbands' service as firemen during the firemen's strike. Not only did it raise their husbands higher in public estimation, but it allowed manageable periods of separation.

The longer periods of separation that came with Belize and Northern Ireland postings were resented much more. Even the most optimistic wife tended to wither in four to seven months, especially when very real worry about safety was added to emotional frustration and domestic inconvenience. Others, too immature to cope, cracked.

'The basic problem,' said the Families Officer, 'is the occasional young wife who can cope, but believes she can't. Nearly a third of my families are aged between sixteen and eighteen.'

The 'problem' wife usually emits the warning signals from the time she joins the garrison. She may reveal that she is playing at marriage by constantly flirting with other men. She may simply find that, separated from her parents and her husband, she cannot be a mother to her baby because she still feels a child herself, and a lost one at that. Suddenly she will disappear from social circulation. No afternoon bingo for her. She will shop at times when the fewest people are about. If she has made any friends, she will lose contact with them.

'I spot this and my staff spot it,' said the Families Officer. 'We make enquiries. We chat to her. She believes she can't cope — not with the children *plus* all the housework that hubby normally does. Wives say, "Can he come back?" If she is only worried about what her kids are doing, I say, "I will be there at five o'clock." I may tell the children what will happen if they don't toe the line. I may get a nearby Bobby from the Community Relations Unit, who will say, "I hear a whisper you have been dipping your fingers into Mummy's purse." Or we can refer her to the social services or home helps. But generally we don't — because she has got to cope herself eventually.' It would be untrue to suggest that such problems come only to the very young wives. Wives over thirty have been known to say they can't cope. But it is usually the younger women, who are trying to cope with the new experiences of marriage and of separation at the same time, who come to the Families Officer. The average soldier in the British Army, after all, is away from his wife half the time.

Domestic problems that occur when the husband is in garrison can be even more fraught. The Families Officer must tread delicately, knowing that there is a narrow line between his being a hero who saved the day and there being a nasty tabloid newspaper story about interference with private lives. Once the Major had to go and see a sixteen-year-old wife who claimed that she had been beaten by her husband. She gave a catalogue of the ill treatment her husband had allegedly given her and ended up with a tearful, 'I'm only sixteen, and it's not my fault if I don't know how to cope.' This girl had been made pregnant by another man when she was fourteen, and the Army man had then married her. The social services were called in, but were not able nor willing to give much help, especially as the girl's attitude was, 'I don't want to know.' 'In the end,' said the Families Officer sadly, 'one could see *why* she was pregnant at fourteen. She went back to Mother.'

Often it is the young male serviceman whose personal attitudes, fanned by the instability of separation and perhaps by the emotional and moral climate of the Army, can cause domestic trouble. What is the aim of the British Army — any Army? Victory. What are the necessary and thus venerated qualities? Masculinity and dominance — indeed seeing masculinity *as* dominance. I speak with amused perception on the point. I was given care and courtesy at every stage of my dealings with the Army; but seldom have I ever encountered so many individuals so masterfully determined to put over their set pieces, whatever I wanted to know. Had I been a woman pushed into hysteria by an unstable home life, I can well imagine shouting, 'Will you let *me* say what I want to?' and perhaps flinging a few Army-issue dishes. The inexperienced young soldier, whose high intelligence is not to be assumed, is easily led into the habit of trying to throw his weight about at home — especially if he had felt himself to be a pawn ordered about by senior ranks, and has tried to compensate by over-assertion with his wife and children.

The results can be unhappy. Some young fathers *order* their baby daughters to sit on their laps when they return home after seven months away. The daughter, seeing a large stranger, doesn't want to. The soldier gets annoyed, both with her and with his wife — she must have been letting things slide in some way while he has been out of sight! He has been made to feel insecure himself, and he fights back in the way he knows — with an attempt at dominance. Result: one crying toddler and one wife who resents being ordered around, after having had to cope on her own with all household problems for the long months of separation.

'My own daughter,' said the Families Officer at Colchester, 'ducked behind the settee when I came back. It took

253

me three days to get her not to. We have never had the same relationship since, in that sense. I was six months in Cyprus. My daughter was two when I went and three when I came back. I had a similar problem with my son when I went to Korea in 1953 to 1954. He was four when I went and five when I came back. I now explain the implications of this to families.'

The institution of the Families Officer is a strange one for the Army. Though the Army itself will not agree, not all Commanding Officers are in favour of it. Some regard the Families Officer as a meddler, and try to use the job as a pigeon-hole for an officer who is otherwise difficult to place. Some ignore the officer as much as possible. As the Army's overall ethic has to be action and dominance, this is not totally surprising but those at the very top of the Army are all too well aware that, even if the Families Officer is dealing in the sort of imaginative refinement that would be unwanted in the battlefield, his presence is a necessity, *not* a gesture, in today's British Army.

'We are all worried about the reason why people leave the Army,' said an experienced officer at Colchester Garrison. 'It has got worse over the years. It is connected with the fact that, in the Army, people can be separated from wives and husbands.'

'And,' said the Families Officer, 'it is not always because the child and the husband are having strains. Perhaps the wife has got herself a civilian job and identifies with it. At five o'clock she goes out of the office, one of twenty clerks. Nineteen of them are getting into their husbands' cars, but she makes her way home on the bus. This rubs like a sore in time. Then she goes into the coffee shop and she sees her friends having coffee with their husbands. And she is on her own. When he comes back, she says, "I want my own house." Then he is under pressure. She says, "I want you home." The biggest reason for men leaving the Army is that wives get fed up with separation. I don't think being able to buy their own houses would have that much effect, quite honestly. In the main, they are too young and they haven't got enough money.'

One of the wives said that civilian employers weren't keen on taking on Army wives for civilian jobs. Once they knew, from a barracks address, that the woman was married to a soldier, they tended to discriminate against her.

'One big store,' said a wife, 'didn't know we were in the Army, and so they took us on. The others do tend to discriminate.'

'I have had a lot of jobs,' said another, 'and the only ones I could keep were cleaning jobs. I went for a job at an advertising office, but as soon as I said my address, they didn't give me the job. I have been potato picking because we could take the children there. That is about the only sort of job they are willing to give you.'

Many officers believe that the one-parent family problem would be best tackled by getting rid of all barracks which are too far outside towns — like Weeton outside Blackpool. Here the problems are apt to be even worse than at Colchester Barracks, which is on the edge of the town and, moreover, within an hour or so's train journey of London.

Equally important are the amenities with which the Families Officer is connected. One is the Telephone Centre of the type arranged at Colchester. In this building were four public telephones for the use of wives — two for outgoing calls and two for incoming calls. Wives could use the social amenities of the building, including the bingo afternoons, while they waited to make calls to their husbands or take calls. This amenity had been known to backfire when calls were being made from Northern Ireland. Immediately there was a casualty among the soldiers there, the outgoing telephones were automatically cut off so that no one could relay any information until the next-of-kin had been told. Several times the Families Officer had gone round eight telephone boxes, not only in the Telephone Centre but in other parts of the garrison, telling wives trying to take or make calls that the casualty wasn't from their unit, or was an unmarried man.

But the policy had become, in general, that wives should be told as much as possible, as quickly as possible. Sometimes this had taken the form of a party of wives being flown over to Belfast to see what their husbands were doing on the streets of that riven city. Sometimes, in areas where wives were allowed to be with their husbands, it had taken the form of sending out an advance reconnaissance party well before a battalion was due to move, and making sure this party had a much broader social structure than it would have done only a few years ago.

'A few years ago,' said the Families Officer of the 1st Battalion, Worcestershire and Sherwood Foresters, 'the advance party would be a Second-in-Command to the Battalion, a Quartermaster and one other officer. They would have to look at *all* aspects. It took four days and on the *last morning* they would have a quick whip around the quarters in a Land Rover, and that would be it. Nowadays they realize the importance of the wife's point of view. I have spent eight days, as Families Officer, looking through all the quarters and suchlike. I will work out what school uniforms there are. Do they have school meals? What are the medical facilities? How many of the children are educationally sub-normal? How many are disabled? Is the air good, or not good, for people with asthma? I make up a complete shopping basket, so that the wives will know all the products sold in the NAAFI.'

Communication has always been a problem. Some wives are not good letter writers even though the postal service is free to Northern Ireland if the letters are written on the appropriate form. Perhaps the form has been regarded as a chilling deterrent. Many wives do not *need* to write letters; they send their husbands recorded cassettes. One officer was horrified when he heard that only four wives had come forward to take advantage of the special cassettes-to-husbands service at Colchester. 'Oh, we do our own,' said the wives casually.

256

The only thing most wives couldn't do individually was produce video tapes of the sight and sound of coffee mornings, special visits, outings and quarters. The Army did that for them.

These facilities might be thought to have narrowed the gap in social advantage between the wives of officers and the wives of other ranks. In a material sense, they have. But pyschologically and socially? Operationally, officers and men are now automatically brought more into everyday proximity, but it does not automatically happen in the case of their respective wives. Talking to two wives sitting at one table in the Colchester Telephone Centre with their children, I asked them how long they had been friends.

'Only recently,' said one. This seemed strange, as both had been in the garrison for some time, and both were wives of Sergeants. 'But mine,' said the other, 'was made up to Sergeant only this month.'

Some social distinctions have bred even wider mental chasms. One wife of a Private complained: 'I really can't manage all the household chores and the children on bath night.' Told this by the Families Officer, one officer's wife remarked, 'My god, you mean they don't bath their kids *every* night?'

The answer she got from the Major, who was brought up in a council house himself, was, '*You* have always lived in a house with a bath. Where that girl comes from, the bath hangs outside on a nail.'

'To this day,' explained the Major, 'this sort of misunderstanding happens — but not so often.'

Gradually officers' wives have been coming to realize, on postings and in quarters, that they share many of the problems of the once condescended-to other ranks. Some officers' wives have even regarded themselves as a sort of neglected minority — the female version of the sort of grievance public school boys in Britain had when they occupied cold and draughty buildings at a time when the new state secondary modern schools had central heating and all mod cons.

257

They have felt, in short, that a Private's wife could make a fuss and call for the help of the Families Officer if she had problems, but the officer's wife was expected to cope with all *her* problems on her own, and possibly advise wives of other ranks as well. When I asked the Families Officer at Colchester how high in the ranks his help could go, he said, 'Well, I have sometimes *spoken* to Majors' wives.' When I asked him if he had ever helped the wife of a Lieutenant Colonel or rank above that, a glazed look came into his eyes and the question was avoided.

The Army has been increasingly imaginative and bold in the way it has dared to attend to the welfare of wives of other ranks; perhaps because this area has lent itself to a more collective approach, and because it has been assumed that they would not resent this. But it has addressed itself to the wives of officers, in a changing social climate, more hesitatingly, if at all. The officer's wife is still half expected to be the Shining Light and Example she might have been in Simla at the time of Queen Victoria's Jubilee, and to preserve a decent silence about it if she feels the role is not for her.

Quite right too, say the more traditionally-minded Army officers: an officer of the British Army, and everything connected with him, must be looked upon as the custodian of the most prized and useful object of the whole Army: the common or garden soldier. It is the soldier's feelings (and by inference his wife's feelings) which must be safeguarded, not the officer's (and by inference the officer's wife's).

There is a rough justice about this stance, especially at a time when in much British civilian life the 'officer's' status is often measured by the extent to which he may abuse his position to cream off benefits for himself and his family, and devil take the hindmost. But more and more wives of officers regard themselves as separate entities (even separate professional entities) from their husbands. Without endorsing the vague dogmatisms of Womens Lib, they wish at least to be regarded as such. Allowing the wife of the young officer her own identity while not prejudicing her husband's concentration on, and effectiveness in, his own job, may prove one of the most challenging tasks of the British Army in the 1980s and for the remainder of this century.

The choice could be a stark one: complete and pointed severance from the Lady Bountiful psychology of Simla, or Army wives successfully persuading their husbands to give up the officer's seldom-seen cane for the junior executive's always-seen plastic attaché case.

Fortunately, men who like the Army life tend to like it not tepidly but tenaciously. Even when men sever their links with the full-time Army, it is not always the end of their connection with military life. And even men who have always felt that their lives would not fit into the Army full-time can become a very important part of it — a part even more vital to the pruned and lean British Army of the era when both Empire and illusions have departed.

13

The Part-timers

'The problem in the Territorial Army is that there aren't enough Court Martials. I say that half jokingly, but it is true. It can be a problem keeping discipline when you are dealing with volunteers.'

— Major in Territorial Army.

'You can drive them harder than you can the regular soldier. The more you drive them into the ground the more they like it. If you get a criticism at camp, it is because it is not hard enough. Sports were organized, but they went down like a lead balloon. They would rather have been soldiering in the mud, lying in the bracken, because that was hard.'

— Commanding Officer of Territorial Army Battalion.

There had been a minor mix-up. The Colonel of the Territorial Army Battalion had been away for ten days. The Colour Sergeant had been detailed to deliver four bulky files and a pile of letters to his private house on Friday night, so he could do his homework before he met his part-time soldiers the next day.

The next morning the Colonel arrived at the TA headquarters still unbriefed. Surely Sir had received his correspondence? No, Sir hadn't. Where was it? Word went down the line to the Colour Sergeant, and came back up the line again. He had certainly taken the correspondence to the Colonel, but there had been no one at home. So he had left it with the people next door.

The Commanding Officer decided on direct action. He phoned his wife. 'Darling, would you do a smart bit of recce? Are the people across the road in? Could you nip over and see if they have got my correspondence?'

Was it, perhaps, just as well there was no Third World War on, especially if the next door neighbours had sympathies with the Fifth Column? Even if it was very unlikely that the CO expected sensitive documents, the anecdote, though entertaining, did not augur well for the modernity of the willing band of 63,000 part-time, adequately but not ostentatiously paid, purely voluntary soldiers who form what is called the Territorial Army. The incident happened not in 1907 (when Lord Haldane formed the part-time Army as the Territorial Force); not just after the First World War, when it was retitled the Territorial Army; not even at its safe heyday in the 1960s (when it ran to ten Divisions and four independent Brigades); but in 1980, when its defensive role did not look quite so theoretical.

Did the affair of the misrouted correspondence reveal that Britain's Territorials were still what some people think they were in the first half of the century — the opportunity for a weekly social get-together at the local TA Hall, in circumstances in which retired Colonels and nostalgic Other Ranks could live out their social observances in a way that they themselves, at least, could regard as being useful?

My first view of a fairly typical TA unit, the 7th Battalion the Royal Anglian Regiment, part of the 7th Field Force and based at Leicester in the industrial and rural East Midlands, rather reinforced the hoary old stereotype. On the parade ground, part-time soldiers with fixed bayonets were marching ceremonially up and down, while Sergeant Majors looked vigilantly at buttons on tunics. In the main hall of the building, there was an enormous regimental tapestry or painting reading: *Relief of Ladysmith, February 28, 1900*. The balcony ran all around the rectangular hall and from it hung a pink canopy acting as a colourful ceiling for the hall underneath. Candles set in bottles rested on red paper tablecloths, and revealed that the famous Relief

261

would not fail to be celebrated as usual exactly eighty years after the event.

'Misleading,' said an officer. 'We are rehearsing for the presentation of our first new Colours by Princess Alice later this year, which is thoroughly untypical. I don't expect to see another ceremonial like it in the rest of my period of service. We don't spend a great deal of time on ceremonial these days. The party preparations are for a company dinner, which is valuable because it brings people together.'

Like all other TA units, the 7 Royal Anglian has been grouped, regrouped, renamed and thoroughly confused in the post-war years, when the chances of another war involving Britain directly seemed infinitely remote. In the 1960s most of the time-honoured regiments of the TA, with their strong local roots and connections, were shrunk to cadres, mere skeletons which kept only the names alive. The government wanted defence cuts and the Army decided, with some ruthlessness, that they should fall chiefly on the part-timers.

But when, in the 1970s, the government decided that there would be some growth in the TA, 7 Royal Anglian was reformed as a General Reserve (guarding the homeland) Battalion. And what diplomatic niceties were necessary, what fine concern for regional pride! A Company of the 7th Battalion covered Grimsby and Scunthorpe, where during the militant steel strike of 1980 some strikers manned the TA Hall in the hope they might be able to do something useful. B Company covered Lincoln, and also Gainsborough and Boston, places which insisted on having their own individual platoons. There was no C Company at all. Into this administrative slot was put no mere number, but The Leicestershire and Derbyshire Yeomanry, Prince Albert's Own Regiment, who were centred on Loughborough.

'Thoroughly peculiar, that,' said the incumbent Commanding Officer of the 7 Royal Anglian. 'Thoroughly a TA thing.'

True. The Yeomanry were gentleman farmers who

brought their own mounts and saddlery to battle. They were credited with a much more autonomous spirit than other sections of the British Army, and those who followed them (though without saddles and horses) were not without similar pride. They could not be allowed, in the TA, to form their own Rifle or Cavalry Regiment. That would have been a bit much, thirty years after the first atom bomb explosion; so they had their own autonomy in lieu of C Company, 7th Battalion, Royal Anglia Regiment TA.

'The only way you could revive the TA was to make them semi-autonomous,' said the Commanding Officer of the Battalion, with a hint of admiration in his voice. 'If you ask me whether there is a price to be paid in real terms for these sort of fine distinctions, my answer is simple. You discard these traditions at your peril. They are valuable. The more you foster the regimental spirit and the company spirit, group psychology benefits. The Americans are always trying to work their way towards the British regimental tradition.'

What the Americans are *not* trying to work their way towards is the disciplinary position in the British TA. Their own National Guard is run on different lines. A National Guardsman, once he signs on, is considered to be under military orders. If there is a civil emergency, he is *ordered* to turn out, and may be punished under military law if he does not, just as he can be punished if he fails to turn up for a drill or an exercise. If a British TA man fails to turn up for even the Princess Alice presentation of the Colour, his seniors can do little more than give him a nasty frown.

'He is not committing an offence,' said the Colonel. 'I haven't got any sanction over the guy. If he is a Company Commander, I can say, "I expect you to take it seriously." If he is a soldier further down the scale, the less I can do about it. If he says, "My children have German measles," it is something I have to accept.'

The point is not merely theoretical. Though TA officers say they have no doubt that, in an emergency, civil or

263

military, the men would be at the TA Hall as soon or sooner than they could be called, a fairly high absentee rate is not uncommon. At Leicester when I visited, it was a sixty per cent turn-out, though on non-ceremonial occasions, an eighty per cent attendance had been more usual.

'Frankly,' said a Major, 'we know that a man, after this TA weekend, can point two fingers at us and go home. You can't continuously discipline him. And the men are divided up into separate companies and may be very distant geographically. So you have to give the local Commanding Officer discretion, and he tends to protect his chicks like a mother hen.'

Things went a bit far when a Corporal relieved his sense of grievance at a local shopkeeper by letting off a TA thunderflash in his shop. He appeared before a civilian court, accused of a breach of the peace. But the civil authorities had discovered that the Corporal should not have had a thunderflash in his car. So this had to be investigated militarily, in the knowledge that powers of sanction were limited. In the end, the Corporal was reduced from a full Corporal to a Lance Corporal by 'military administrative action'. Even if a man backed his truck into somebody else's Land Rover on TA property, doing £2,000 worth of damage, there would probably be no more than a board of inquiry and, as the Commanding Officer put it, 'an invitation to him to contribute to the cost of the bump'.

Against this background, the dedication and increasing professionalism of the present-day TA, in practice, is all the more remarkable. And yet it certainly exists.

At Leicester, the 7th Battalion of the Royal Anglia Regiment has a *Regular* Army man as its Commanding Officer for the first time: before regrouping the COs of the various parts that made it up were all volunteers. The Training Officer was a Regular Major. The Regimental Sergeant Major was a Regular — and very insistent that he expected as much of volunteers, if not quite so soon, as he did from Regular soldiers.

One of the Company Commanders, a solicitor who had been in the TA for seventeen years, starting when he was eighteen, said the whole character of the TA had changed in that time. 'It is tied up with this professional approach. Things like equipment and uniform and attitudes. There is the feeling that we are very much part of the Army, instead of being a sort of Rather Super Cadet Force. It is more demanding, especially of time.'

The TA soldier of the 1980s must expect to devote about forty (some say as high as seventy) days a year to TA activities. It will usually take the form of every other weekend, one drill night a week, and, in the case of officers, possibly about half an hour a day on the telephone, tieing up arrangements. For this he will receive a training bounty of £100 for the first year, £200 for the second and £300 after three years with additional pay of so much per full working day. The solicitor Major, who had no Regular Army experience, said he would be drawing £22 for a full day. This was obviously far less than he would make in an average day practising as a solicitor.

The Major had fought two General Elections as a Conservative candidate. 'I am very much a Thatcher person. I would like to think that the traditional values are right for the sort of society I want to see. I support the idea of meritocracy. Through their own endeavours, people should prosper, but I don't believe in huge amounts of inherited wealth.'

No nostalgia about Poona from this Major, who didn't want to see soldiers joining the TA for the money; but thought that they were entitled to be properly recompensed. His Command was in Scunthorpe; and civilian pay in the steel town was ahead of TA rates. In a high wage town like Scunthorpe, there was a difficulty. 'The problem,' he said, 'is not that they feel let down. The problem is the young chap who is buying a house on mortgage, has got high liabilities and finds he can't afford to miss shifts.'

Though the 1979 pay award considerably improved the financial lot of the TA soldier, the incentive remained more moral, idealistic and, above all, professional. Some TA battalions had been pushed further in this direction by the designation of certain battalions for roles alongside the Army abroad in case of war. 7 Royal Anglian at Leicester was assigned a role alongside Regular Army men in Germany under NATO. The 5th Battalion had already been given a NATO role, and the 7th, originally in competition with the 5th, was temporarily low in morale after its defeat in this contest for preferment. It was much happier when it caught up.

One Major, aged thirty-one, a grammar school boy who became a marketing manager after leaving the Regular Army, said the role of each battalion was much more clearly defined than it had been ten years ago when he had joined: 'There are a few chaps about who do like playing at soldiers, but that is not generally the case. They have stronger motives than that. It starts as a very enjoyable hobby and then develops into seeing that they have a role to play as the second part of the Army. I think there is a greater feeling now that one might take up a rifle in anger, because people have a better idea of what they would do if anything actually happened. The battalion used to have a home defence role. You would tend to attract the sort of officers, particularly in the rural counties, who thought joining the TA was the Thing To Do. Now you will find a fair cross-section of occupations. At one time it was all solicitors and accountants. Now there are a lot more people involved in industry, which reflects the attitudes of employers.'

There had been one sad effect of appointing some TA battalions to NATO roles while leaving others in the business of defending the home country. The TA Colonel of the 7th Field Force (to which the 7 Royal Anglian is assigned) said, 'The basic problem with home defence is that, though they know they have a worthwhile job, they can't escape the fact that in the TA they are the Second Eleven. Their equipment is not so good. They haven't got the same manning levels of Regular Officers and NCO's.

They are much lower down the priority scale, for instance, if they want helicopters for training.'

Plainly it is unhealthy that the people who have to guard the native soil should be left so relatively low in the pecking order. The Ministry of Defence, according to TA men, has taken the point and is trying to raise the level of both equipment and manning in the battalions responsible for home defence. General reserve (home defence) battalions are in the process of receiving a new type of radio which will put them on a par with the battalions earmarked for NATO.

'Public opinion is turning a lot; emphasis is being put on it at the highest level; and one can see things actually happening, instead of a lot of talk,' said the TA Colonel of the 7th Field Force: a civilian, of course, but with the seasoned military man's salty mistrust of mere talk.

Fortunately for the TA, there is a swing generally towards matters military in the universities and schools. Students at universities are joining the Officers Training Corps in greater numbers. Nottingham University started a girls' platoon. 'We are rich in the age group just above seventeen, and we have plenty of officers aged about forty-five,' said the Commanding Officer of the 7th Battalion. 'I am somewhat short of young officers. What I am after is the dedicated bloke with, I hope, some military background. That is the fellow I want, aged around twenty-two or twenty-three. Absolute magic! But the bloke I am after is at the most crucial stage of his own family life and working his way up in his career. He is trying to get his foot into the property market, and his wife may be going out to work to help pay for that. When he has got through that barrier he is probably twenty-seven or so. If he is a bachelor — magic!'

The TA still has certain monastic attitudes. Some units like the 7th Battalion at Leicester have lost a high proportion of West Indian soldiers, and girl friends are blamed by some of the older TA men. One Corporal said that West Indians and Indians made good soldiers, 'But we have about six in the whole battalion, and we used to have thirty or forty. Some go into the Regular Army — we are just a testing ground. I don't think it is the TA that puts them off. It is their own way of life that does it. They have got girl friends and wives. That is a lot of the cause of the trouble, girl friends. He might come here for two years and then meet a girl, and doesn't have the time to give to the TA. We call them, jokingly, coons. They don't take the least bit of notice, because they call us anything they like. We had one of the Regular Staff who was an Indian who had done twenty years in the Regular Army. His colour made no difference at all.'

How sensitive West Indians and Indians are to ragging, Army style, is of statistically less importance to the British Army than how sensitive *everyone* is to discipline. There have been some surprises.

An eighteen-year-old Private, who was a woodwork machinist supervisor in his working life, confirmed (rather to my surprise) the view of the Commanding Officer (which he had not heard) that people who had to take orders were no less keen on the TA than people who gave them. 'At work I am dealing out discipline as well as giving it. I don't enjoy it, but it has got to be done. Discipline has got to be there. The TA would be of even more value to the country if people saw more of its discipline. They would change to conscription: conscription to the TA. People say young people do not know how to look after themselves. It is better to teach them *now*, before things start to happen. That is how it happened in two World Wars: we weren't prepared. We should have learned from our mistakes.'

Is the sense of urgency there? In human terms, probably. But there have been bottlenecks in getting the right equipment — sometimes in getting the most basic equipment. 'There is really nothing that irritates me about the TA,' said the Private, 'except for the waiting around for uniforms. I have been waiting seven months, and I have only got mine this morning. You feel left out, having no uniform on. Going out at weekends with the others, you don't feel the same. It gives you a certain amount of self-respect, a uniform.'

But the Private thought his uniform meant more than just a means to self-respect for him: 'I *do* think I might be asked to defend Britain. You might as well have the gun ready now. If the Russians carry on the way they are, there is going to be nothing left of the world. I expect to be fighting the Russians if it carries on. It is chaos at the moment. We want to get down to something positive. It has been done before and should be done again.'

The Private had touched on the most crucial single question facing the TA: if it did come to war, could the Territorials take up their posts, and *would* they?

Apart from the possibility of disruption at the embarkation ports, there is the simple issue of whether there would be an adequate turnout in the first place. A TA Major at Leicester reckoned that he could get a Company together in six hours, by telephone or by sending a dispatch rider round to their homes. Perhaps they would not need six hours, because the men would be watching television news or listening to the radio, and they would probably be there before he could summon them. But it might take two days to get them across the water.

'If a man is not in within a few hours, he is not coming in at all,' said another Major. Other officers pointed out the tug of loyalties any TA man would feel, setting off from home at a time when other husbands were returning to look after their families. But he thought the turn-out would be overwhelming.

The Regimental Sergeant Major, less obviously paranoid than his traditional stereotype, insisted that he believed in *telling* soldiers rather than shouting at them, and that discipline was at present quite tight enough in the TA. But he thought perhaps the basic rules should be more like the American National Guard.

There was some feeling among the officers that he could be right. The Battalion's Second-in-Command, a Major, said he was confident the TA had discarded its 'Dad's

Army' image when it came back invigorated in the early 1970s. 'And,' he argued, 'there is a lot of scope for the TA, provided they change the ground rules. The sort of rules I would like are that the TA is voluntary until you sign, when you are subject to military law in the same way as a Regular soldier, and your employer is legally obliged to allow you time off. At the moment you do have problems with administration and training, however good the TA is today. All these problems would disappear overnight if the rules were changed. I think this is a more realistic approach than woolly thinking on the subject. But it requires the will, it requires the willingness on the part of politicians and soldiers, and it requires the law.'

The Commanding Officer courteously walked with me to the gates as I left. He was non-committal about changes in the law, and enthusiastic about the calibre of his men, but plainly none too happy with that weekend's sixty per cent turn-out.

Why this comparatively low turn-out? Perhaps because the Britain of post-war years has not been generous in its view of the Army, in the best and safest of all possible worlds, in which war was always something that happened to other people?

My assumption, when I went to visit a battalion of the Territorial Army given over to the age-old, more typical and perhaps more unfashionable purpose of home defence, was that the weekend turn-out would be even lower. My assumption was wrong.

The equipment of A Company of the 2nd Battalion of the Wessex Regiment may not have had the complexity and sheen of a NATO-designated unit. It may have had only one professional Army man, a Colour Sergeant, on its strength. Its Land Rovers may have been a bit noisy and smelly and the Commanding Officer of the Battalion may have said that if he had £200,000 or so to spare, he'd ditch all his old two-wheel-drive lorries and have four-wheel-drive ones that could be driven practically anywhere on ice, mud or slush. But eight out of every ten men turned out for a testing, hot and uncomfortable exercise on Salisbury Plain, a typical exercise for TA men designated for home defence. Those who didn't almost always had a valid reason — a mother dead, serious domestic trouble to sort out.

'On Monday morning I couldn't care less how knackered the men who've turned out may feel,' said the Commanding Officer, an ex-officer of the Royal Hampshire Regiment, now in his early forties, who went into the wine trade when he retired, but kept a fiery-eyed devotion to military values. 'I will only be worried if on Monday morning they turn round and say, "Well, and what the hell *happened?*" Because that will mean they have been bored.'

On Salisbury Plain the company I joined *did* know what the hell was happening. About thirty soldiers of the enemy (or, as some officers more baldly put it, Russian) Diversionary Brigade — their version of the British organization for covert operations behind enemy lines, the Special Air Service (SAS) — were holed up in the ruins of Thornecombe Farm near the village of Imber. They were well armed with semi-automatic weapons and they were elite troops in good morale. They must all be eliminated.

No doubt many civilians would have seen such an operation as purely academic, and its title, Exercise Hothouse, no help in dispelling the impression. The first sight of the TA Centre in Portsmouth, home of A Company, where the preliminary briefings took place, might not have helped, either.

The Edwardian building, directly across the road from the central railway station, resembles — at least from inside, looking out — the roof of St Pancras railway station. It is leased to the Territorial Army by a trust established by the Duke of Connaught, which ensures that the use of the hall will remain military. There is a thriving bar off the cast-iron balcony, where ladies of TA men play darts on Thursday evenings — part of a conscious attempt to involve women in the atmosphere of the TA, which removes menfolk from view for alternate weekends and many evenings during the week.

271

It soon became clear (perhaps clearer than some wives and girl friends would like to think) that the centre of interest was not the bar but the briefing room. Once in the briefing room, it became more evident why the company was prepared to spend the weekend eating at field kitchens fired by petrol, sleeping in their clothes inside sleeping bags or the backs of lorries, and performing urgent calls of nature either behind trees or in the solitary thunderbox.

Adrenalin began to flow once it was established that Exercise Hothouse was not an updated version of whitewashing regimental coal, but a task stemming from a credible set of circumstances. 'The Russians,' said the briefing officer (lapsing from calling them merely 'The Enemy', as officers are apt to do, though this is the official term), 'have moved across Germany at a fast rate. At first they made substantial gains but they have been stopped 125 kilometres into Germany. In Britain, diversionary brigades of the enemy have already been set up, little cells to blow bridges, radio stations and so on. They may have been here for years, posing as ordinary members of the population, but they are the enemy — highly-trained and very tough soldiers, very much like our SAS. They had great successes initially and caused great confusion, but now police and Army activity has made it difficult for them to operate. The Diversionary Brigade troops we have to deal with have been using the village of Imber. There are about thirty of them at Thornecombe Farm, tough soldiers with good morale and armed with semi-automatic weapons.'

The officer paused and then said three times in precisely the same tone of voice: 'You will eliminate that enemy.'

The TA men set off for Salisbury Plain in Land Rovers and lorries in the small hours of Saturday morning, snatched an hour or so's sleep in their sleeping bags, and at 4.50 in the morning were behind the last of three hedges the enemy (men of the 1st Battalion, the Wessex Regiment) could see in front of them as they looked down the slight slope which was their visible landscape. In a real war, the storming of the gutted farmhouse would have been staged *before* dawn. But from the training point of view, there was an advantage in doing it in the light of a damp, dewy dawn. One of the latest refinements, a video camera, could be used; and the taped event, mistakes and all, could be played back to the Territorials later.

Hence the video cameraman, the Colour Sergeant and I were lying flat on our stomachs, in tall wet grass on a bank by the farmhouse, as the men down the hill formed up (they hoped unseen) to begin the attack.

The Colour Sergeant was a professional jewel — the sort of a man who could be in ten places at once, pushing everyone on with a turn of repartee ('Are you trying to tell me something, or are you just chewing on a brick?') and pointing out errors with a candour that was quite memorable, but inoffensive because quite impersonal. This was the man who before the attack started assured me he never forgot that Territorial Army men had to be *better* than Regulars to learn as much in the limited time available; that their standard, though it could not match that of the Regulars, was very high: and that when he had inherited a company down to forty-five men, twenty of whom never turned up, he brought back *in* many men his predecessor had thrown out — and later recommended some for promotion. 'You can't just fling people out if they don't match Regular Army standards right away,' he had said.

Now that his charges were about to storm the farmhouse, across land that offered little cover except that of lateral hedges and occasional tiny clumps of bush, he was growling exhortations and imprecations to himself as the action unfolded itself, at first silently. 'They are either not there at all yet or they are better than I bloody thought.'

'By Christ! They *are* there! They *are* better than I thought. You clever little sods, you!'

(I myself still could spot absolutely nothing.)

'There's one there — lazy devil! — on his knees instead of his belly, so you can spot him.'

(I couldn't.)

'Well, ten minutes gone and I've seen only ten of them,

273

and there are a good sixty men there somewhere. Still, one is enough to give the game away. The enemy must be bloody asleep!'

(I could still see nothing at all except hedges. Then the men below started to advance more visibly.)

'A bit too much like The Thin Red Line! Too straight a line, too visible! Still, it is just cheeky enough, you may get away with it!'

'Bloody hell! Look at those on the left. They weren't supposed to break cover for another hundred metres.'

'Six of you coming through an obvious gap in that hedge! What if I have just mined the gap, you twats?'

At this point the enemy in the farmhouse saw the soldiers coming up the hill and started firing.

'Take cover, you idiot! Get down.'

'Oh, look at them bunching together so they can all be taken out at once! Jesus Christ! Have you learnt nothing?'

'Too many of you up at one time. Look at you! One man fires while another runs zig-zag and then the man who ran drops down and fires to let the other by! That's the *proper* way! Look at you!'

'If you can't run faster than that it will be the last run you ever make!'

By this time, the TA men were into the little wood immediately surrounding the farmhouse, firing blanks; and the Colour Sergeant and his video camera were trying to follow them as they shot at each other from behind trees at twenty feet range, followed the enemy into the farmhouse itself and shot them in the living-room and upstairs. The Colour Sergeant was still full of imprecations which could not then be heard (but which would certainly be heard later when the inquest was held during a weekday session).

'Look at you! Already calling for an ambulance for your own men! You should be checking to see the enemy are all dead, you twat! What if they aren't?'

As the men split up into individual platoons to go on to the next stage of the exercise — eliminating little groups of four or five Russian Diversionary Brigade men in nearby woods, with the help of a helicopter hired from the Royal Air Force at about £2,000 an hour — the volunteer Army men gave their own impressions of the way a typical home defence exercise had gone.

The Major who was Officer Commanding A Company — an ex-RAF man and now an executive officer at a computer centre — thought the chain of command had worked well, but that some of the younger lads had been a bit lost. The professional Colour Sergeant tended to agree. And the younger soldiers thought that dropping down into tall grass and immediately rolling over and over (so that when they popped up again it wouldn't be in the spot the enemy expected) was a bit more tiring than *they* expected.

'I didn't think I was moving fast enough over that difficult terrain,' said an eighteen-year-old volunteer with four months' experience. 'I shall do better next time.'

Plainly a great deal of adrenalin had been circulating, enough to induce forgetfulness of the (also considerable) quantities of perspiration. Perhaps among the very young recruits the potential reality of the situation they were dealing with was not as apparent as it was to the officers, who tended to be in their thirties or early forties. But experienced Territorial Army men thought that such an impression would not be correct.

One officer who recently helped to form an Officers Training Corps in a university in the South of England said the task was getting easier and easier — the problem was ensuring that standards were not watered down. 'Anti-Army militants are now in a very small minority,' he said. 'There seems to have been a 180 degree turn in attitudes. This must be good for the Territorial Army as well.'

Officers and men said they could not see the exercise itself as purely theoretical. Several mentioned the Russian invasion of Afghanistan as the reason they felt personally less safe. British feelings of safety have almost certainly tended to isolate the Army, full-time and part-time, in the postwar years, Britons regarding it as a luxury rather than a necessity. In turn this has bred a certain insularity in the Army — or at least inflamed an insular mistrust of civilian thinking and civilian ways that was there already.

This isolation has never been total. How it will develop in a harder era (or whether it will continue at all) will be one of the most fascinating questions for the remainder of this century. The British Colonels in Downing Street, even — will they remain a fantasy or could they become a newspaper headline?

PART THREE

How They Mix with the Rest of Us

14

No Coups, Please, We're British

'If a militant picket got between us and an ambulance or some other necessary public utility and refused to get out of the way, and it was our orders to go through, then if a violent picket insisted on a rifle butt over the head, they would get it. Would my men go along with that? Are you kidding? It would be them who would be pushing me to give them the order.'

— Major in the Infantry.

'Could the military stage a coup on Britain? Quite impossible, my dear chap. Could you imagine the Grenadiers and The Blues and Royals combining in anything, let alone a coup?'

— Company Commander in the Guards Division.

In the past, the British Army has austerely detached itself from ordinary civilian life with almost the zeal of a monastic order. It seemed as if it wanted its own code to remain forever virgin.

Northern Ireland, the carrying out of vital services for civilians during industrial disputes, and the kudos both these have gained for the Army in terms of public relations, have greatly changed this attitude. So has the campaign for more pay in the late 1970s, which encouraged both officers and men to speak their minds publicly with a positive edge not seen before.

Largely as a result of these different factors, four questions have latterly been posed about the Army's future behaviour. Is there scope for the introduction of more civilian philosophy in methods of operation? Is there room for trade unionism in the Army? If the ordinary soldier were ever called upon to tackle unruly strikers or unlawful pickets with a riot stick or rifle, would he do so? And perhaps most important of all, is the first coup by the Army since Oliver Cromwell now possible in a Britain which is becoming increasingly difficult to govern?

The idea of the coup is the most dramatic and, in the opinion of many intelligent officers, the most farcical. Sometimes they emphasize its absurdity almost too much, like men trying to shout above an increasingly freshening wind. If they have a fear, it is that the mistrusted breed, politicians, will try to enmesh them in their power struggles; and if there is one thing the British Army does *not* wish to be involved in, it is political power struggles. Public order is another matter and, at least among officers and men talked to, I could discover little reluctance to come to the help of the police, should they ever be asked to. Unless a substantial number of the British Army are such good actors that they deserve membership of Equity, the actors' trade union, the British Army as a whole would be embroiled in a coup only if it were sucked into one by a series of tiny steps which got out of hand — a 'holding of the ring while the politicians sorted themselves on normal democratic lines', as one officer expressed it (as a hypothesis rather than as a possibility).

Even at Camberley Staff College, where the high-fliers of the Army go for a year's practical tactics instruction and contemplation of sophisticated Army philosophies, the staging of a coup does *not* feature in the curriculum. Shortly after a television programme was made about life at the college, there were newspaper reports discussing the possibility of such a coup, and suggesting that the Special Air Service Regiment (SAS) could be used. The speculation ran thus: the SAS (that mysterious body which can spend a week immersed in water and dine off slugs and neighbourhood cats if required — at least according to rumour, which is all that is forthcoming from the Army on this subject), could go from Chelsea Barracks to Downing Street in a matter of minutes, to turf out terrorists who were trying to take over. So, they could just as easily (ran the speculation) turf out, instead, the Prime Minister and Chancellor of the Exchequer, and place their own posteriors around the Cabinet table.

Instructors at Camberley were greatly surprised, afterwards, at how a few snippets of officers' conversations while thinking aloud in the bar, so to speak, could have been magnified by some of the media into an Army preoccupation with the possibility of a military coup. 'It is true that, if you asked the 120 United Kingdom students here how the Army could in future be involved in civil disorders, you would get 120 answers. This might not have been a true a few years ago,' said one student. 'But I have never heard a military coup in Britain discussed seriously here.'

'The SAS in Downing Street? Absolute rubbish,' said an instructor. 'There has certainly never been a Staff College exercise on those lines. It is the sort of thing young Army officers will joke about in the bar, but it is not part of our curriculum. Perhaps we talk irresponsibly in some instances, as other people do in the bar, but it isn't in our syllabus, nor can I ever imagine it would be.'

It is perfectly true that in their final terms, the high-fliers of the British Army go on to talk about chemical and nuclear warfare, Northern Ireland and peacetime operations and training. But they do not discuss military coups. Neither have coups featured prominently even in the home-made pantomimes that students put on at the end of every course for the benefit of themselves, their relatives and local civilians, in which all sorts of things can be shown for a laugh.

But in the sophisticated corridors of Camberley the subject *is* discussed privately — 'just,' as one officer put it, 'as it might be discussed in a university room late at night.' (Some senior officers say they doubt this.) In Northern Ireland, where the adrenalin circulates without the need of intellectual speculation, the subject comes up more rarely. A senior officer at one military base said he had thought about it and would be surprised if a coup by the Army, as such, ever came about. 'I haven't heard anywhere, at any time, any sort of talk on those lines, not in messes and not anywhere else,' he said. 'Obviously one hears the young Captain after dinner exploring the theory, but only in the sort of way you would hear it in the common room at a university. One of the strengths of the system is that the *fear* of getting involved in political power games is *encouraged*. You are taught to see your relationship to the state as a whole, *not* to a political party. If you think of yourself in Northern Ireland, for instance, as part of the *law* and *order* forces, your path is clear.' He meant that the proper role of the Army must be to aid the police in protecting lives of all persuasions and property of all types.

Could this, transferred to the mainland, lead to a more direct intervention of the military in civil affairs? Soldiers and cautious men in the corridors of the Ministry of Defence will speculate with a great deal of reluctance and *never* for public consumption.

One line of reasoning is that if there were a revolution in Britain, and the legally-elected government were to be deposed and physically taken out of Downing Street by the rebels, then in the last resort the Army might find itself in the position of having to defend that government. The possibility is looked upon as unlikely, because it is thought there is no way a revolutionary group could get itself firmly enough entrenched to be able to count on popular support if the legal government were to be deposed.

Any action by the Army, such as in Chile — in which soldiers helped remove the legally-elected Allende, after inflation had reached insupportable proportions and the constitution seemed to be in danger — is regarded, in military circles, as even more unlikely. 'The British system is such that you would not get the chain of circumstances,' said one MoD official. 'No doubt, in the past few years, some people in the Forces have been very unhappy about some of the decisions that have been taken. But you don't get them going off at half-cock against governments. They accept decisions. Maybe the British character has a different approach to things than in Latin-American countries. Here everyone in the Services would accept the parliamentary will.'

About the only situation soldiers themselves, and the men who control them, can see as likely to involve them in the business of government is a World War Three. A war, moreover, in which the civil government had been wiped out and the country was therefore ruled by regional authorities with sweeping powers quite unheard of in normal times. In these circumstances, the regional authorities would in all probability have to draw on both police and Army to protect such services as were possible, and to keep order generally.

'It would be a matter of pure survival, with *everything* so different to what we can imagine today,' said one man with military experience. 'The situation would require people to collect and distribute food and make sure that local barons did not take it over. Presumably that would involve the Army.'

So it might; but that involvement would be about as unlike a military 'coup' as it would be possible to imagine. My contacts at all levels of the British Army led me finally to believe that an Army coup would only be of two types. The first, an *imaginary* one conducted by bright sparks at military colleges or by faded sparks being greeted with yawns in latenight messes. The second, a real one and a partial one, consisting of the Army, against its will, traditions and etiquette, being finally prevailed upon to do *something* because people were starving in a war, or because pickets were sitting in front of fire stations and citizens with homes burning were hammering on the doors of Army barracks.

Such reactive action would hardly be a coup as commonly understood: not only the Army, but the majority of the country would by then see it as assistance to the civil power; and that civil power could be drawn from any political party. The assumption that it would necessarily be a right-wing British government that would need to draw on the Army in this way is, arguably, based on a habit of thinking rather than an imaginative awareness of the actual possibilities. Who, in Britain, would be seen as having the most widely-accepted moral authority to call in the military as the last resort?

Ask any Army man to comment openly on such matters, and he will mumble 'speculation' and change the subject. Of course, many men destined to become sound and constitutional Army high-ups will have discussed Army coups in the bar at Camberley, just as many university students will have discussed revolution before going on to become reliable bank managers, computer programmers in search of promotion, and steadfast readers of the *Daily Telegraph*. The blazing certainties and intellectual games of youth rarely persist.

The SAS as the agent of a political coup may be a concept far ahead of any easily imaginable reality. Its mysterious ability to lay low is part of its mystique and its efficiency and these would be severely compromised if it involved itself in civilian politics. It was formed by Colonel David Stirling in 1942 to operate in the North African desert, carrying out acts of sabotage and guerrilla warfare that would persuade the Germans to think they faced more manpower there than they in fact did. It remains a very hard-edged instrument to be used against an enemy, with no holds barred, rather than in civilian matters, where the lighter touch is usually what is required.

Usually, but not always. In the mid-1970s, a number of armed IRA gunmen occupied a flat in Balcombe Street, West London, and held the tenant and his wife hostage for several days. They gave up and handed themselves over when they knew the SAS had joined police marksmen in staking out the flat. The presence of the SAS on that occasion was not a matter of great public comment.

In 1980, it was rather different. The SAS moved much further into the public arena, and into what would normally have been thought of as civil affairs — indeed, they achieved what is almost the ultimate accolade in post-

Empire Britain: television stardom, albeit behind masks and blacked-up faces, as they carried out an operation.

Iranian gunmen forced their way into the Iranian Embassy in London in protest at the policies of the regime which had taken over from the deposed Shah — a regime with which Britain's relations, in common with the rest of the West, had been, to say the least, touchy. They took hostage not only the Iranian Embassy staff, but also two British BBC newsmen who happened to be in the Embassy, applying for visas, and an armed British police constable who moved in to investigate what was happening at the Prince's Gate mansion that housed the Embassy. It stands in the middle of a private road in the Kensington foreign embassy area, almost within shouting distance of the Royal Albert Hall.

For several days, police mounted a siege in a way which had produced success on two previous occasions. These had involved armed would-be thieves holding hostages at a Knightsbridge restaurant called the Spaghetti House, and the IRA men in Balcombe Street. For some days it seemed as if tempers were calm and that the police might succeed in talking-out the Iranian gunmen. Then, almost immediately after the Commissioner of Metropolitan Police, Sir David McNee, had sent in a personal message, assuring the gunmen of their safety if they did not harm hostages in their care, they shot one hostage and dumped his body outside the Embassy door.

For days, the SAS had been studying the structure of the Embassy buildings and photographs of the hostages. Blasting their way through adjoining walls, crashing themselves through windows on ropes lowered from the roof, and hurling stun grenades into the building, the black-overalled SAS men shot all gunmen except one, and saved all British hostages and all except two of the Iranian hostages. These had been shot before the SAS attack.

It was a coup of a non-political sort that won the SAS an enthusiastic Press, even extracting from those who are no friends of the British Army praise that was as tepid as they could in decency make it. The police constable, Trevor Lock, had his photograph deservedly over the front pages of newspapers, having saved the life of an SAS man by grappling with an Iranian gunman who was about to shoot him as he crashed through a window. The two BBC men gave long interviews to the newspapers and to television.

The SAS men, variously estimated at between eight and fifty-five in number, disappeared without a trace. They were interviewed by no one. The Prime Minister, Mrs Margaret Thatcher, insisted on going to their temporary barracks in Regents Park and congratulating them as they celebrated their achievement modestly in lager; but almost certainly the SAS men would have been just as happy if they had not had to show their faces, even to the Prime Minister.

Good standard journalistic practice required feature articles on the SAS. The pieces that appeared were bromides, which shuffled round in varying order the few available facts about the SAS which are in the area of public knowledge. That the emblem is a dagger on wings. That the motto is 'Who Dares, Wins'. That the depot is at Hereford. That the men often serve under a pseudonym. That they rarely win medals individually, only as a regiment. That they are all specialists — in explosives, or any other aspects of anti-terrorist operations. That the proper name for the regiment is the 22nd Regiment, SAS. That it is organized into four operational squadrons, each with six officers and seventy-two men. That they wear no badges of rank, call one another by their Christian names only, and are trained not to rely on fixed patterns of procedure. That their final test at the Hereford depot includes trekking nearly forty miles across the Brecon Beacons in twenty hours while carrying over one hundred pounds of kit on their backs. That some of the successes of the security forces in Northern Ireland have been thanks to the very presence of the SAS in border counties such as South Armagh, used or not (and when I was with the Army in South Armagh, no trace of the SAS was discernible to the naked eye).

Not being visible to the naked eye is one of the arts of the SAS, who now enjoy the reputation of being probably the most highly trained and effective anti-terrorist force anywhere in the world: the force that is called in when, and *only* when, the talking has to stop. When the Home Secretary, Mr William Whitelaw, said after the freeing of the hostages by the SAS, that Britain 'would not tolerate' acts of terrorism on her soil, and praised the SAS for their action, it was a sign, and almost certainly intended to be a sign, that Britain would no longer be a 'soft touch' to those who tried to live by the gun and the bomb. Civilians rejoiced at their intervention in what would normally have been solely a police matter. But between this and intervention in political matters there would be a huge chasm, which would be avoided by the Army itself no less than by the politicians (except perhaps those who were under concerted violent attack of a quite unconstitutional kind).

Nevertheless, the British Army's increasing involvement as the operator of vital public services in time of industrial dispute has been, willy-nilly, a training for an increasing role in civilian affairs. Troops who had been rather demoralized by the low pay in the Army until just before the end of the 1970s had a great but ambivalent boost to morale when they appeared before the public as last-minute providers.

'The public has noticed us at last,' said one soldier. 'Before that, we might have been the Invisible Force. We were always abroad or in barracks.' But soldiers also saw how much some militant workers earned already, which did not endear them in their eyes.

The most unfair and untypical reflection on the British Army's capacity to help during labour disputes — an expanding part of British life — came during the strike of firemen at the beginning of 1978. A party of soldiers with an old Army Green Goddess fire engine spent hours climbing a tall tree and coaxing a pet cat down. Then they drove off, running over the cat.

Militant trade unionists were apt to seize on this anecdote as an example of how the Army could never deputize satisfactorily for civilian workers on strike, and *could* only be amateur dustmen, firemen, ambulance men or power house men. But the fact is that the Army has been increasingly used, in recent years, as an alternative to the regular labour force in a large number of activities made vulnerable by strikes, lock-outs and go-slows. It has proved itself in the public estimation as a result, without stirring up commensurate hatred in the rank and file trade unionist. Often its value has been that it can *underwrite* vital services, and keep up civilian morale, even if its services have not actually been called upon.

A microcosm of this social involvement, and a scene rather more characteristic of military finesse and patience than the run-over cat, came in late January, 1979. Most of Britain, during that most depressing and demanding week, had been hit by both bad weather and strikes. Snow was falling in heavy drifts in Westminster. Big Ben was coated in what looked like coconut icing, while the politicians below, in the Mother of Parliaments, debated once more which party was more responsible for the situation than the other. Just across Westminster Bridge Road, a stone's throw away, I found the Life Guards standing by, in their berets and camouflaged battle dress, at the forecourt of Cannon Row police station. The police kept up their morale by throwing snowballs at one another in the slushy courtyard; the troops by having a rest on their camp beds inside the building whenever they could.

It was a day when morale generally was low. The weather was the worst for sixteen years. British Rail trains were not running, London Underground trains were disorganized. Buses were running full, most ambulancemen were out on strike, and food was rotting at the ports because of a strike of lorry drivers. There was every reason for everyone to work hard at keeping up their own morale. They did not always succeed. Tempers among civilians sometimes visibly slipped. People who normally went into work by train were frightened to take their cars instead. They feared that if they skidded on the ice and slush — not gritted because public service workers were also on strike — and had an accident, in which they were injured, they might be unable to get to hospital. Ambulance men might not arrive at all at accidents, though some — a vague and unreliable number — had said they would attend emergency calls. Some civilians had an almost morbid fear of being hurt. A man who was careless with the sharp end of his umbrella while walking down the steps of the subway at the bottom of Whitehall had it snatched away from him and thrown to one side in a way worthy of a Jacques Tati film.

In John's Cafe (which stood opposite Cannon Row police station from the days when it was the original New Scotland Yard) parties of valiant winter tourists shivered over their cups of tea. Passing taxi drivers, the weather so bad that they were having to tout for customers, were apt to swear at pedestrians who didn't get out of the slush-covered way as quickly as they might have done.

Inside Cannon Row police station, morale was rather higher. Four field ambulances, with equipment, had been driven down by Life Guards during the preceding weekend (together with twenty-six others to different destinations) from a field depot eighty miles from London. The Life Guards were based at Windsor — a prestigious place to be in view of the proximity to the Queen's home at Windsor Castle. But the sixteen of them drafted to Cannon Row (two men in every crew, a driver and a medical orderly, and two shift crews per field ambulance) took over a storeroom at the police station and plumped their camp beds down in it, with every intention of eating there and sleeping there until the emergency was over. The young Lieutenant in charge of the party, which was supported by the Royal Electrical and Mechanical Engineers, slept on a camp bed on the floor of the room taken over as his office. Always he was only an arm's length away from the telephone.

Other factors, too, did not appear to be ideal for morale. Some volunteer civilian ambulance services were functioning: the Army was there only as back-up, often a dispiriting thing to be. They had been there seventy-two hours when I went to see them, just before the regular ambulance men accepted their union's request to go back to work, and they had not had to answer a single call. In all this time the young Lieutenant, who had been in the Army less than three years, had never left the police station; but he seemed to be in fine form.

I asked him what he and his men thought of the task of civilian back-up, expecting a resigned, if determined, answer. I got an unequivocally cheerful one. 'We have done it so many times that we now *expect* to get called out if there is any kind of strike,' he said. 'There is no resentment against anyone who is the direct cause. Quite frankly, it is in the line of duty — and, looking on the bright side, it makes a change.'

The Lieutenant must have seen a shimmer of scepticism in my eyes: normally the cobbler doesn't like to be separated from his own last. 'No, it's true,' he insisted. 'The thing that really browns people off is the lack of equipment, due to defence cuts. They have limited training. There are things that can make up for the fact that we do not get very well paid, but if at the same time we can't train properly, because we don't have enough ammunition or petrol to drive the tanks . . . well, it's a bit much. So when we do things like this, in industrial disputes, some of the men quite enjoy it.'

They were still enjoying it a month later. On 21 February of the same year, ambulance men in London said they would not operate even emergency services. The following day, negotiations were to be held between their employers and their union. Union officers advised them to work normally, pending these negotiations. In the event, about half of the ambulance men in London attended to emergencies, leaving the rest of the work to police and Army ambulances.

This time, the thaw had set in. London streets were clear of ice and snow, though not of rubbish—the dustmen were still out on strike. There were, however, few accidents; if the troops fretted about anything it was the lack of activity.

At Cannon Row police station, it was principally the bandsmen — brought in for the first time to help medical men in an ambulance dispute — who were irritated. Three of them from the Coldstream Guards turned out from Chelsea Barracks, with three men from the Medical Corps and six Grenadier Guards as drivers. They arrived well before midnight, when the strike was due to start, and took over a room on the fourth floor of the police station, directly over the canteen and beside the field training and traffic warden sections. There were twelve men altogether, working four to a shift. Three ambulances were always available. A rota of men was drawn up and, once a man had answered a call, his name automatically went to the bottom of the list. Sleep was snatched when possible.

Some of the musicians lost money as a result of helping out in the strike. 'We have what we call private enterprise jobs, but these have been restricted because of the industrial disputes,' said one musician. Some Coldstream Guards musicians play at civilian functions in their own time, which is regarded as a legitimate 'perk'.

The musicians had a last-minute briefing in first aid by a Warrant Officer who was in charge of the party, a State Registered Nurse. He said afterwards that all he could teach in the time available were the rudiments of the subject, but that in every ambulance there was a skilled medical man — skilled even in midwifery. One musician said he had been in the Army seven years and never previously been taught first aid; but the Warrant Officer pointed out that he would have done stretcher-bearing as part of his basic training. The musician agreed, but still seemed pardonably nervous about the possibility of a pregnant woman crossing his path.

'It's the soldier's lot to chop and change,' said a Coldstream Guardsman stoically. 'You have to accept that if you are in the Army. You will find yourself praying that something will happen. If we were called out a bit more often, I would like it. The trouble is that it's quite a build-up actually *coming* here, and then it's an anticlimax.'

Cannon Row was one of the many quiet areas on this occasion. Ambulances were called out more often from Fulham, Croydon and Sutton. By late afternoon of that day, Chelsea Barracks reported that Army ambulances had gone out over fifty times in the capital. Forty-nine Army ambulances were available in London on that day. All but ten were used. The rest were held in reserve at barracks, to be put into the field if any of the others broke down.

The striking ambulance men had declared that they would not obstruct the Army, nor any other emergency ambulance services, and no friction developed. It could have been very different, and possibly would have been, in many other countries.

I asked the Warrant Officer in charge at Cannon Row what *feelings* he had about manning ambulances during a strike. 'I am a soldier,' he said, 'I have no feelings. I certainly have no personal feelings about the dispute. It is just another job to a regular soldier. You must remember that a soldier comes off one tour of duty and on to another, and he does it regularly. He automatically copes.'

It became apparent, from the number of times soldiers emphasized, during the dispute, that they had no 'personal feelings', that this had been inculcated into them carefully before each operation. What happened was very British, very impersonal. One got the feeling that if anything *un*pleasant had happened, that would have been very impersonal too. Certainly no one would have accused the Army of being an *agent provocateur*.

What happened in the ambulance men's strike was only one example of what was happening to soldiers generally in an era of regular labour disputes. Shortly afterwards, soldiers were acclaimed as heroes when they rescued people, and saved property, as floods badly hit the North of England. That this produced public praise was not remarkable; the lack of animosity displayed by workers to troops in the labour disputes *was* remarkable.

Did the troops see the striking workers as what the militant trade unionists hoped — brothers under the skin? Hardly. All the signs were that they hardly saw them at all; they merely did the task allocated to them, with some relief at being able to stretch their limbs. But the strikes aimed at vital services in this period gave more credence to what officers repeatedly claimed in conversations with me: that the men were actively relieved to be in the Army, because there they were free of the power of the unions.

'You will find more of the men frightened of the unions than you will find officers who are,' said one officer. Men did tend to say so, whether as an echo or not it was sometimes difficult to judge.

Lack of enthusiasm for trying to unionize the Army itself has been visible even in many trade union leaders. On one occasion, an important official of the Trades Union Congress was invited to Sandhurst to talk on trade union matters: the modern British Army likes to keep abreast of more than military affairs. All went smoothly until question time, when a new recruit in the hall stood up and asked the direct question: 'Would trade unions be a good thing here in the Army?'

In such a way might a novice have walked into a synagogue without a hat, or into a Muslim temple with his boots on. Breaths were sucked in, audibly. Friends of the new recruit wondered if his military career would take on an irreparable blight from that moment. Officers admitted afterwards that they wondered if the lad was mad, inviting trade union propaganda like that. It was like asking the Devil, 'Tell me, would sin be a good thing?'

There were gasps of relief when the trade union official said, 'No, I don't think they would be a good thing — after all, you do look after your people already.'

Even moderate opinion in the Army insists that obedience must be absolute; this means there must be no power of strike and that, in the absence of this power, a union would be a eunuchoid farce. There has not been a significant body of opinion in the ranks wanting trade unions, and there have been voices very loud and rancorous against them. When a rifleman was driving a dust cart in the middle of the dustmen's strike, one of the strikers shouted through the cab window, 'You are a worker.' To which came the unsympathetic reply, '*You* aren't — you're an animal.'

The Army in Sweden, Holland and West Germany have versions of trade unions; but the British Army has always been able to avoid any move in that direction. The low pay of the 1970s could have been a new foothold; but a new government immediately agreed to substantial increases, long before there was any coherent call for unionization.

'And you must remember,' said an Army man in Whitehall, 'that the Army has well-defined procedures for dealing with grievances and complaints. Some trade union leaders have said these procedures do not handle grievances quite as impartially as the Army makes out. My instruction to my staff when dealing with a grievance is, "You will put yourself in the position of the *complainant*, and assure yourself that every aspect of *your* complaint has been answered quite justly and accurately, even if it is not to the Army's advantage." You must also see, to the best of your ability, that decisions at unit level are fair.'

Another Army man in the corridors of power said that, in the technical corps, there might be some feeling for a trade union, partly as a craft organization. But not for the majority of the Army. 'I would say, almost the exact reverse,' he claimed. 'The men would be much more positive in saying they didn't want a union — certainly in the front-line units.'

And yet another powerful Army voice in the rabbit warren that is the Ministry of Defence chipped in with the observation that, during one industrial dispute, a soldier had told him, 'If you want us to hammer through the picket, we would be happy to oblige.'

Political action and trade union action seem to be equally

discounted at all levels of the British Army. Other Armies react differently. In the South American countries, the Army traditionally plays a role in political conflict, at least to preserve its own ideas of stability. This would *not* be taken as a commendable model by critics of the British Army. But the experience of other countries who have trade unions in their Armies is often quoted as an example for Britain.

Especially Sweden. Is it a valid parallel?

At the beginning of the 1980s, three trade unions had members in the Swedish Army. The NCOs were the first in the field, starting a union in 1908. It was not well received, and was disbanded in 1912. For six years after that, there were organizations only at unit level, which did not have the right to negotiate nor take any industrial action. In 1918, a trade union proper was created under a central organization, and NCOs belonged to that. Officers formed their own union in 1932. It was a section of the Swedish Civil Servants National Organization, which merged with the academics' trade union in 1972. Between the officers and the NCOs in the Swedish Army, there was a union for Company Officers — a distinct rank unknown in the British Army — which was formed as long ago as 1912.

This complex system, both of ranks and of unions, was being rationalized in 1980. The Company Officer and NCO levels were in the process of being abolished and a Professional Officer Corps created, including everyone from Corporals to Generals. It was to exclude only Privates because, in the Swedish Army, these are all conscripts and so in the Army for a limited time only. It was hoped that one union for the Army would be a by-product of this revision of the ranking system. All the unions involved agreed in principle that one union, and one union only, would be the best solution. But they found some difficulty when it came to agreeing on *which*. The officers did not want to leave their amalgamated civil service and academic union. Nor did the other two ranks want to leave their own union.

This dispute could well provide ammunition for those in the British Army who regard a tendency to inter-union disputes as one reason why Armies and unions don't mix at all. The fact that, in Sweden, the Army unions have had the right to negotiate and to strike might alarm them even more.

But this right to strike is not quite as simple as it might look. It is, in fact, where the parallel between the Swedish and the British Armies begins to break down. The right to strike has required, and received, a discipline which might, or might not, be acceptable to trade unionists in Britain. In Sweden, government and unions have agreed that a certain number of officers are not allowed to go on strike and that the employer cannot lock them out. The unions agreed never to withdraw the labour of those engaged in the training of conscripts, the day-to-day defence of Swedish territory and sea space, and Intelligence operations.

In point of fact, there has never been a Swedish Army strike by any of the unions. When the merged unions of the academics and civil servants, to which the officers belonged, took out on strike some civil servants employed on the Swedish railways, the government itself actually threatened to *lock out* a certain number of Army officers as a reprisal — a circumstance which may, to British militarists and trade unionists alike, sound like Alice in Wonderland. In fact, it made sense, precisely because the social fabric of Sweden, which allowed unions with teeth, was rather different in other important ways from that of Britain — different in ways which continue but which are *not* emphasized by those who most readily quote Sweden as a model. If unions call a strike, the unions, not Social Security, must pay the strikers. If the government had locked out the Army officers, their union (which also included the striking railwaymen) would have had to pay them. With the pay already due to the striking railwaymen, it would have been a prohibitive burden.

Would trade unionists in Britain regard such an arrangement in Britain as a step forward, from their own point of view? Two facts must be borne in mind. The Swedish Army unions have had full powers of industrial action since the early 1960s. They have never once used them to strike in twenty years; even in the so-called General Strike in Sweden from 2 May to 11 May 1980, there was no question of the Army being included, though other members of the unions to which Army men belonged *did* go on strike — including civil servants, but *not* civil servants in any way working for the Army.

'The unions tried to find sectors where a strike would be immediately felt by the general public,' said one Swedish military man, 'and this was mostly in the area of civilian transport. A strike in the Army would not have been noticed so quickly by the general public. As far as I know, the Army was never even discussed as part of this strike at all.'

These two facts — that the power is *there* but that it has never been *used* once in twenty years — may show either that the Swedes are an eminently sane nation or that trade unions tend to think twice about striking when they, and not the taxpayer, have to foot the strike pay bill. But the mere fact that their system seems to work cannot, in itself, be fairly used to establish a case for trade unions in the British Army.

Could the Swedish arrangements for conscripts have lessons helpful to Britain? Conscripts are permitted to form associations. These can talk to (thought not negotiate with) the military commanders. There is also what is termed a yearly Conscript Parliament, which can pass resolutions about what it does and doesn't want. The fact that proceedings of both these bodies may be reported in the media gives them some influence, if not power. No negligent commander likes being called negligent in public.

'In the long run, they would probably persuade a commander to change,' said a Swedish military man, 'because in Sweden the Services are a firm part of society. The professional Army in Britain is not really kept completely beside the civilian community. The system of having military people living in married quarters, inside the gates, is a sort of incentive for being kept aside from the civilian community.'

In the Netherlands, where there are military associations which do *not* have the right to strike, there is a fairly sophisticated and well-proven arrangement of consultation between the Defence Ministry and the organization of the men. It goes back to 1922, when a committee known as the FC (Committee for Formalized Consultations) was set up. The committee has survived in various updated forms and now consists of a government delegation appointed by the Secretary of Defence and a personal delegation appointed by the associations. It cannot deal with individual cases of grievance, but it can discuss procedures in general.

For many years in the Netherlands, conscripts had no association, unlike Regular officers and men. The Association of Military Conscripts (VVDM) was founded in 1966, covering all ranks doing their National Service commitment. At first its dealings with the government were on a largely informal basis. In 1975 it alarmed some military top brass by being integrated into the Committee for Formalized Consultations. Later it alarmed them even more when its control got into the hands of young radicals who seemed bent on confrontation with the government. The extremes of alarm proved unfounded. Though the VVDM is still the largest organization of military personnel, it lost ten thousand members in two militant years (1974 to 1976) while, in the same period, a more recently launched and more moderate association of conscripts, the General Association of Netherlands Soldiers (AVNM) increased its membership from three thousand to eight thousand. The milder organization had been started as a direct result of what some conscripts saw as the excessive militancy of the older organization — an indication that even when men are forced to do their Army service compulsorily, they are not unanimously eager to throw in their lot with an anti-establishment line.

Neither the Netherlands nor the Swedish experience is a valid parallel for Britain, but they do tend to show that the idea of having the Army 'integrated' with civilian labour procedures is neither all profit nor all loss.

The argument about how healthy it is to think of the Army as part of the general community, and how politic it is to have it living entirely by its own (necessarily special) rules will go on into the twenty-first century and no doubt beyond. But though the very idea of either political or trade union action will raise temperatures and lower drink in any British Army mess, there have been mild flirtations with civilian philosophies and methods and in at least one of them the ardour was reciprocated.

The Army recently arranged an exchange of a young officer for a young executive in private industry. A marketing director went into the Army as a Major for six months, and a Major went into the private firm as a project officer with the special aim of examining communications within the company.

Some soldiers concluded that the Army had agreed to the scheme because it thought industry had a lot to teach it about efficiency in the modern world. In practice, there was some feeling, at the end of the exercise, that it was rather the Army which had a lot to teach private industry, certainly about how to make men motivated enough to work efficiently. At any rate, though both executive and Major recommended more exchanges, their suggestion was not acted upon. This seems a pity.

Does the Army deliberately cultivate its private language and its irritating plethora of strange initials in the hope that civilians will remain mystified and keep their distance? It may well have been true up to the Second World War and perhaps some time beyond it. But the Army's need to be understood and appreciated by a public increasingly manipulated by public relations experts and pressure groups in other spheres (a need made crucial by Northern Ireland) has had a significant effect on Britain's soldiers. They have become much more ready to put parts of their house on public view, and to welcome some civilians and civilian ways which might hitherto have been looked on with resentment or suspicion. Hence, perhaps, the exchange scheme, which may not remain on the shelf for ever. It *may* not have been repeated because of the Army's traditional suspicion of civilian involvement on anything except social lines; but equally it may not have been repeated because the Army felt it did not have much to learn by such means. One way or another, the ancient reticence asserted itself.

'I think that, because the Army still tends to be a bit remote and reticent, they don't present themselves very well to the public. The picture they conjure up is very different to what appears actually to happen in the Army,' said the seconded industrial executive afterwards. 'The Army's basic management philosophy is that *people* are generally important. I found that the fundamental thing about the soldier was that he really did believe that he was important, that things worked out better with him than without him. He had a sense of purpose and he felt he belonged.'

The idea for the revealing exchange came as the result of a discussion, at the Royal United Services Institute Leadership Seminar of 1977, between the Commander-in-Chief United Kingdom Land Forces and the Chairman of the holding company of the Bulmers Cider firm. The Commander-in-Chief thought it was a good idea to get men out and about, learning more about the world outside. The Chairman of Bulmers, which is a medium-sized firm, with a record of good staff relations, thought that the answer to Britain's problems lay in the field of 'personal leadership rather than scientific management'. He also thought that authoritarian management may have worked before the arrival of the welfare state in Britain, but that leadership was now essential to promote industrial achievement.

John Hings, the executive chosen for the exchange, was working as marketing director for Bulmers. He was thirty-four when he became an honorary Major attached to 6th Field Force, one of the Army's elite groups. He soon came to the conclusion that the remarkable thing about the sense of purpose in the Army was that it had been fostered in peace time, when the aims of soldiery were bound to be a bit nebulous. 'I am sure you can go through a whole life in the Army without ever seeing a bullet fired in anger,' he said. 'It must be significant that you can create this great sense of purpose without an end product, as it were — and you can. You can create this incredible will to win with fairly intangible goals.'

The reasons for this? They will bring very little comfort to those who believe that good labour relations require everyone to participate directly in decisions at every level — the blueprint for industrial democracy fashionable in some quarters.

'It is delegated authority, and giving people the opportunity to make decisions and influence things,' said John Hings. 'Also in the Army, there are very clear areas of demarcation. I favour that. There is the concept elsewhere that if you break down barriers you get closer to people. But, human nature being what it is, when you break down these barriers, artificial ones are put in their place automatically, because that is human nature.' Clear areas of authority could lead to better human relations, not worse.

The Army Major who was seconded to the firm reported at the end of the exchange that above the level of supervisor, loyalty within management was less apparent than in the Army. 'Managers sometimes seemed loyal to their company only to the extent that their personal aspirations matched those of the company,' he said, in a tone of surprise which might itself surprise many civilians. He felt that corporate loyalties would be much more solid if managers were to 'appreciate more the value of human resources, and the need for close and genuinely caring relationships'. In other words, as any entrepreneur in Britain's years of business success might have agreed at once, there *is* room for sentiment in business — a fact which has become increasingly clouded by Pavlovian enmity.

Both men thought that trade unionism, as it existed in civilian life, would not work in the Army. But John Hings said, some time after he had collaborated in the joint report, that although this might be true, it might not be quite the end of the matter. 'Perhaps trade unions as such wouldn't work,' he said. 'But there are opportunities for the equivalent of Employee Councils and that sort of thing. There could be forums created, whereby all ranks could have the opportunity of greater freedom of speech on certain matters, especially concerning welfare.'

In general, the Army still seems happier when dealing with human beings it can categorize in its own ranks and subject to military discipline on time-honoured lines. Many jobs are done for the Army by civilians, but the Top Brass of the Army is still troubled by 'Ifs'.

What *if* civilian workers alongside the Army went on strike? Civil servants, after all — and civilian workers with the Army are civil servants — *have* shown interest in industrial action. What *if* there was a sudden emergency that conflicted with the routine of civilian workers, which is to stay on one site and not follow the flag wherever it goes, like the soldier? After all, what would have happened when British soldiers were sent to police the second set of elections in Zimbabwe-Rhodesia, as it then was, *if* civilians had been doing vital jobs for them? Soldiers would have had to be found very quickly to do those jobs abroad — for the civilians would not have been posted overseas.

Even in non-sensitive jobs, the British Army is more comfortable when dealing with ex-soldiers who 'know the form' rather than with civilians with no military experience. Such ex-Army civilians pop up all over the place. The hotel for servicemen and their families and other visitors in West Berlin is called Edinburgh House. It is a mile or so from the Brandenburg Gate and East Berlin. The manager, when

I stayed there, was a retired Major who had been in the now defunct East Surrey Regiment for eighteen years and in the Royal Army Rifle Corps for four, before being retired when the Army was deliberately whittled down in the 1960s. His mother had wanted him to run a restaurant. He had pointed out that a restaurant would not provide an income for his whole family, and had suggested a hotel instead. He ran one on the south coast which got into the *Good Food Guide*. Later he took catering jobs in Kenya and Tanzania. When conditions got too difficult there, he went to the Officers Association, who were 'absolutely fantastic' and mentioned the Edinburgh House job. 'Gets you back into the Services orbit,' said the Major, in those clipped military tones so beloved of the older Army man and so rare among the high-fliers of today.

An ex-Major was certainly more likely to be attuned to the fine social distinctions of Edinburgh House, a hotel which otherwise could pass without comment as a quality hotel in a chain. Officers go to one part, Other Ranks to a (rather plainer) part of the establishment. No difficulty there; the dividing line is clear cut. Visiting civilians are a different matter. As a writer, I was considered 'of like status' to an officer, and put in the officers' part of the hotel. So I would have been as a schoolteacher. Had I been a miner, visiting my brother who was a Private soldier, I would have been put in the other ranks part of the hotel. What would have happened had I, as a writer or school-teacher, been visiting a brother who was a Private soldier, I cannot guess. Possibly the Major would have had a nervous breakdown.

Or possibly not. The Major had been able to draw on his considerable military and civilian experience to interpret military rules in the modern world. 'Status — awful word, wish we could get rid of it,' he said. 'We had a film crew staying here the other day — long haired weirdoes, some might say, but quite harmless, and no problem. Stayed in the officers' part, of course.'

An ex-Army man could be relied upon to make light of

such situations, and to keep the establishment on a steady course in all circumstances. When a vital zip fastener on my suit broke, the ex-Major's well-disciplined staff searched out a supply of safety pins with military thoroughness. Charterhouse and the Rifle Corps 'zip a chap up', as the ex-Major rather unfortunately put it, and give him a polish in carrying out the most unlikely tasks.

The demand for ex-Army people in civilian jobs connected with the Army is likely to expand, with unpredictable results. But in a Britain given increasingly in recent years to strikes and other industrial unrest, the Army may well be tempted to *encourage* its own exclusivity rather than make more gestures towards civilian ways. That outcome, not necessarily for the best, is more likely than the opposite: a rash meddling in social and political matters.

Fortunately for the Army there are other ways, colourful if less crucial, in which it can keep in contact with the British public and, indeed, the larger world.

15

For Queen and Tourist

'Occasionally there is a gang of passers-by who will criticize your boots in your hearing, to degrade you in front of their lady friends.'

— Coldstream Guardsman of The Queen's Guard outside St James's Palace.

'Ceremonial parade really calls for steadiness. If you can do this sort of thing, then when you go into battle it helps discipline.'

— Guards Major.

A piece of thread shorter than a little fingernail protruded from the top buttonhole of the Coldstream Guardsman's grey topcoat. In a few minutes he was due to be on guard outside Buckingham Palace, at almost the very time the Queen herself would be arriving. Definitely *not on!*

The Sergeant Major with the Inspecting Officer on the parade ground of Wellington Barracks, a stone's throw away from Buckingham Palace itself, made this view clearly felt. It involved a forefinger-to-chest harangue, in a growling purr that tourists in front of the railings couldn't hear, but which was calculated to send shivers down the spine of the nineteen-year-old Guardsman, with its suggestions of names being taken and charges being made if it happened again. The erring lad's face grew red and sweating under his tall black Bearskin.

'In ceremonial duties,' said the Sergeant Major afterwards, when the removal of the big black Bearskin from his head, and the insertion of a cigarette into his mouth, had reduced him to mortal proportions, 'people may sometimes get a little lackadaisical. You have to watch that. I told this one his coat must not show a single thread again. Yes, after they have been in the Queen's Guard for two or three years they may get lackadaisical. If they have threads showing *all over the place*, you would have to tell them to get the coat re-tailored.'

Take, said the Sergeant Major (eyeing my, to me, well-polished shoes carefully), boots. 'Look at my own,' he demanded. 'They wouldn't do for the start of a Guard, because I have been wearing them for three hours. When I come off duty in an hour's time, they will be cleaned again.' It was a dry, dustless day.

I said his boots looked fine to me; indeed that you could not only see your face in them, but also whether you were looking flushed or pale. 'Ah,' said the Sergeant Major sharply, bending his ankle, 'that's the toecaps. You can see they have dulled down at the *sides*. I consider your own shoes to be *clean*, but I wouldn't wear them if I were on Guard duty for the Queen.'

Every day of the summer, and every other day in winter, the Household Division of the British Army mounts Guard on the Queen at Buckingham Palace, and also on the Court at nearby St James's Palace. They do this irrespective of whether the Queen and Court are there or not: the main difference being that when she and it *are* there, the sentries do not stand alone but are doubled up. And every day, twenty-four hours a day, the Bearskinned (by day) or peak-capped (by night) Guardsmen mount Guard within the railings of the two Palaces, watched by hundreds of tourists all the time and many thousands of tourists when the Guard changes at the end of the two-hour spell of Guard duty that will last in all for twenty-four hours in the summer and forty-eight in the winter.

Why *within* the railings of the Palaces? The sentries used to stand outside, where they were easier meat for tourists with cameras. The general assumption is that security must have been behind the change. So, in a sense, it was, though the concern was for the security of the hard-working soldiers rather than that of the Monarch. The person who played the most crucial part in the behind-the-railings decision, if not the final one, was an amorous female. She was not a Queen. She was not even a British taxpayer. She was an overseas tourist, who just happened to be passing Buckingham Palace when she was in a vivacious mood.

'I understand,' recalled a high-ranking Guards Officer, 'that she insisted on what is colloquially called touching-up the Guard outside the Palace. Of course, that's just not on. When she did it for the third time, the Guard's boot or knee — reports differ — accidentally came into contact with her in a way she had not expected. It was too much. The Guards went inside the Palace railings, and carried two-way radios with them in case of trouble.'

This decision was taken by the Royal lady — Her Majesty the Queen — personally. One wonders how they would have explained the issue to Queen Victoria, and how the present Queen managed to keep a straight face when she was asked to pronounce on the difficulty. The incident was twenty years ago, when the Queen was comparatively new to the dignity of the throne.

Though other regiments may be called in to ease the pressure from time to time, the ceremonial guarding of the British Sovereign falls traditionally to what is called the Household Division — the Division, in other words, nearest to the Royal Household. It consists of the five Regiments of Foot Guards — the Grenadier Guards, the Coldstream Guards, the Scots Guards, the Irish Guards and the Welsh Guards, which together are spoken of as the Guards Division — *plus* two regiments which, together, are known as the Household Cavalry, the Life Guards and the Blues and Royals.

This may be a little difficult for the non-military man to grasp at first or, indeed, second reading. The Army has not fallen over itself in the past to make its labyrinthine niceties more accessible to the general public; perhaps, instead, preening itself on its private knowledge. There are further complications in understanding what the uniforms so beloved of the tourists actually *are*. The Guard at Buckingham Palace is called, appropriately enough, the Queen's Guard, and this is normally drawn (or 'found' in British Army parlance) from the Guards Division, though it may be found from any other regiment. The Queen's Life Guard (which might have some slight difficulty guarding the life of the Queen, as it is mounted at Horseguards, where the tourists are, but the Queen isn't) is normally found by the Life Guards and the Blues and Royals. But when the Queen's Life Guards are at summer camp, their deputies are the King's Troop, Royal Horse Artillery, a body which remains very much in force when the Monarch is female and there is no King. Is all that perfectly clear?

Ah, well! The British public probably loves such picturesque complications and inconsistencies: especially as it is not expected to remember them in detail, or even in general. Few could now tell a Grenadier from a Coldstreamer, and might not even *care* if their uniforms were both nice and bright. Pageantry is all: pageantry with a sense of nostalgic national pride for which there is, in modern Britain, an increasing shortage of emotional outlets.

'This morning,' said the Sergeant Major, who had successfully dealt with the matter of the thread, 'I noticed a little old fellow who took his trilby hat off to our Regimental Colours. That means an awful lot to him, to me and to the Guardsmen. Unfortunately there isn't a lot of that happening these days. You don't often see hats doffed to Colours when we are on Guard.'

It was a chilly day in November, with the wind cutting across Wellington Barracks parade ground and ruffling Bearskin furs and civilian hats, when I went to watch a Guard form up to replace those already in front of Buckingham Palace and St James's Palace. It would have been tempting to see the elderly ritual taking place as a sign that the Army itself — or at least the Household Division with its virtual monopoly of Queen's Guard duties — was still buried in its Imperial past and practices.

Behind the whole procedure on Wellington Barracks

parade ground, however, was a physical backcloth that neatly represented the philosophical backcloth to a quite different situation. Behind the ancient and untouched façade of Wellington Barracks, a new super-barracks was being built, with all mod cons, for about a thousand men. This was surely symbolic: behind the façades of the British Army as a whole can usually be found deft moves towards modernity.

All the same, the moves have been slowest in relation to ceremonial and Guard duties — slowest and proud of being slowest. Combine the rules of a shove ha'penny game in a Rutland pub with the ritual of a Masonic Lodge, add the rules of bridge and the figurations of a Viennese dance, and you would still have an inadequate picture of Army ceremonial ritual — the product of a history so long that even the people who act it out in the present day have forgotten half of it, or never known it. And you would be quite wrong if you assumed in consequence that behind the weird configurations and observances the needs of modern life — when even a Monarch's security could be at risk — are not being served.

But weird, if weirdly magnificent, it all does seem at just past ten o'clock on a windy November morning, with the Coldstream Guards forming up in front of Wellington Barracks with the Grenadier Guards band instead of its own — because bands and Guards are on different rotas, and do not necessarily coincide.

'The problem,' said the Major who was doing his best to explain it all to a windswept civilian, 'is that there are battalions who live out of London. All the Coldstream Guards live at Caterham. It isn't possible to mount a guard from Caterham, so they come down to Wellington Barracks and are mounted from here. If you are stationed in London like the Scots Guards, they can mount a Guard from their barracks at Chelsea and march down here.'

Meticulous integration was complicated by another factor. The 2nd Battalion of the Coldstream Guards were mounting Guard with their *own* Corps of Drums (which were in fact drums *and* flutes) and not with the Corps of Drums of the Grenadiers, who supplied the band. 'But, the Scots Guards and the Irish Guards, in addition to drums, have a pipe band, and if they decide to bring pipes on, then the Corps of Drums don't come on. You follow that? There is nothing obscure about it. Why don't bands always play with their own people? Sometimes bands are playing with other battalions somewhere or other. Or they are on an engagement overseas, or are on leave.'

It was now twenty to eleven, and the Adjutant, who is *called* the Captain, but is, as often as not, a Major, was involved in forming up the men with the Regimental Sergeant Major and the Drum Major (who was not, of course, a Major but an NCO). It was at this point that the Regimental Sergeant Major noticed the offending length of thread from the Guardsman's tunic, and I noticed that with the (sensible, it seemed to me) exception of one young man, who had his Bearskin chinstrap *under* his chin, all the rest of the Guardsmen had their straps hanging against the *front* of their chins, where their utility in keeping the Bearskin actually on the head on a windy day was, to say the least, obscure.

The solitary Coldstream Guardsman was, of course, the one who was wrong.

'The Blues and Royals,' explained the helpful Major, 'are the only ones who are supposed to have their chin straps *under* their chins. All the rest have them higher up the chin, with the exception, of course, of some of the flautists of the other Guards Regiments, who keep theirs lower so they can play their flutes better.'

Why the habit of *not* wearing the chinstrap in the way most likely to keep the Bearskin on the head?

'It is regimental custom. It has *always* been,' said the Major, politely veiling his impatience at civilian inability to understand. 'Probably they have got them a little lower today because of the wind,' he conceded. 'The Adjutant can give permission for this alteration to be done according to the weather.'

The next thing to be explained was the bringing on of the Regimental Colour. This was done as the band played incidental music which, though from a prescribed list, had more to do with tourist interest than military ritual. Army bands are justifiably proud of their repertoire, which they employ for civilian, as well as military, occasions. The Regimental Colour — a flag — was brought on by three Guardsmen walking briskly like clockwork toys, arms swinging rigidly as if made of wood. If the Nazi or Soviet goosestep conjures up mental pictures of rigid brutality, this British carrying of the Colour suggested the more genial atmosphere of Toy Town.

Was it quite, well, *military* enough for such a display? 'The Colour,' said the Major, 'is *always* brought out as quickly as possible on parade. The Colour, like all important things, is always protected very carefully. It is always brought into the picture in quicker time than anything else would be. Footguards march at 120 paces to the minute. They would bring on the Colour at around 130 paces a minute. The Russians, don't forget, do exactly the same sort of thing. All countries have their ceremonial Guards, and here it is also for the protection of the Monarch. *And* the Household Division has its two roles — it takes its place as fighting soldiers in Northern Ireland and elsewhere, as well as helping in the ceremonial role.'

The Guard, having formed up on the parade ground of the barracks, started to march over to Buckingham Palace. They met the usual scene in front of the Palace: a crowd of people, several lines deep, up against the railings, hugely enjoying it all in spite of the chilly wind. Inside the railings, the Guard who were about to be relieved were forming up into rows, at right angles to the Palace. They were Scots Guards, and their Regimental Colour, carried by the Ensign, had a laurel wreath on top of the pole.

'Today,' said the Major, 'there must be a battle honour due to the regiment. If a regiment mounts Guard on a day it can claim a battle honour, there is always a laurel wreath on the Colour.'

It was when the Coldstream Guards marched through the gates at the other end of the Palace forecourt, facing the Scots Guards like an opposing football team, that the discrepancy in the decoration of their Bearskins became apparent. Some men had red plumes, rather like dyed fox's tails in appearance, on the sides of their Bearskins. Some did not.

The explanation, it appeared, was 'straightforward'. The Coldstream Guards *always* wore red plumes on the right of the Bearskin, and the Scots Guards didn't have any plumes at all, the one cleaving with pride to its deprivation as the other did to its red display. The Grenadier Guards, on the other hand, had white plumes on the left side of their Bearskins, the same side as the Welsh Guards had their white-green-white plume; while the Irish Guards had a St Patrick's blue plume on the right. The fine points of the Queen's Guard extend from dress to etiquette. Woe betide the Guardsman, albeit a little bleary from a forty-eight-hour spell of duties or a late-night celebration, who does not remember it.

As it happened, at the same time as the two Captains of the Guard — the old one and new one — were going forward for the handing over of the ceremonial key (which does not fit any lock, but is purely ritualistic), the Queen's Life Guard (mounted) was returning from Horseguards, at the other end of The Mall, to Knightsbridge Barracks. This required the Life Guard to pass the Palace while the Changing of the Guard was going on in the forecourt.

It is vital to remember, in such a situation, who salutes who and who doesn't. As the Queen's Life Guard (though mounted and with all the bravura of a Cavalry history) was commanded by a non-commissioned officer, and not by a commissioned officer, it was the junior guard. As such, it had to give an eyes-left as it swept past the Palace railings, a sort of genuflection in the direction of the senior Guard inside the railings.

At this moment, the Queen herself was not actually in Buckingham Palace — she was due back from Windsor within the half-hour — and the nearest thing to actual Royalty on the forecourt was a lady from the Palace public relations department, charming and helpful as always in the face of questions from those unversed in Palace protocol.

Had the Queen actually been in the building at that time, it was gently explained, the etiquette would have been rather different. Both the Guards — old and new — in the Palace forecourt would then have presented arms *to* the passing Queen's Life Guard.

'If the Queen were in residence, the Queen's Life Guard would be the senior guard, because they would have an officer in command and they would have a Standard. And their Standard is senior to the Foot Guards' Colours. You must understand that Standards and Colours are the be-all and end-all, and are treated with great reverence. They are based on actual history, which still has a reality today. When President Nixon tried to dress up the White House Guard in different sorts of ceremonial uniforms, it didn't last long, because it had no real tradition.'

And, said the Major, tradition had to be adhered to, even when it was not strictly commercial. 'Otherwise,' he said dismissively, 'you might as well go along with the travel agencies who say, "Why don't you have this Changing of the Guard three times a day?" If we did that, against all real tradition, we might as well have television actors playing the Guards, with drum majorettes in front of them, and so on. It is tradition that matters. And look at all these people who have come to see it, even on a November day.'

Admirable sentiments in an often plasticated world. But the dividing line between tradition and wasted time is not always an easy one to delineate, for all that. Two Corporals, one from each Guard, hurrying along the Palace forecourt, while all the other Guards stood immobile, created great interest among the tourists. What were they doing? Going to inspect the sentry boxes to 'make sure they are not damaged in any way'. The vandalization of sentry boxes, since they were placed two decades ago *inside* the Palace railings, where only Guards themselves could get at them, is not believed to have been extensive. But the two Corporals still buzz around for the delectation of the public. And of course there *is* a practical benefit in it, especially since the security of the Monarch ceased to be taken for granted as the planted bomb became less of a stranger to London.

The sentries outside Buckingham Palace and St James's Palace, once the new Guard has been mounted, do not have an entirely ceremonial role. Though their guns are unloaded, they have 'access to ammunition', and would be available in an emergency to assist the Metropolitan Police, who have charge of all security matters. Not only are sentries doubled up when the Queen is in residence; after dark they abandon their comparatively clumsy Bearskins in favour of peaked caps and even carry walkie-talkie radios so that their patrol of the Palaces becomes, effectively, a security operation.

But at all times practical utility walks hand-in-hand with fine points of etiquette that would grace the *inside* of the Palace. To the casual eye, they have their quota of innocent comedy.

The method by which sentries, working as pairs, signal to one another is difficult to describe with a straight face, yet undoubtedly it works, and works with a commendable economy of means. When two sentries patrol, one is *always* the senior, even if he is senior by only a single day's service in the Army. If they are marching and the senior wants to halt in front of the other when they meet, he will extend one finger of his hand, and the next time around, the junior sentry will come to a halt in front of his senior. If an officer is seen approaching, the senior sentry will extend two fingers — not in the way that might be assumed by the light-minded, but by dangling the fingers down towards the ground. The junior sentry picks up the code. Both Guards go to their own sentry boxes, and salute the officer as he walks past.

The drill for ordering marching up and down, if both men are standing by their sentry boxes, is based on the ear rather than the eye. One tap of the rifle butt on the ground means: 'Do the ordinary Slope Arms and begin to march up and down.' If an officer is passing by, two taps indicate that they must get ready to salute as they stand in their boxes. And if the Queen herself comes back, or goes out, she gets three taps and a Present Arms.

The origin of these tappings and finger-extensions is lost in history. 'Just as much,' owned the Major, 'as why the Coldstream Guards have a red plume and a white band round their forage caps, while the Grenadiers have a white plume and a red band round *their* forage caps. No one has ever been able to tell me that, and I can't find it in any history book.'

Things — at least *some* things — about the Palace Guards have changed. As the Major put it: 'Before the war, when the Captains of the Guard went into Buckingham Palace, there was champagne for them. Now there is water.' But the Captain of the Guard, if there is an investiture, is still formally presented to the Queen, just as in pre-war days, when there were levées at the Palace and the King would probably swap military jokes with the Captain. And the officers' Bearskins are still reputed to be made from female bear (smoother) fur, while the men have male bear (though it is possible that both will have to accept plastic substitutes one day, if bears contract in number faster than the British Army and the price becomes ruinous).

The whole Changing of the Guard takes about an hour. Thereafter, the Guard maintained at the two Royal Palaces usually consists of one officer and twenty men when the Queen is there and one officer and seventeen men when she is not; two officers and twenty men at St James's when the Queen is there and two officers and fourteen men when she is not. One officer and twenty-one men mount Guard at the Tower of London — the number never varies because the Queen is *never* in residence there. At Windsor Castle, the Guard is one officer and twenty-one men, constantly. All this presents a very minor 'bill' for military personnel, compared with the tourist interest generated — quite apart from the practical utility in security terms. Only at the Bank of England has harsh modernity banished the Guardsman as sentry. The last Guard was mounted there by the Scots Guards in July, 1973, after which electronic eyes took over. Whether they have been more successful as deterrents is incapable of proof. They have certainly been inferior as tourist bait.

After the Changing of the Guard at the Palaces is over, the crowds outside thin out. The Colour of the new Guard is marched to St James's Palace, where it is *lodged* (heaven help the recruit who says merely *put*) in the Officers Guardroom of the Officers Mess Block. The Captain of the Guard works from St James's Palace. By tradition, provided one officer stays in mess there, in case of emergencies, other officers can walk across to Pall Mall and have a game of squash on the courts of the Royal Automobile Club. It *must* be the RAC. Once again, tradition and utility go more hand-in-hand than might, at first sight, be expected. The club sets the right sort of regimental tone, while being conveniently close to the Guardroom of St James's Palace should anything go amiss.

I was not allowed into the Guardroom at Buckingham Palace. This, I gathered, was partly because it was not thought seemly and partly because the arrangements there bear directly on the security of the Monarch. But I was told that accommodation in the building — to the left of the Palace itself — is fairly spartan. There is a telephone, ammunition, living accommodation with television set, a rest room and — believe it or not in a Royal Palace — a NAAFI. There is also a small kitchen with six tables.

At St James's Palace, there is rather more room for the men who do the hard work. The Officers Mess has a rather nice rest room, with plenty of regimental silver and plenty of young ladies popping over for lunch or tea to talk about the weather or other decorous matters. They have to be out by seven forty-five in the evening, when the mess becomes an all-male preserve. The men have fewer facilities for entertaining than the officers. Twenty of them sleep in one big room during their one- or two-day Guards; the Corporals, at four to a room, enjoy comparative luxury.

Do the men like the work? 'With soldiers straight from the Depot it is extremely popular work,' said a Guards Officer in the St James's Palace Officers Mess. 'They write home to Mum and tell her what they have been doing, and Mum comes down at the weekend and photographs them outside Buckingham Palace. It is extremely popular with them, at the start. But when battalions come back from abroad, having been three years away, there is no doubt that it is only human nature that, after what they have been doing abroad, the novelty of ceremonial wears off. And in the winter months, when there aren't vast numbers of tourists and pretty girls watching them, it is not quite so popular.'

A 2nd Lieutenant who had just changed out of his topcoat and was sweating profusely ('I'm just one of these revolting people who *do* sweat, I'm afraid — don't blame the dear old Bearskin') said that the whole emphasis on respect between officer and men had slightly altered in the Guards: 'One has to strive to maintain their respect by example and so on.'

The Captain of the Guards was a Major with eleven years' experience, a father who had been in the Army, a public school education and a quiet contentment with spending an estimated twenty per cent of his Army life on ceremonial (compared with fifteen per cent of it in Northern Ireland). He said that the day began at five-thirty. At that hour, the two Captains of the Guard — the one about to sign off and the one about to be mounted — would breakfast together. The day then involved inspecting the sentries at least twice; visiting the Guardrooms; television; meals and bed. 'We are very proud of the fact that we are fighting soldiers as much as the rest of the Army. We can shoot, do sports and go into battle like everyone else. But we can *also* do this ceremonial as well. Properly regarded, it is a demonstration of military efficiency.'

In the Guardsmen's room, there was something of the same keenness, though standing on sentry duty for two solid hours must inevitably become boring at times. What does the human being inside the tourist-trap uniform *think* about all that time?

A twenty-eight-year-old Guardsman with eight years' experience of the Guards volunteered the opinion that it was best not to 'get into too deep thoughts'. 'I have got to keep my wits about me,' he said, sitting rigidly to attention on the chair. 'The thing I tend to think about is my family, what I could be doing round the house, things like that. But I avoid deep thought. If something moves, my attention is there.' When Princess Anne was shot at in the early 1970s, when in her car in The Mall, this Guardsman was on duty at St James's Palace. He heard the shots. He stayed rigidly at his post, as is the rigid rule. But he could have been called upon in this very real emergency, even though his presence is ostensibly purely ceremonial.

The Guardsman admitted that if he was tired the two hours he was on sentry duty seemed like six: 'You have to listen to the clock chimes. That keeps you within some time limits. Sometimes at night and in the winter it is rather like being in a black box. You can't look at a wristwatch. But when there are tourists in the summer, it is quite interesting. You learn the customs of other peoples and their attitudes.'

The attitudes of strangers to London must indeed sometimes be difficult for the Queen's Guard, young men who *do* have highly stylized and strange uniforms but do *not* yet have the mellowness of maturity. One Guardsman gave his assessment of how the Queen's Guard of modern Britain was looked upon by other nationalities. Japanese were very polite. Italians were 'ignorant, and regard you as a clockwork soldier'. The Americans? 'One or two, you can see, are terrified of you, as you stand there with their wives posing beside you.' The French: 'They all seem to be children, and they giggle.'

Then there is a British domestic product, albeit a

minority: 'the young yobbo'. He is the young civilian who tries to prove his virility to his girlfriend by poking fun at the sentry, goading him to answer back. The yobbo's theory is that he will look brave because he is facing a fixed bayonet, irrespective of the fact that for the Guardsman to use his fist, let alone his bayonet, is about as likely as it is that the Monarch will herself get out of the brown Royal car for a bout of fisticuffs.

Sometimes honest, but too-confident, ignorance can sting the practitioners of British Army ceremonial more than quite deliberate baiting. A young Guardsman at St James's Palace admitted that he had once, and once only, lost his patience to the heinous extent of actually *talking back*.

The innocent offender was an American. 'Paw,' said the American's son, 'why are his boots so shiny?'

'Because they are made of patent leather.'

That was *too* much. The maligned robot pointed to them, and actually spoke. 'They are made,' said the Guardsman, 'of spit and polish.'

The visitors nearly collapsed. A Queen's Guard *talking?*

'I broke the code, I know,' said the Guardsman, as if admitting to a murder at very least. 'Not because I spoke, because we *are* allowed to speak, contrary to what people think. What we are *not* allowed to do is to gesture with the hand.'

The average Briton, tired and irritable after standing only fifteen minutes on a commuter railway station platform, must concede that, under such provocation, he would have made a *very* unforgivable gesture. But in Army ceremonial, as in battle, discipline is all and excuses do not exist. How many other occupations could claim as much?

16

In Conclusion

It would be misleading to leave the British Army to the sounds of a ceremonial fanfare. Ceremonial is just the icing on the cake.

What of the cake itself? Civilians in Britain, other NATO countries and the potential opposition will want to know whether, and in what ways, the British Army has changed since Britain ceased to be a colonial power. Is the British Army man of today and tomorrow essentially different in character, calibre and class from the one who fought to keep the American Colonies, won the Crimean War, guarded the old North-West frontier of India, inspired Kipling and others, died at Ypres and survived at Dunkirk? And how well suited is he to assure Britain's safety in a much changed world?

In one sense, the British Army man is no different at all. He is still constantly faced with instant yes-no decisions that may mean life or death. It is the essence of his job. Mercifully, it is not the essence of the writer's. To come to rapid conclusions about the British Army with the same decisiveness that a soldier might have to display in Belfast or Belize today, or Bielefeld or Bournemouth tomorrow, would be rash. It is too diverse for easy generalization. What may be true about one section (most Guards Officers come from public school) may not be true of another (in the technical corps, more officers are coming up through the ranks). Nevertheless some threads of thought did emerge. After exposing oneself to the danger of being shot or blown up in Northern Ireland, or being bitten by something nasty in the jungles of Belize, to go in fear of intellectual sniper fire would be a sad anti-climax.

From the point of view of involvement with the lives of British citizens, the Army's role, in what remains of the twentieth century and beyond, is likely to become more rather than less significant. For years the Army has been almost invisible to the eye of the average civilian, until to some it may have come to seem a little-needed anachronism. Right or wrong, this view is unlikely to survive.

The Army has been drawn willy-nilly to public attention in several ways. It has manned vital public services such as ambulances, fire engines and dustcarts during industrial disputes and been seen in this context, by the general public and by many trade unionists themselves, as a convenient and benevolent force. The more militant trade unionists, whatever their intentions, have *de facto* given the Army publicity worth millions of pounds in public relations terms. It has come to public attention in Northern Ireland where, whatever the British public may think of the rights and wrongs of the situation politically, the British soldier has been seen to be steady, temperate, firm and courageous in his professional response to that painful scene.

Perhaps the most basic reason for the heightened awareness of the importance of the Army has been the train of events in Afghanistan, Poland and elsewhere; events which have dramatized the bald statistical fact that the Warsaw Pact countries have now more or less got the three-to-one advantage in conventional warfare methods that any invader needs to be reasonably sure of success (or about nine times what is necessary for mere defence). They have got this advantage, moreover, in conditions where it is unlikely that Russia will strike directly at America with a nuclear bomb because her own cities would be at risk; unlikely that America would strike directly at Russia with a nuclear bomb because of a similar retaliatory fear; and correspondingly *likely* that conventional forces, such as the Army, would be more important in the nuclear impasse, not less.

Any discussion of what sort of animal Kipling's heirs are today will arguably take place against this backcloth: that the British Army's importance in the next fifty years will be seen as increasing rather than diminishing, perhaps considerably so.

The focus of this book has been people rather than weapons, because the identity of people tends to be more enduring than that of machines — especially machines of war, which become obsolete fairly fast, sometimes faster than they can be used. One type of soldier, too, has become obsolete: the military twit, the one with a vacuum between his ears and air where his chin should be. He is dead or dying and the Army itself is doing much to speed the parting guest. Indeed it could be argued that the Army has done as well as the rest of Britain — in some respects rather better — in adjusting to the fact that Britain is no longer a colonial power with world sway. It has cut its coat according to its diminished cloth with some ruthlessness and lack of self-deception. It has become smaller, leaner and far more professional; while at the same time consciously striving to retain the individuality conferred by its traditions. It still tries to implant the thought, '*Our* regiment is the best', because of its conviction that men will still fight better for a 'family' than for a large impersonal organization. Unless the human brain and heart have conveniently altered their shape in a generation or so, to tailor themselves to the nuclear and micro-chip age, can the Army be dismissed as quite wrong on this point? It has been possible to pooh-pooh the regimental or school House spirit at a time when war has been, quite rightly, abhorred and when, perhaps less correctly, the prospect that war might be forced on even a contracted and peaceful Britain has not been taken seriously. It will be interesting to see whether the desire to cheer 'our team', and believe in its history and personality, will seem quite so ridiculous, even to intellectuals, as the character and standards of the West come increasingly under siege, and the real effects of it are felt. It is interesting that the Americans are considering the introduction of some sort of regimental or regional system into their Army.

The British Army is now an amalgam of very old traditions (such as the virtual autonomy of The Regiment) and much newer concepts (such as women carrying guns for personal defence and the development of the SAS as a long range penetration group with obvious if incidental uses in anti-terrorism). In general, the social dividing line between the officers and the others is just as absolute in the 1980s as it was in the Boer War. It is still unthinkable that either part of the Army could use the mess of the other. The fence is still firmly there. But it can be, and is, vaulted more easily and more often. A far higher proportion of commissioned officers have been NCOs and 'crossed over' than was the case thirty years ago. But such officers are almost always in Support roles rather than Combat roles. Effectively, unless he became commissioned very early, there is no chance that a private soldier could ever become the Chief of General Staff — a post that needs a personal background including a great deal of Combat Arm experience.

There seems little doubt, too, that selection of officers still rests greatly on the 'right' school; and in practice this means boarding school, which in turn almost always means public school and, in some regiments, a major public school. Of course such schools may, as it is claimed, do most to foster a knock-about toughness of spirit which the Army needs, but is there really a simple and almost *magic* connection between the particular institution and the particular human quality? At least to one civilian it did seem that rather too many people who were to screen officer recruits in arduous practical tests were told *beforehand* what school the boy had gone to. Why not let performance speak rather more for itself? Nevertheless it is true that a large minority (forty-five per cent) of those who pass the Regular Commissions Board come from state maintained schools.

It could hardly be claimed that the British Army reflects the whole of the present-day society in which it exists; but then no profession does. It is still an occupation for fairly tough, extrovert and non-self-analytical personalities who can rig up a temporary bridge with planks, scale a high fence that would defeat the average civilian and, in the last analysis, take on any enemy face to face and with bare hands. It is no mystery that the average soldier is not the most appreciated citizen of the average academic or other person whose life depends on communication rather than action.

If the social background of many male Army officers is a fair subject for debate, the way the Army has used women will commend itself to the proselytizing Ms. It has set itself, so far, against using women as combat troops, though in November 1980 it was announced that women would in future be armed for personal defence only. This decision was well in line with sentiments expressed to me by members of the Women's Royal Army Corps previously: many said that they loathed the thought of picking up a rifle to shoot somebody, but could easily imagine themselves in situations where, although they were not combat troops, they might have to shoot to protect themselves. Other countries, including some within the Warsaw Pact, use women as combat troops. How the situation will develop in the British Army during the rest of the century must be a matter of some speculation. The fact remains that I did not find one woman soldier attracted to the idea of being a combat soldier.

I did not find many woman soldiers, either, who were seriously dissatisfied with their present lives in the Army. Some wives of soldiers were a different matter. Given the fact that more women in civilian life are insisting on being judged on their own qualities, and not on the status of their husbands, it is not becoming easier for Army wives to accept the life of an hierarchical institution (even if a strictly defined hierarchy often makes it *easier* for a man to adjust). Army wives are still apt to be treated according to their husbands' rank. The Army points out, justifiably, that the same sort of thing happens in civilian life: would the wife of a junior manager really be on Christian name terms with the wife of the chairman? Perhaps not; but the issue might present itself only once or twice a year, at the office party.

In the Army, wives are more apt to live on top of one another, and correspondingly more likely to have any latent irritations aggravated. The problem of how to maintain necessary military discipline while allowing Army wives to be 'more themselves' (including having more freedom to choose their own curtains and carpets) may be one of the most important ones faced in the next few years, as women's influence becomes more pronounced in surrounding civilian fields.

Adjusting to trade union power may not be so difficult. Though the idea of trade unionism in the Army has been canvassed by some trade unionists, it has not got very far, and is not likely to. Some officers and men claimed that one of the reasons they joined the Army was to get away from the power of the trade unions, which they saw as being more unpredictable than that of the Army itself. The Swedish Army, the most often quoted example, may have trade unionism of a kind; but it is not generally understood that there are restrictions on trade union power there which make direct comparison invalid.

Nor is the highly theoretical possibility of a military coup to take over political control of Britain likely to present much of a problem in practice. Presented with a politician or a political issue, the British Army man's instinctive reaction is to stiffen his upper lip so much that speech is impossible, or dive under the nearest table. Non-involvement in politics is inculcated more than precautions against venereal disease. It is possible, however, that the Army could be drawn more into the defence of a democratically elected government threatened by violence of any kind, including violent revolution. But my impression was that it would have to be *dragged* into even this by, as it were, a clear public demand that the police should have support in their normal duties of keeping the peace.

There can be little doubt that the British Army's relations with the civilian public are improving. Its public relations techniques are better and its will to put itself across effectively is increasing. A pendulum swing in public mood, away from the assumption that passive postures always ward off trouble, and towards a greater respect and admiration for the man of action as distinct from the man of (often discredited) words could help bring about a radical change in the view taken of the British Army.

It could well help bring the Army back to an honoured place in British society, a place it has not perhaps known since Britain started sadly disengaging herself from the biggest empire the world has ever seen or (if the world is careful) will ever see again.

17

Falklands Epilogue

I was proved right sooner than I expected. In the last chapter of *Soldiering On*, I predicted that international and even domestic events were shaping up in such a way that the British Army could again achieve an honoured place in British society after well over a generation of near invisibility and public neglect. The Falklands conflict, in a quarter of the world neither I nor anyone else had expected to be explosive, gave a great and possibly decisive thrust to that change in public status.

'There is nothing worse,' said an officer in the highest echelon of the Army, 'than an Army which has to say, "We haven't actually fought since 1582." The Falklands campaign certainly removed us from that danger.' A General told me, 'The most important result is that at present there are a lot of Army chaps on the Army Board (the Army's highest link with Parliament) who have seen action in Cyprus, Kenya and so on, but have never seen action in a real war. In future there will be a leavening of people on the Army Board who *have*. That has tremendous implications'.

The Falklands narrative has been told and re-told time and time again already. No doubt it will be told many times more for the benefit of incredulous grandchildren. But the long-term significance of the whole operation was that it was a proving-ground British soldiers have not known since the Korean war. That was just after the Second World War, well over a generation ago.

'The post-colonial activities of Cyprus, Aden and so on were not all-out modern war as it is understood,' said an officer lower down the hierarchy but with Falklands experience. 'Neither are the Army's activities in Northern Ireland, which have been in a security, peace-keeping role. Yes, modern weapons have been used, but it is not modern warfare as it is thought to be. In the Falklands, there was experience of being under bombardment, in mine warfare and in air contact with the enemy. You had people growing up very quickly and understanding how they had to handle a cold, hostile environment and a professionally-equipped enemy — because they *were* professionally equipped, whether they were capable of fighting or not.'

What had been proved, said this officer, was that 'the British young man today is just as fine as he ever was in the days of his grandfather' and that the realistic training faced by British troops was justified.

The Falklands also put one more nail in the coffin of the comfortable theory that, in the so-called push-button warfare era, the nuclear umbrella is a sufficient protection on its own. Conventional weapons — even those sometimes thought to be out of date — played their successful part for Britain in the Falklands as they have been doing for other nations elsewhere. A battalion of the Parachute Regiment no longer had heavy machine guns on their current inventory, but raided the regimental store for some to take to the South Atlantic.

'They proved,' said one of the officers of the battalion, 'that even in modern warfare you still need something between the heavy gun of a tank and an ordinary rifle if you want to punch your way through.'

Even bayonets were used by some British troops, apparently with success. But was the lesson a false one? Was the Falklands conflict a one-off chain of events which had no real bearing on Britain's ability to defend its territory in more vital areas and to meet its most important defence commitment to NATO in a divided Germany where East and West face one another directly? Officers scoff at the suggestion. They maintain that, on the contrary, the Falklands might even revise the military philosophy of the

British Army, and of others in NATO, along this front line.

In my earlier visits to Germany, talking to British troops, I never came across the slightest suggestion that *offensive* action was even considered, let alone contemplated. Most military men believe that this outlook is valid in its major implication — the West is *not* going to invade the Warsaw Pact countries. But many now believe that the Falklands precipitated an awareness that the concept of offensive action may have a certain value even on the East-West German border. 'If you are going to *re-take* ground which has been lost,' said one high-ranking officer after returning from the Falklands, 'you must be familiar with the concept of offensive action. I wonder if we have borne this sufficiently in mind. Careful thought must be given to this in the training of our troops in NATO.'

British forces re-taking the Falklands had one powerful advantage that was perhaps unusual: the readiness of a rugged and resolutely patriotic civilian population to give what help they could. One civilian who had bunked down with relatives fifteen miles outside Port Stanley after the Argentinians arrived told me, 'One night after a game of Monopoly we turned in for the night. The electricity generator was turned off and was on its last chug when the city was lit up by flares, machine gun and automatic weapon fire. After a few minutes of hugging the floor everyone ended up in the kitchen. Presently there was a loud bang at the door. "Who's there?" we shouted. "Open up — British Army!" came the reply. It must have been the SAS and what a relief! The next day an advance patrol of the 3rd Battalion the Royal Parachute Regiment arrived. We had seen them advance during the afternoon. They slept outside in the clothes they wore and arrived in full the next day with supporting tanks. They had walked across the island. Are you surprised, after that, to hear that the list of materials taken forward by civilians to the front line was endless? On several occasions they came under artillery and mortar fire.'

Such events must stir the blood of those who hear about them, just as they will stay always in the memory of those who actually experienced them. But no doubt there will be many British and other civilians who will dismiss military action on a frozen little group of islands, 8,000 miles from home, as too unrepresentative to have any real lessons for the future.

Military men do not agree. The Marines, who played their part in retaking the Falklands, were used to training in Norway, where conditions can be even worse. One of the commanders of the Royal Parachute Regiment told me on his return that he and his men had not been asked to do anything they hadn't been prepared for in training: keeping going in difficult conditions, in all weathers, by day and by night; and assaulting difficult features of the terrain. It is easy to see that these abilities, perhaps enhanced by the Falklands experience, would have a value elsewhere.

While Infantry can capture territory — and did so in the Falklands — artillery was diagnosed as the winning factor. The Argentinians cracked, it is held, because they were outflanked. They knew that the fearsome Gurkhas were on their way and Argentinian conscripts were no match for them; and, far more significantly, because they had taken 6,000 shells in the previous twelve hours and couldn't take any more. (British soldiers said they were angry with some media suggestions that the Argentinians were tin-pot opponents: it degraded their own efforts to beat them.)

'If you get your artillery and your heavy weapons, then you stand some chance of taking on the best-prepared defensive positions,' said one officer. He dismissed any notion that the Russians automatically would have the winning hand in Germany because they were thought to be capable of saturation barrages ('Could they *really* do this in a mobile war, and would they want to do that to land over which they later hoped to advance?'). But he added, 'In many ways what happened with our artillery in the Falklands is interesting and has to be talked about in the context of the British Army of the Rhine. If you think about it logically, if you are going to recover territory, you must think about offence. The Falklands has opened up this dialogue and encouraged people to re-examine old lessons in the light of experience.'

The lessons were not only in military technique. There were also those in human relations. For the men who took part these may have been just as important. Certainly they were just as memorable.

Some officers in the campaign had to cope with the strains and complications of a civilian organisational life intensified a hundred times and set against a background of acute physical danger. There were moments of truth for many thinking men. Perhaps the most testing moments came after a critical early stage of the battle for Goose Green, with the death of Lieutenant-Colonel H. Jones, commander of the 2nd Battalion of the Parachute Regiment. Jones was a tough and inventive officer whose death left a painful vacuum, especially in the eyes of the Ministry of Defence in London, who at that point were working on less than perfect intelligence. A Lieutenant-Colonel of the Regiment who had been working on the Intelligence side in Whitehall was rung up at the weekend and informed he would take 'Colonel H's' place. He would be taken by boat and plane to the South Atlantic and then be parachuted into the ocean near the Falklands. There he would wait until he was picked up.

In the meantime, Colonel H's number two had assumed command of the Battalion. He had fought a bloody but successful battle at Goose Green where, without the fire support available later, he brought through almost all his men. The arrival of the new man was a situation full of personal and professional explosiveness for both officers: the one who had fought a successful battle after stepping into dead man's shoes during the shooting and the man who was sent out, at no little risk to himself, to replace the man whom the Battalion regarded as their leader by grace of battle, if not by grace of the regimental hierarchy and the Ministry of Defence.

'It took me about forty-eight hours to get down there,' said the Lieutenant-Colonel. 'You take everything one step at a time in this sort of situation. I knew the Battalion had had a hard battle down there. I knew they had casualties and I knew that Colonel H had been killed. We were friends: his wife and children were coming to us for supper that night. I had never jumped into the sea before. I was flopping around in the water in my big orange waterproof suit waiting to be picked up. But when I arrived I knew a lot of people in 2 Para. More to the point, they knew me. When I arrived at Goose Green, they were unshaven, no two soldiers were dressed alike, but it was still like coming home. But I was acutely aware, at that point, that the experience of Goose Green had united them into a close-knit unit and that I was an outsider coming in.'

He employed tact, though under great pressures. 'I had a long talk with him about it. He was quite naturally — though he never said as much to me — extremely disappointed that he was not keeping the command. One of the things that struck me was that there was no way I was going to take over at that moment. Anything to do with the move up to Bluff Cove, which he had planned in detail, he was commander for, and I was learning myself into the situation. My arrival was not a lack of confidence in him. I think we are close friends now, really. We agreed that, whatever one's personal feelings about it all were, it was the Battalion that mattered. In the Army we are different from civilian life. One does have a very strong sense of loyalty both to the Battalion and to your subordinates as well as your superiors — which you don't have in civilian life. It is a family; and the family comes first. And it was war and people were dying out there. If one was going to have friction at the top, more people were going to die — you start making the wrong decisions and soldiers are going to be killed.'

The Lieutenant-Colonel won the confidence of the displaced Major by allowing him command of his own plans to take Bluff Cove; and of the battalion as a whole by telling them that he would not commit the battalion to battle again without the firepower to support their advance.

The Major, whom I later saw at Aldershot enjoying a snifter in the mess bar with the same Lieutenant-Colonel who had deposed him, found the experience just as testing. It was a day after the battle of Goose Green when a soldier asked him: 'Are you going to stay as CO, sir?'

'Until then it had never occured to me that someone would replace me,' admitted the Major. 'When the Colonel actually arrived he said, "I am terribly sorry this has happened." I said, "It doesn't matter, you are here and we have a job to do. Let me do the operation on Bluff Cove and when we get established in Bluff Cove I will be a loyal second-in-command." He came, with humility, to understand very clearly the delicate situation that existed.'

The Major, an ascetic-looking man with prematurely white hair was sustained by his Catholic beliefs. He told me that he thought General Galtieri was invested with evil and that evil must be resisted. He told himself, when the bullets were still flying, that whatever happened to him would be a happy outcome: if he died he would go to heaven and if he lived he would go back to his family. Few civilians are as philosophically and morally proofed against the dangers and pitfalls of their trades. 'I regarded the whole affair as very valuable spiritual experience, and I regarded it as such while it was going on,' he told me. 'There is no doubt that, through suffering, one does spiritually develop.' He dismissed the idea that his personal professional disappointment had been part of the suffering ('I honestly didn't think about my future. I am still not concerned in the slightest about how it will affect my personal career.') but he would be less than human if that were totally true. He would be less than human too, if he did not enjoy the high decoration for gallantry which he was later to receive.

Officers of the Battalion assured me they were largely too busy thinking and planning to feel afraid, but for NCOs and men the professional and personal problems faced were more directly concerned with sheer physical courage. 'The men did their jobs without chaos because of the drills taught to them,' a Platoon Sergeant told me. 'But it is good for people to know they can actually work under fire. You can be the best soldier in the world, but until that has happened, you don't know what you will do if you see men shot around you. At Wireless Ridge when the artillery came in, I just hit the deck and I know it sounds silly — I covered my head with my hands although I had a helmet on. I got up and one of the soldiers of the platoon was dead. I had lost two men before that, at Goose Green. You feel mournfulness because you knew the person, and you start to feel hate for the enemy, but you just carry on.'

The reaction of a Section Commander, a Corporal, was similar. He was injured in the back by a shell on Wireless Ridge: 'I remember crawling into cover. The adrenalin was still running in my bloodstream; you don't feel the pain. There was so much happening; you don't know what has happened to you till after. The adrenalin started to flow, and I didn't care a damn. That is what the name of the game is. We are about the best fighting soldier you will get, this Regiment. We are all screwballs, squibs, fireworks. These blokes don't give a damn. We call anyone who is not a Para, Crap-Hats. We call the Marines Cabbage-Heads.'

But the man at the very sharpest end in battle — the Private Soldier — was far from totally thoughtless about the danger, even in the Parachute Regiment. It was just that the specific effect of danger, and the sight of death and mutilation, varied sharply from man to man.

At one extreme, one twenty-three year old Private told me: 'I have changed. I am not interested in the Army any more.' I probed for reasons. He had been machine-gunned in a valley when moving up towards Darwin and seen one man killed and two injured. But that did not seem to be the reason for his apathy. He thought there was a need in the Parachute Regiment for more specialised training in the ranks. But that sounded more like a rationalisation than a reason. Finally he came out with the remark that seemed to me to be significant: 'It has lost all its shine now, the

Army. When I got back it took me ten minutes to decide — the first parade. It wasn't for me. I had the feeling I had been here before. I feel I am wasting my time now.' Battle, it seemed to me, had made him full of ironical scorn for spit-and-polish.

A twenty-one year old Private who had been wounded in the chest and buttocks in the 'worst experience of my life' thought it was 'just a job to do, and you get on with it. I am still the same soldier, just a bit more experienced, that's all.' He too, was machine-gunned at Goose Green. He had four years of a six-year contract in the Army still to run, which did not seem to depress him. But he said he would not sign on again. 'I think six years is enough. I wouldn't get married in the Army, because of the chance of anything that might happen.'

The third Private soldier felt that the Falklands had been a positive experience. He was nineteen and had just signed on for nine years, *after* the Falklands campaign. 'The Falklands affected my decision quite a lot,' he told me. 'I have always wondered which way I would behave under fire, and whether I would be able to keep firing back. I found it just comes naturally. I was under fire just outside Goose Green. I was just thinking it was an exercise, only then I saw people being killed. And then I realised they were trying to kill *me*. It made me feel more aware. I was excited more than anything, and frightened at the same time. I was sweating and breathing heavily. It lasted for ten minutes. I have grown up an awful lot.'

In what way? 'I suppose I was more violent down-town before I went out to the Falklands. Now you just laugh in people's faces when they try to take the piss. Now I wouldn't get involved with anyone who wanted to get violent. There's no point. I have proved I can do my job.'

A twenty-two year old Lance Corporal said he was more sensible about money matters since he came back from the Falklands; drank less; played more squash and looked after himself better. A Company Commander was sceptical about public-house fights being a thing of the past, but thought the men had definitely matured. 'Yes, there are fewer fights than there would have been. But on the other hand, the public response to these men is different to what it would have been before. They find the police are more tolerant, and so are the general public, who might previously have taken offence and provoked fights. Certainly around Aldershot, there used to be a distinct feeling that the Army people were a bloody nuisance, for all the fact that Aldershot owes its living to the Army. I think that, now, a lot of the local population are *proud* to be associated with the Army.'

There is no doubt at all that the Falklands conflict hastened to an unexpected degree the British Army's slow march to the greater public appreciation I foresaw. This could have a practical value to the general public as well as to the Army itself. An Army with a spring in its step is a vital component of any country's defence, even in a nuclear age. The Falklands are hardly the worst trouble zone for Britain that could be imagined, but even the Falklands could lead to future problems.

They have certainly led to problems — and great resource in the officers and men who have had to solve them — in the present.

What, then, is it like for the 3,000 or so men of the British Army on the Falklands, who in some areas outnumber the local population by well over two to one?

For those who guard important installations and monitor air movements it can be, as one officer put it, 'like working with World War Three equipment in World War One conditions'. They live in trenches for their period of duty and when off duty adjourn to one of the alternative modes of living that the Falklands offers its servicemen; the portable cabins like those used as builder's site offices or lavatories at gymkhanas: aboard ship, or on floating accommodation modules like those seven-storey living cubes used on oil rigs in the North Sea.

The conditions in which these particular men live are probably the most demanding experienced by the perma-

336

nent garrison there. But the merest glance over the terrain is enough to make any civilian realise that the conditions and the demands must sometimes be claustrophobic and confining.

Getting there is a gruelling experience in itself. The people who do it more easily are visiting Ministers or men (and supplies) in top-priority demand. They fly by VC10 to Ascension Island, which takes them eleven hours. At Ascension Island they have an overnight stop in portable cabins. Then they are taken on to Port Stanley by Hercules troop carrier plane, refuelling in the air once or twice on a 10,000 foot controlled dive, which can be a nerve-racking experience for Prime Ministers and Privates alike. They land in Stanley thirteen hours after take-off on the way out and ten hours on the way back to Ascension, since for the return journey they are assisted by the trade winds.

These are the lucky people. For the average officer or soldier on his way to a posting, its maximum five months may include nearly a month's travelling time. He will have the eleven-hour flight to Ascension Island like the VIPs, will stay in the portable cabins there but will then go aboard one of the two ships that ply between Ascension and Port Stanley, for a journey that will take ten days. He will then face a terrain which in bad weather would strike the average civilian as woe-begone and, even in good weather, not immediately inspiring.

There are five identified wrecks in Port Stanley Harbour, one of them a three-masted sailing ship, others acting as reminders of more recent perils. Moody Brook Camp, near Wireless Ridge, which used to be the garrison for the forty Royal Marines Britain mistakenly thought sufficient to symbolise the British commitment to the Islands, is a pile of rubble with a single square chimney stack — the only recognisable thing left — standing bizarrely on its unsupported own like a totem pole.

The men who march in or march out at Port Stanley — rather as they would do at the beginning and end of their duty in Northern Ireland or anywhere else — observe that there is only one 'good' road ('*Good* is a relative term,' pointed out one officer) on the Islands. This runs six miles from Port Stanley, would be classed as an average country road in Britain, and has taken a heavy battering from heavy military vehicles — first by the Argentinians' and then by the British.

It was handy that the Argentinians left behind them a number of Mercedes four-wheel-drive vehicles similar to British Land Rovers; but in practically everything else the Army has had to graft onto the islands (which have less than a 2,000 civil population) a garrison and back-up equipment for 3,000 men — slightly more than that in the Antarctic summer, when major building work is are carried out.

Even apparently simple things could conceal logistic trip wires. There was no laundry on the islands because much of the laundering was done in Argentina. The military created a tented one near Wireless Ridge. Here heavy washing and dry cleaning can be done where it has not been possible for the Ministry of Defence to get the work done under contract by local citizens.

There were never more than three pubs in Stanley; there are now only two. This means that units have had to arrange their own clubs. Usually this has been done in one of the massed portable cabins which have become a conspicuous element of island life, and will probably remain so until Whitehall makes up its mind about long-term accommodation — a decision which may take two or three years.

Months after the end of hostilities, more than half the soldiers on the Falklands were living on a ship moored in the middle of the harbour, having to be 'bussed' backwards and forwards to duty. Hundreds of others were in the portable cabins, eight to ten men to a cabin, with only a locker and box for personal belongings and an outdoor walk for any man wishing to go to the washroom or lavatory (usually arranged in a separate portable cabin within a hundred feet of the other cabins).

The reason for this was not, I was assured, that the Army had not vigorously attacked the problem of providing decently for its men. It was because they had had to start from scratch. Around Christmas 1982, a floating accommodation module, similar to the ones used on oil rigs, was in use, moored alongside land and housing 300 soldiers. A further one was on its way. But in the foreseeable future, some soldiers may have to accept a life within a portable cabin or a ship as the status quo, easing their frustration with the two-pints-a-day beer ration.

Senior officers point out that it is not totally dissimilar to what has been going on for years in Northern Ireland; indeed, that in some ways, it may be better than life in Northern Ireland. First, no one is likely suddenly to snipe at them. Secondly, because of this factor, accommodation can be spread out more, whereas in Northern Ireland, a military post has to be as small as possible to present the smallest target to an attacker, and so men are often crammed together cheek by jowl.

Two thousand men of the garrison are now in the Port Stanley area, but spread out in a way which probably makes it better both for them and for the local population who are doing their best to assimilate them: with grateful cordiality on high days and holidays, with occasional irritation at other times. There are only 900 islanders in Port Stanley and at the end of the fighting, they were living side by side with about 4,000 British troops, most of them now withdrawn or dispersed to other areas.

One officer said defensively: 'It may seem to civilians that we have been very slow in getting things off the ground. But, bearing in mind the state the place was in, and the fact that 4,000 troops were here with housing adequate for the 900 citizens, it is not too bad. There was a parallel situation at the end of the Second World War. I lived in Portsmouth, and it was four years after the war ended before they cleared all the defensive minefields and six years before a road closed to the public at the beginning of the war was reopened for public use. I would say we are now moving as quickly as we possibly can.'

Given the difficulties, it is small wonder that there are

occasional grumbles by troops. One wrote anonymously to a newspaper alleging that officers had swiped their beer and food to give a party for the local population to which they themselves were not invited. But senior officers said they had no evidence to support the assertion and that they would be surprised if men's beer had to be taken to entertain other people. They had never seen anything to make them think such allegations could be true.

What does appear to be true is that, although soldiers are kept pretty busy (it is the written command from on high that every man should have 'not less than one half-day' of his seven day working week free for leisure activities), there is little for them to do in their free time except sit on their beds and read (books have been flown in by the hundred) or drink their beer ration, or brood on the possibility that they have drawn the short straw and that other people in the Army are having a rather better life than they are.

'It is quite simple really,' said one officer. 'There are no girls on the island.' That is to say, those on the island are local civilians who are probably either married or betrothed and in effect strictly out of bounds for the soldier wanting an evening out or more. The mere thought of having a brothel or anything approaching it on the Falkland Islands, especially in the winter, is as ludicrous as the thought of open air Morris Dancing in the Arctic. Weekend trips to the nearest towns are out, as these happen to be in Argentina.

In these circumstances, grievances can receive a powerful physical impetus, which the Army is trying its best to soothe by keeping possible pretexts down to the very minimum. But there is no doubt that, for quite some time, conditions will be more like field conditions than is normal in the British Army, and that four months' stay on the islands at a stretch is about as much as any man can be asked to do. For some men, the turn-around is even quicker than that; specialists may be there for only a matter of a fortnight or so.

At the higher levels of command, life is rather less

physically challenging. The Commander himself now lives in a wood chalet which used to be the offices of the Argentine airline. The military headquarters itself is located in one of the few big buildings which was already on the island. This is a hostel for boarding children at Port Stanley. It was never accepted for that use, and had stood empty for some years. It looks rather like a provincial telephone exchange; but, at a time when at least 300 British soldiers were still living in tents, its aesthetic shortcomings were not widely commented upon. What is much more depressing is the fact that practically the only beautiful trees left on the islands are those around Government House.

Housing the headquarters was less of a problem than housing the injured and ill. Port Stanley's single hospital was barely adequate for the local population, let alone the 3,000 troops sustaining the usual 'industrial' injuries or stepping occasionally onto mines that remain the sick heritage of the brief Argentinian occupation. The hospital has now been ringed around with the ubiquitous portable cabins and is run by a civilian doctor and an officer of the Royal Army Medical Corps.

The winter of 1983 shaped up as a critical point of the British Army's presence in a part of the world almost forgotten until the Argentinians tried to take the law into their own hands by using military force. There was a summer race to get a hard covering over every man's head before the dismally cold, wet and windy winter (April to November) set in, making further building work difficult. And the roads were demanding some attention too: 'The bitumen surfacing is of noticeably poor quality,' said one officer. 'I remember being on a road on a day that was about as sunny as a Scottish Spring, and the bitumen was showing signs of melting, which shouldn't happen. The roads have suffered an amount of damage during the hostilities and our own vehicles have made the problem worse.'

Throughout all these difficulties, there has been a general assumption that the Falkland Islands must now be added to the list of postings which is part of the British Army's permanent routine, along with Hong Kong, Northern Ireland, Belize, West Germany and Berlin.

But the most exciting off-duty activity the troops can indulge in at the present moment is watching video in the portable cabin which serves as their unit's club and cinema. There may be one of these clubs to every dozen or so cabins; and though all the cabins are 'temporary' and have a book life of two years or so, temporary measures frequently exceed their expected time. The floating modules, especially if moored to shore, are much better. They are medium-term expedients. At the back of his mind, what every officer and man must be waiting for is a decision on long-term garrisoning policy, which can hardly be postponed beyond the expected life of the temporary measures.

In the meantime, the British Army in the Falklands is having to play a waiting game in conditions very far from armchair ease. There is some feeling — life might be *more* grim if it were not so — that the waiting game may not be a long one; and some noises coming out of Argentina have tended to support this assumption.

Even at the time of their defeat, some Argentinian officers hinted that they might come back for more. One Argentinian officer with fluent English contrived to keep a personally commendable cool irony in his prison enclosure when questioned about the war by a British Brigadier. 'Well, I'd call it a Semi-Final, wouldn't you?' he said suavely.

The point was well taken by his British interrogator. But the lessons of the South Atlantic may well play a vital and even decisive part in the British Army's actions in quite other parts of the world, in that upgraded era I predicted for it when the Falklands were known to the public at large, if at all, as an irrelevant and run-down remnant of empire.

500,000 DIED IN THE WARSAW GHETTO.

Jack Eisner IS THE SURVIVOR

When the Nazi blitzkrieg hit Poland Jack Eisner was 13, a choirboy training for the Warsaw Music Conservatory. But he would never hear the choir. Instead he heard the wail of sirens, the crash of bombs and the screams of butchered fellow Jews...

Within weeks the choirboy was an expert smuggler risking his life daily for the starving ghetto. As a teenage racketeer with a flick-knife up his streetwise sleeve he killed to bring in food, medicine and guns through the sewers and over the rooftops. Jack chose to fight, to live, even to love in the hell of the ghetto and the camps.

Half a million Jews died in Warsaw, but Jack Eisner lived. His story is their monument, a tale of unbelievable courage in the face of total, inhuman depravity.

THE SURVIVOR

AUTOBIOGRAPHY   0 7221 3267 0   £1.75

THE MEN WHO HOLD THE WORLD'S FUTURE IN THEIR HANDS

THE NUCLEAR BARONS

Peter Pringle and James Spigelman

This superbly researched and forcefully argued account tells for the first time the full story of the nuclear era and its architects. It details the tests and exposes the deadly accidents, cynical cover-ups, ruthless profiteering, megalomanic ignorance and wilful evasions of democratic control which characterise the nuclear industry.

Peter Pringle, a correspondent for the Sunday Times Insight Team and James Spigelman, who held several high-level posts in the Australian Government, have used a worldwide network of sources to trace the devastating tale of nuclear build-up which has led to today's situation.

'There is no shortage of books on all things nuclear, but if you want to read just one . . . this is the book to read.'
New Statesman

WORLD AFFAIRS   0 7221 7029 7   £3.50

The Cambodia File

JACK ANDERSON AND BILL PRONZINI

A posting to Cambodia was like an invitation to a carnival in hell. Diplomat David Foxgrove thought that the Asian war would end when the last American Huey lifted off from the scarred and devastated war zone that had once been Phnom Penh. His Cambodian mistress, Kim, stayed in the ravaged city to face the murderous rage of the Khmer Rouge. For the generals the war was over, but there was no easy exit for the people who had lived a season in hell.

In THE CAMBODIA FILE Pulitzer Prize-winning war correspondent Jack Anderson and novelist Bill Pronzini have created an awesome tale of the cost of war and the price of love in the front line. Out of the battle-torn lives of a dedicated man and the woman whose nation he has betrayed, the authors have forged an epic tragedy of our time.

GENERAL FICTION   0 7221 7024 6   £2.25

A selection of bestsellers from SPHERE

FICTION

THE RED DOVE	Derek Lambert	£1.95 ☐
DOMINA	Barbara Wood	£2.50 ☐
A PERFECT STRANGER	Danielle Steel	£1.75 ☐
MISSING PERSONS	C. Terry Cline Jr.	£1.95 ☐
BAD BET	Roger Longrigg	£1.95 ☐

FILM & TV TIE-INS

BY THE SWORD DIVIDED	Mollie Hardwick	£1.75 ☐
YELLOWBEARD	Graham Chapman and David Sherlock	£2.50 ☐
STAR WARS	George Lucas	£1.75 ☐
THE YEAR OF LIVING DANGEROUSLY	C. J. Koch	£1.75 ☐

NON-FICTION

THE FINAL DECADE	Christopher Lee	£2.50 ☐
THE DOCTOR WHO TECHNICAL MANUAL	Mark Harris	£2.50 ☐
A QUESTION OF BALANCE	H.R.H. The Duke of Edinburgh	£1.50 ☐
SUSAN'S STORY	Susan Hampshire	£1.75 ☐

All Sphere books are available at your local bookshop or newsagent, or can be ordered direct from the publisher. Just tick the titles you want and fill in the form below.

Name _____

Address _____

_____

Write to Sphere Books, Cash Sales Department, P.O. Box 11, Falmouth, Cornwall TR10 9EN

Please enclose a cheque or postal order to the value of the cover price plus:

UK: 45p for the first book, 20p for the second book and 14p for each additional book ordered to a maximum charge of £1.63.

OVERSEAS: 75p for the first book and 21p per copy for each additional book.

BFPO & EIRE: 45p for the first book, 20p for the second book plus 14p per copy for the next 7 books, thereafter 8p per book.

Sphere Books reserve the right to show new retail prices on covers which may differ from those previously advertised in the text or elsewhere, and to increase postal rates in accordance with the PO.